THE POP CULTURE PARENT

Helping Kids Engage Their World for Christ

Ted Turnau, E. Stephen Burnett,
and Jared Moore

New
Growth
Press

newgrowthpress.com

New Growth Press, Greensboro, NC 27404
newgrowthpress.com
Copyright © 2020 by Ted Turnau, E. Stephen Burnett,
and Jared Moore

Unless otherwise noted, Scripture quotations are from the ESV®
Bible (The Holy Bible, English Standard Version®), copyright ©
2001 by Crossway, a publishing ministry of Good News Publishers. Used by permission. All rights reserved.

Scripture quotations marked (NIV) are taken from the Holy
Bible, New International Version®, NIV®. Copyright © 1973,
1978, 1984, 2011 by Biblica, Inc.™ Used by permission of Zondervan. All rights reserved worldwide. www.zondervan.com. The
"NIV" and "New International Version" are trademarks registered in the United States Patent and Trademark Office by
Biblica, Inc.™

Scripture quotations marked (NLT) are taken from the Holy
Bible, New Living Translation, copyright ©1996, 2004, 2015
by Tyndale House Foundation. Used by permission of Tyndale
House Publishers, Inc., Carol Stream, Illinois 60188. All rights
reserved.

Scripture quotations marked (KJV) are taken from the King
James Version.

Cover Design: Faceout Books, faceoutstudio.com
Interior Design and Typesetting: Gretchen Logterman

ISBN 978-1-64507-066-5 (Print)
ISBN 978-1-64507-067-2 (eBook)

Library of Congress Cataloging-in-Publication Data on file

Printed in Canada

27 26 25 24 23 22 21 20   1 2 3 4 5

From Ted

To two of the most important women in my life: Vivian W. Turnau (1937–2019) who raised, guided, loved, and prayed for me constantly, even in the messy times; and Carolyn S. Turnau, an unbelievable gift of God, a wise, beautiful spirit, and a wonderful partner in the journey of marriage and parenthood. I would be so much less without these two.

From Stephen

To my parents, Eric and Jane, who embraced radical-missional ideas such as biblical faith and homeschooling and introduced me as a child to Christ-exalting popular culture; and to my beloved wife, Lacy, who not only loves the best stories with me but encouraged me to try writing nonfiction until finally I listened.

From Jared

To my children, who are gifts from God: Caden, Ava, Ian, and Jude. You've changed my life for the better, becoming one of the primary avenues through which I enjoy Christ. May this book provide us with the tools we need to enjoy God through pop culture as you prepare to engage your world for Christ.

Contents

Five Simple Questions to Ask about Popular Culture

1. **What is the story?**
   Play "Tell Me a Story"
2. **What is the moral and imaginary world?**
   Play "Show Me the World"
3. **What is good, true, and beautiful in this world (common grace)?**
   Play "Find the Common Grace"
4. **What is false and idolatrous in this world?**
   Play "Spot the Hooey"
5. **How is Jesus the true answer to this story's hopes?**
   Play "Find the Real Gospel"

These five questions, used throughout this book, are adapted from those created by Ted Turnau in his book, *Popologetics* (Phillipsburg, NJ: P&R Publishing, 2012).

Chapter 1
Why We Need Pop Culture Parents

Popular culture lives everywhere. Stories, songs, shows, games, and images all flow into our eyes, ears, and imaginations. They come from television screens, books, and radio stations. Even more often, they're reaching us over our computers and mobile devices.

As a parent, you already live in this inevitable world of popular culture. So do your kids.

If you're on a family vacation and you pass something as simple as a billboard, that's a bit of popular culture. When your young child comes home from church talking about a TV show, or your teenage child shares photos on a new social-media app, that's even more popular culture. As the internet grows, this popular culture–filled world will become even larger for your kids. On the internet, movie fans of all ages share news and art about their favorite stories. Music fans download songs, video gamers swap tips on beating the most difficult levels. Book fans follow their favorite authors and order new volumes from retailers.

In fact, by reading this book, you're engaging in (Christian-made) popular culture yourself.

Popular culture is like the very air we breathe. We can take it in and give it out and not even think about it.[1]

In this book, we define popular culture as human-created works that occupy common spaces, such as TV, the internet, music, and beyond. Popular culture is everywhere. We can't resist it or escape its influence.

Or can we?

Should Christians try to defend ourselves against popular culture, screening out its influence in our families? How many TV shows, movies, or games are too much for our kids? What about certain movies with violent or sexual content? Or is popular culture neutral? Is it "just entertainment" that is ultimately harmless as long as parents avoid legalism?

These questions have launched many discussions, books, and blog articles. We've read movie-review websites and picked up discernment resources. And from academic sorts of Christians, we've seen articles that promise to find the gospel or a redemptive theme in a popular movie franchise or streaming drama series.

All these can help Christians, but they haven't explored the most crucial need of all. As parents, we need to *understand* popular culture and parenting according to God's Word. Only then can we avoid both (1) fearing popular culture and (2) embracing it with little discernment. And only *then* can we apply this truth to our parenting and to the entertainments our children love. That way, we can best glorify God as we fulfill our incredible and biblical calling as parents.

That's why this book isn't only a "tips and tricks" guide for helping your kids handle specific types of popular culture. Instead, we created this book to give you a stronger and more biblical understanding of your calling as a parent and what popular culture has to do with it.

We will challenge several assumptions about kids, parents, and their relationships to popular culture. Once you understand these relationships, you will be better able to enter your children's favorite worlds—the popular culture they love—so you can lead and serve your children in fantastic, Christlike ways.

Ted's story: How I entered my children's favorite world

One day in 2006, my son came home from middle school absolutely excited. He told me, "Dad! Dad! You've *got* to watch this Japanese anime series with me! It's called *One Piece*."

I asked him what the series was about.

"It's about a pirate named Monkey D. Luffy who wants to find a treasure called the One Piece and become king of the Pirates!"

Honestly, it sounded like the dumbest thing ever. I didn't jump in right away, but I noticed he was watching a lot of it and that he'd also gotten his younger sister involved.

Eventually I sat down with them to give it a try. After five or six episodes, I found that I liked the over-the-top, very stylized, and goofy visuals. I found the characters growing on me. I developed an affection for this show that obviously meant a lot to my kids. They even went back and started from the beginning, so my wife and I could get the whole story from episode 1. *One Piece* has been part of our family life ever since (and it is *still* running).

Yes, the show includes some elements we don't agree with. We've often talked about the characters' moral choices. After all, they *are* pirates, even if they engage in little piracy! We've also explored the artists' decision to portray characters (especially women) in revealing attire. But we've delighted too in the story's deep excellence. *One Piece* includes signs of grace as well as idolatry, like most popular cultural works. And the stories have provoked many interesting and important conversations about all sorts of moral and spiritual topics. These conversations would have never occurred if we as parents hadn't decided to step into our children's world to share something that delighted them so.

A Pop Culture Parent's Basic Questions

This book is practical but perhaps not in the way you might expect. It isn't meant to feed you specific reviews and talking points about particular TV shows, movies, or games. Instead, we will give you clear examples of how to explore these stories, songs, and more for yourself, so you can sense how to help your kids do the same. This will prepare you to help your kids grow in the gospel as you train them to engage their world for Jesus Christ. That way you can help your children better understand their life's purpose: to live as God-worshiping members of Christ's church who are called to love, serve, and teach our neighbors in the world that so desperately needs the gospel.

Our approach will often differ from some existing Christian materials. For example, some resources about Christian parenting and popular culture do not usually explore the big question, *Why in God's world are people making and sharing all this culture in the first place?* Other resources may respond to human stories and songs as if they're a hostile force—an enemy that's dangerous to a biblical worldview and the hearts of your children. Often such resources attempt to limit the damage of popular culture.

Still other books and articles may act as if only we as "professional" Christians should watch, listen to, or play popular cultural works—so we can better connect with our neighbors. Sometimes they reframe the gospel in terms of whatever is hot in popular culture. They may have titles like (we made these up) "The Gospel According to Yoda" or "Finding God in the DC Universe." These resources assume readers have grown to maturity and can resist the tempting lies and false worship of popular culture without too much trouble (if we need worry about its deception at all). But these materials do not usually address Christian parents or explore how parents can raise children from the training stage to biblical maturity.

This book takes a different path. In the chapters ahead, we will (1) define popular culture according to its original, biblical purpose in God's world; (2) review our special calling as gospel-centered parents; and (3) propose clear, practical, and *biblical* strategies to understand these stories, songs, and beyond, asking questions about each cultural work, so we can start guiding our kids to do the same. From there, we will (4) explore how to do this for children as they grow to maturity, providing three age-appropriate examples (from two popular movies and one video game). In this way, we hope to provide parents a way to enter their children's cultural worlds to talk, to enjoy, and to equip kids for reaching into their friends' cultural worlds.

As this book's authors, we've spent lifetimes wrestling with these challenges of human stories and songs, particularly in light of the gospel, and relating to our families:

As a teacher and parent, Ted Turnau has trained to enter the worlds of anime, television drama, and video games with his three (now-adult) children. Ted and his wife, Carolyn, have spent years in ministry in Europe. They have also often hosted university students at their home to explore the grace-filled moments *and* idols in popular movies and songs.

As a storyteller, E. Stephen Burnett is just beginning his parenting journey. He has spent years not only creating stories but reviewing popular movies and other fantastical stories from a Christian perspective. Stephen and his wife, Lacy, are now facing these cultural challenges with the foster children to whom they have been called to minister.

And as a pastor, Jared Moore brings a uniquely pastoral *and* parental view to this topic. He and his wife, Amber, are raising four children. Despite their busy lives of church ministry, parenting, and teaching, Jared has a special interest in finding helpful ways to introduce young children to popular culture and train them to explore each story's graces and idols.

Welcome to Our Post-Christian World

We especially need this training in the post-Christian culture our children will inherit. As Christians we find ourselves living among neighbors who show less interest in our faith than ever before. Between 2007 and 2014, the number of Americans claiming no religious affiliation jumped from 16 percent to 23 percent.[2] In the UK, recent statistics show the religiously unaffiliated have grown to more than half the population.[3] In the rest of Europe, the statistics are worse, not better.

Not surprisingly, this secularization leads to deep chasms of distrust between Christians and non-Christians, some of whom openly distain biblical Christianity. On Twitter, a Christian author remarked that she was rejected by multiple publishing houses when they learned she was Christian. On university campuses, Christian groups have been denied access to college facilities because they affirm biblical sexual values.[4] Many non-Christians say they believe Christians (particularly evangelicals) are bigoted, intolerant, greedy, anti-intellectual, anti-science killjoys.

Our Children Are Like Sheep Sent Out to Raid the Wolves

This is why many Christian parents feel that exposing their kids to any popular culture will also expose them to many evils: unbiblical worldviews, sexual imagery, exploitative violence, and ideas designed to undermine the family and undermine their children's faith. As parents, we may fear that these wolves will prey on the little lambs under our protection. We may feel we must constantly beat back the wolves. Or we might try to ignore these threats, just teach and live out the gospel, and hope our children will learn to stay true to Jesus despite the wolves.

Jesus had quite a different response to a hostile culture: "Behold, I am sending you out as sheep in the midst of wolves, so be wise as serpents and innocent as doves" (Matthew 10:16).

Jesus intentionally sent his disciples *into* wolfish territory to heal and bring good news. Jesus also prayed for his disciples in John 17:18: "Just as you sent me into the world, I am sending them into the world" (NLT). Jesus's response to a hostile world was not to withdraw in self-protection but to serve as a missionary and train his disciples to do the same. In Jesus's mind, the sheep aren't victims; they're the raiding party.

The famous preacher Charles Spurgeon put it this way: "The wolf leaps into the midst of a flock and rips and tears on every side. It matters not how many the sheep may be, for one wolf is more than a match for a thousand sheep. But lo, here you see sheep sent forth among the wolves, as if they were the attacking party and were bent upon putting down their terrible enemies! It is a novel sight, such as nature can never show, but grace is full of marvels!"[5]

Do we have this confidence? Can we train our children to be fully committed to the gospel in dovelike simplicity while also being wise as serpents, familiar with the ways of their neighbors' culture? We believe that as God's people, working out the gospel, we can.

To be sure, all these shows, movies, games, and songs that reflect the cultures of our lands often appear like terrifying wolves. But in Christ, we need not fear them. If we are willing to engage this world *with* our children, using God's gifts—his Spirit, his Word, and his church—we can equip our children to grow into this maturity. The mission Jesus gave his disciples is our mission today, and it also belongs to our children. If we wish to train our children for a disciple's life beyond the shelter we provide, we should start now. You can teach your children wisdom to prepare them for a lifetime of wolf-wrangling.

OUR CHILDREN THEMSELVES HAVE WOLFISH HEARTS

To complicate the sheep-versus-wolves picture, we must also recall that our kids aren't simply sheep. Our reality is messier: the "wolves" also already live inside our children.

Jesus affirms this in Mark 7. He explains why he rebuked the Pharisees after they chided his disciples for ignoring ritual purity codes. Jesus outright condemned these religious leaders' habit of believing that external objects, such as the wrong kinds of foods, spiritually defile us. Jesus says our disordered hearts are the real problem:

> "There is nothing outside a person that by going into him can defile him, but the things that come out of a person are what defile him. . . . Do you not see that whatever goes into a person from outside cannot defile him, since it enters not his heart but his stomach, and is expelled?" (Thus he declared all foods clean.) And he said, "What comes out of a person is what defiles him. For from within, out of the heart of man, come evil thoughts, sexual immorality, theft, murder, adultery, coveting, wickedness, deceit, sensuality, envy, slander, pride, foolishness. All these evil things come from within, and they defile a person. (Mark 7:15, 18b–23)

By understanding that the heart is a well, poisoned at its source, Jesus cut to the chase: don't get hung up on externals, but look to the state of your own heart. No one catches sin, like a contagion, from outside influences such as food, or even popular culture. Rather, the idols within our hearts already threaten to defile us and our children.

Even if we could create a popular-culture-free bubble for our children, we could not secure their spiritual safety. Children take the evil within them wherever they go. Yes, popular culture can entice hearts, hook into our idols, and tempt us away from God's purpose. If that is so, and we are called into the world by Jesus, our path is clear. Instead of keeping our children ignorant, we learn to gauge their level of maturity and guide them to further maturity as we intentionally train them to discern idols—the ways culture entices us to serve and worship that which is not God. We teach our children how the gospel outshines the fool's gold offered by the idols!

Otherwise, once children leave home, they will be unprepared and might be blindsided by temptation. Plus, if they were raised disconnected from culture, they will likely prove to be poor ambassadors, unfamiliar with the mind-set of the neighbors they are trying to reach.

We want to help you teach your children how to refuse heart-seducing idolatry and answer this temptation with the greater beauty and power of the gospel. When we form and guide our children's heart affections in the very midst of our surrounding culture, they can learn how to be wise as serpents and single-hearted (*not* simple-minded) as doves.

POPULAR CULTURE IS A MESSY MIXTURE OF IDOLS AND COMMON GRACE

As we recognize our children's sinful heart issues, we also need to affirm the good things God has left in human stories, songs, games, and more. Theologians call these good things *common grace*. This refers to the gifts God gives to people in the world, even if they never believe in him. We find this concept based in several biblical texts. In Matthew 5:43–48, Jesus teaches about love for enemies by talking about how the Father gives rain and sunshine even to his enemies. In Acts 14:15–17, Paul points the people of Lystra to the blessings around them, such as rain and crops, "satisfying your hearts with food and gladness." These, Paul says, are witnesses to God's goodness and generosity. The principle behind Paul's saying is this: anything that gives human hearts joy is ultimately a gift from God. Such gifts give witness to the beauty, love, and power of the Father. Popular culture offers a dazzling collection of these gifts.

In the following chapters, we will explore how Christian parents can search for common grace in popular culture.

We'll also explore how parents can teach their kids to disentangle these good things from the real idols that also inhabit stories and songs and beyond. Even better, we'll learn how we can start to answer these human longings—which no other story or song can ever truly fulfill—with the promises found in Jesus alone.

GOD MADE KIDS, AND ALL OF US, TO SHARE IN CULTURE

At this point, you may still have concerns about engaging popular culture with your children. Isn't being a pop culture parent simply optional? Don't you have more important things to teach your children, such as biblical worldviews, apologetics, or career readiness?

Later we will answer these concerns in more detail. For now, we'll provide the main reason cultural engagement is a vital part of our parental calling. This "impossible" mission—which we must choose to accept—is a way to glorify God by enjoying him forever *through his gifts*. We do this in three ways: by worshiping and enjoying personal relationships with God through Jesus by the Holy Spirit, by reflecting his grace in relationship with our children and other Christians, and by letting that grace shine to those who need to know God—that is, bringing his gospel to our friends and neighbors. We can't do any of this apart from making and engaging culture.

1. God made us to worship him through culture.

As human beings, we've been created in God's image. God has made us to be creative. He called Adam and Eve to create culture, even as he called them to fill the earth with children (see Genesis 1:28). Of course, sin has since entered the world, warping our culture making. But even now, we find goodness reflected in culture because it is created by people made in the image of their Creator. Humans may bend and distort and even deny God's image, but we cannot erase it. Nor can we avoid reflecting the beauty, love, power, and awesomeness of God in the culture we create.

Popular culture is not popular because people are lazy, ignorant, and wicked. It is popular because our works include awesomeness that reflects our awesome Creator and Redeemer. People hunger for that grace without knowing quite what it is they truly hunger for. Popular culture is popular precisely because of the grace to be found in it, however distorted. We and our children can find this grace if we are willing to look for it.

True, these reflections of grace are twisted by sin. But even then, we can train our children to expose these false gospels by comparing them with Jesus. In the light of his glory and grace, idols will grow strangely dim as the true gospel light shines in our imaginations.

Whether a popular entertainment reflects grace or reflects idolatry—either way—we and our children can respond by exploring the gospel more clearly. We can actually catch glimpses of God's glory *through* popular cultural works.

2. God made us to enjoy healthy relationships through culture.

Whatever we do, our children will grow to love culture and entertainments of some kind. As they mature, they'll also become nostalgic for their favorites—not only from their family home but their cultural home. If we as parents make the effort to enter into this world, we will find that over time we can build healthy relationships and deep communication with our children. We and our children will have the same cultural landmarks. We'll get the same references and share inside jokes. And we'll have the memories of discovering imagined lands together, comparing their graces and idols with the gospel, and glorifying God as we've enjoyed the creations of humans made in his image.

This is precisely what Jesus did. When he wanted to rebuild the ruined relationship between him and us, he entered our territory to live with us. Popular culture gives us the same chance. We can enter into our children's worlds, look through their eyes, and discover what they see as awesome and worthy. Engaging popular culture with our kids builds the kind of relationships needed to discuss the deep and serious challenges of life.

We also have relationships that extend beyond our families. Christians belong to churches. The local church is called to disciple saints as the gathered people of God. Churches can be an excellent resource for guidance in engaging culture together. We can be "iron sharpening iron" for one another *if* we are willing to engage together. In this way, the church as a whole grows in wisdom.

But apart from the church's labor, enjoying popular culture should be part of our patterns of collective rest. We glorify God in our work (our own jobs and the church's mission) but also in our recreation. Enjoying popular culture is part of our rest together. It has always been so for the people of God. Both Old and New Testaments include many examples of bountiful celebrations. No God-exalting party brimming with rest, happiness, and feasts is complete without popular culture. We were meant to share stories, songs, games, and other popular cultural works, whether spoken around a campfire or shared on a smartphone.

3. God made us to take his gospel to a world that needs him.

As we engage culture together, we become equipped as ambassadors to our culture (2 Corinthians 5:20). Christians call this the Great Commission, the command Jesus gave his followers: "All authority in heaven and on earth has been given to me. Go therefore and make disciples of all nations, baptizing them in the name of the Father and of the Son and of the Holy Spirit, teaching them to observe all that I have commanded you. And behold, I am with you always, to the end of the age" (Matthew 28:18–20).

As sons and daughters of the King, our Great Commission is to serve as ambassadors of Jesus to people around us. Wise ambassadors get to know the culture of their host country, studying the heart and soul of the people they are trying to reach. Our homes should become extensions of our churches—Kingdom embassies. These are our mission headquarters. We should be *intentional* about enjoying popular culture in the home. We don't only recreate and enjoy stories together as families. We also engage popular culture to train for our God-given mission in the world.

As we engage our world's favorite stories, songs, and games, we become familiar with our neighbors' cultural categories. We grow to discern their desires, hopes, dreams, and fears, finding natural doorways into their worlds. So, as we worship God by sharing in acts of creation and build relationships with our children and others in the church, we're also training for Christ's mission to the whole world: to love non-Christians wisely, speak into their lives winsomely, and serve them by bringing healing into their lives.

Training our kids for this mission—that's the challenge and *privilege* of Christian parents. In your hands, that challenge of popular culture can become a natural ally in this calling.

Your Mission: Become a Pop Culture Parent for God's Glory and Your Kids' Growth

We write mainly for Christian parents who want to apply the gospel to *every* part of their parenting, including the swarm of popular culture works that literally whiz about us using invisible signals every day. But we aim to provide tools not for only parents but also grandparents, child and youth workers, teachers, friends, older brothers and sisters, aunts and uncles, coaches, or *anyone* who invests in the lives of the kids around them.

We prayerfully hope this book will equip you to engage popular culture with your kids. And we pray that with this book you will gain a deeper appreciation for the awesomeness of the gospel of grace, and our awesome Creator and Savior who provides grace for us, by enjoying the awesomeness of popular culture. We were made for delight, and we would love for you to be able to share that with your children!

By now, we hope you're eager. You're ready to watch *Frozen* with your kids, enjoy that story of Anna's seeking and sacrificial love for Elsa, and connect it to our longing and need for the seeking and sacrificial love of Jesus—all while you also expose the idol of authentic self in the song "Let It Go." Well, we love that you're eager. And we're going to get to all of that and much more. But the process of doing it really well, so that you become a highly skilled pop culture parent who can do it for yourself with any movie or song or game, takes longer than just jumping to the answers. There is groundwork to build: We must understand culture. We must rejoice in the gospel. We must embrace our role as parents and know our children. We must respect the movie itself enough to describe it well before leaping to conclusions. And yes, in the end, we will then understand *Frozen* like never before.

All of that wonderful journey lies ahead. To start down this path of helping our kids engage their world for Christ, in the next chapter we will learn why on earth God made people to make all these popular-culture works in the first place.

Chapter 2

The Purpose of Popular Culture

When we want to define the gospel, God's holiness, or marriage, where should Christians go? If we're wise, we go first to the Bible, so we can understand the origins of these truths. Only in the Scripture can we find God's revelation about who he is, why he is, and why he gave his people certain gifts.

However, we've found one concept that often escapes Christian explanation according to the Bible. That's the concept of culture, which includes popular culture.

Instead, even good, faithful, gospel-centered Christians carry their personal preferences into their discussions about popular culture. These oversights can affect how we as Christian parents approach the topic, usually without our realizing it.

Some leaders don't discuss the topic of popular culture except to offer passing condemnations based on its assumed triviality. For example, one theologian characterized modern popular culture as "anti-culture." He dismissed this with the example of "a posturing Lady Gaga or the 'artistic contributions' of some slack-jawed twenty-something with ill-fitting trousers, a pair of over-priced sneakers, and a recording contract."[1]

To an extent, we understand this writer's concern. As we explore later, enjoying popular culture does carry risks because Christians *can* be absorbed by worldliness. We must take seriously James's warning that "friendship with the world is enmity with God" (James 4:4).

However, we too often form our views based on personality or preferences. Or we might respond based on our personal history. For example, if you came to Christ as an adult, you may react against your parents' "anything goes" approach to popular culture. So you might instinctively clamp down with your own children when it comes to popular culture. Whereas, if you were raised in a too-strict Christian home, you might tend to let your own kids roam freely with their gaming systems or social media.

We need to clear aside reactionary and personal attitudes about the messy topic of popular culture. Instead, we need to seek out a *positive* definition, based on Scripture, about why popular culture is even a part of our world and how God expects us to engage this gift.

What Is Culture?

Before we define *popular culture*, we must actually begin by defining the word *culture*.

When humans make new things, as we follow our God-given calling to be faithful stewards of his world, this is *culture*. It includes all our science, technology, art, literature, music, traditions, networks of symbols, forms of government, business, worship, habits of speech, educational systems, agricultural methods, and more. Culture is everything we do to make the world *our* world.

We also create and enjoy culture to express meaning. Tim Keller puts it this way: "Culture is the shared beliefs and values, the shared conventions and social practices of a subgroup or an entire society in which we are taking all the raw materials [of creation], everything in life, and rearranging it in order to express meaning, in order to express what we think is the good, the true, the real, and the important."[2]

As Christian parents, we must hold fast to this insight. However else culture (popular and otherwise) challenges Christian parents, it still presents a serious view of the world. That's what culture does, and should do, according to God's plan. That's reason enough for us to take any cultural work seriously.

Because of the fall, we must also keep in mind the mixed nature of culture. Because culture is made by humans who reflect God's image (Genesis 1:26–28), human culture will reflect God's character. Because culture is also made by those who harbor sinful hearts, it will be tainted with sin. Every human is both a reflection of God and sinner. Therefore, culture is inevitably a complex, messy mixture, and this mixture is our world as we have (re)made it.

What Is Popular Culture?

Popular culture is a subsection of culture. As we use the term, it is a type of artistic expression. Art is the part of culture humans most directly use to engage with questions of meaning.

When we think of art, we usually imagine symphony halls or museums. These kinds of spaces can be called "elite culture." *Popular culture* is simply art that occupies common spaces such as streaming television, musical artists and bands, the internet, and comic book stores.[3] These things give us art with easy access—expressions of the human heart that everyone can reach.

Most of the time, businesses make these cultural products for profit. They often mix this art with marketing. But this fact remains: popular culture is still an art form and has been for a long time. Popular culture is woven into the fabric of the grand human story, from African tribal dances, warriors encamped around a fire telling tales of monsters and heroes, Greek poets weaving tragedies told by stone-faced choruses, and medieval troubadours singing love songs. Popular culture captures stories, songs, images, and games, and it shares these with the broader public.

That's a solid sociological definition. However, we also need to show how culture, especially popular culture, fits into *gospel history*. For Christian parents, we must see how these stories, songs, images, and games are not only things humans made up. They are also a gift God has given us. He *wants* us to make and enjoy culture. Making these things is an essential part of being human—part of God's will for us on earth.

God Created Us to Enjoy Culture

How does human culture, and even popular culture, fit into the overall biblical narrative?

1. In Genesis, God commands us to make and enjoy culture.

God's Word affirms that human culture is not a man-made idea or some neutral concept found outside Scripture. God did not just make humans who *could* make culture. God specifically says that humans *should* make culture to reflect him as Creator.

Most Christians are familiar with the Great Commission. This is Jesus's command to his disciples to go out, share the good news, and make disciples of all nations (Matthew 28:16–20). But long before that, God gave another commission. It was his very first command to the newly created humans, known as the Cultural Mandate. It is the command to go out into the world, create culture, and enjoy what we have made of God's creation.

> So God created man in his own image,
>   in the image of God he created him;
>   male and female he created them.

And God blessed them. And God said to them, "Be fruitful and multiply and fill the earth and subdue it, and have dominion over the fish of the sea and over the birds of the heavens and over every living thing that moves on the earth." (Genesis 1:27–28)

Note how God calls people to have children and raise them right alongside his call for people to steward his world and make culture in it. In other words, if we accept the biblical truth that God wants families to have children, then we must also accept the biblical truth that God wants human beings to make culture in his world!

In fact, without God's Cultural Mandate, we have no context for the Great Commission. When we share Jesus with others, it is always in the context of a specific culture. The Great Commission calls us not just to evangelize but to "make disciples." This means we teach others how to apply the gospel to a whole way of life—that is, within particular cultures. Discipleship always involves cultural engagement.

Genesis 1:28 says we must "subdue" and "have dominion." These words may sound harsh to modern ears, as if God wanted us to beat creation into submission. But to an ancient Israelite, these words would have sounded unmistakably royal. They proclaim a call for humans to bring the planet under their ruling authority as God's representatives on earth. And when you consider how Adam first uses that authority, the supposed harshness evaporates. He doesn't beat anything. Rather, he cares for and nurtures the plants in the garden (Genesis 2:15), and he shows wisdom and care by giving the animals names and identities (vv. 19–20). In effect, God commanded the first humans to take his creation under their wing to bring out its true glory. It's the way a wise and good royal couple would bring glory out from their subjects.

In the Cultural Mandate, God calls us to act as stewards, carefully nurturing and developing creation's hidden potential, filling it with creations of our own. In fact, by planting the garden for Adam and Eve to develop, God had started creating and enjoying culture before they did. As writer Andy Crouch reminds us, a garden "is nature *plus* culture."[4]

This means human culture is rooted in God's good creation. Culture was originally *God's* idea. Our original purpose is to glorify God, love other people, and nurture the earth, and we do all of this *culturally*. Culture forms our worship of God, our community as his people, and our stewardship over the world.[5] Making culture is the human response to God's divine call to develop the world God has generously given to his image-bearers.[6]

What then about *popular* culture?

This is part of the Cultural Mandate. Though Genesis gives us no specific instructions concerning popular culture, if we consider the glimpses the Bible gives us of the ordinary life of his people, popular culture's role begins to emerge.

For example, take the first few verses of Ruth 3, where Ruth goes to Boaz after he eats and drinks during a harvest celebration. Or consider Psalm 45, a love song to help celebrate the king's wedding. Or Jeremiah 31:4, where God promises the exiles that there will be tambourine music and they "shall go forth in the dance of the merrymakers." Popular culture is a normal part of the rhythm of life. It celebrates, entertains, and adorns our common cultural life. Popular culture doesn't sow the seed or reap the harvest. Rather, it provides the songs that accompany the harvest celebration, the tales that would be passed on, the games played. It helps a person woo his beloved or adorn the wedding. It is the way God's people relax and enjoy him, his world, and one another. If Adam and Eve had not fallen, we could *still* enjoy the musical works of Jubal, "father of all those who play the lyre and pipe" (Genesis 4:21).

2. By making culture, we glorify God and reflect his image.

This perspective on culture may strike some Christians as too earthly. Enjoying popular culture to the glory of God? Really? Actually, we are *made* to share such communal enjoyment of the Creator, creation, culture, and each other. That's the point of Paul's command to Timothy, insisting that believers should not reject God's good gifts of sex and food: "For everything God created is good, and nothing is to be rejected if it is received with thanksgiving, because it is consecrated by the word of God and prayer" (1 Timothy 4:4–5 NIV).

There is nothing "spiritual" about rejecting the good gifts God offers. Enjoying culture with wisdom and thankfulness is good spirituality. It is part of the God-ordained rhythm of work and rest, creation and recreation.

The Bible's creation account also teaches us that we are created for creating. Christian thinkers have argued over what it means to reflect or "image" God. In the context of Genesis 1, the most obvious meaning is that we create because we are made to imitate the Creator. God creates and enjoys his creation, and he hardwired us to do the same. Creating and enjoying our creations comes as naturally to us as breathing.

This means we cannot escape culture anymore than we can escape our humanity. If we wish to be real Christians— that is, redeemed *humans* living in the real, everyday world— we must be willing to engage the popular culture that is woven into our world. If we try to avoid partaking in popular culture, we will starve part of our own human nature.[7]

3. We make culture not just in response to sin but in response to God's good creation.

Culture, including popular culture, is not a consequence of the fall—the entry of sin into the world. Yes, our sin stains our works. But even in a broken world, we make culture as our response to God's creation.

You've likely noticed that some Christians will only tolerate the idea of popular culture if a popular culture item proves to be "useful." We assume a useful story or song teaches good moral lessons, educates children, reduces our stress, or preaches the gospel. But each of these uses treats human culture merely as antifall therapy. None of these uses appreciates popular culture as part of God's original creation order.

Scripture says popular culture's purpose is rooted in the order of creation. That means our grateful enjoyment of stories, songs, games, and images is legitimate *quite apart* from any of these reactions to our fallen world. In other words, it's OK for us to simply receive and enjoy popular culture with our kids. It's even OK for children to grow up and make popular culture by creating movie scripts, songs for a pop star, or code for a game studio. God has always meant for us to enjoy these good gifts with gratitude to him and joy with each other.

When Humans Rebelled, Our Culture Fell with Us

Sadly, this world is now broken by the effects of our rebellion. Now that human beings have rejected their God-created purpose, our sinful nature affects all the culture we make. As theologian Albert Wolters asserts, this means that while God's created structures are good, the way humans orient these structures may not be good.[8]

For example, God created the structure of sex, and this gift is not sinful. It is a good and necessary gift. If we wait until marriage and stay faithful in marriage, we've followed the good and proper orientation of that structure. But if we pursue sex outside of marriage or try to redefine sex or marriage, we have sinfully reoriented sex to suit our desires, away from God's will, and we have distorted the good gift of sex toward evil. Similarly, artistic drawing is a good creation structure. An artist who explores creation by expressing her talent gives a good orientation for the structure of drawing. But artists who make rude or demeaning drawings sinfully distort that good structure.

This same principle applies to popular culture. Media technologies like television are not bad, but humans can bend them to bad purposes. Social media is also a cultural good; we can use it to share biblical wisdom or establish friendships. But humans can also put social media to bad uses, such as by slandering others or even sinking into depression because everyone else's lives look better than our own.

Obviously, today's popular culture structures do not align with God's revealed will. Why not? Because we don't align with God's will either. Adam and Eve rebelled against God, corrupting their relationship with him. That stain, and that irresistible tendency toward selfish rebellion (what Paul calls the flesh, or sin nature), was passed down to all their descendants. The result: our hearts are now distorted by the fall. We begin life alienated from God, wanting to reorient all of life to ourselves. We actively seek alienation from God. Because of the fall, our hearts' default mode is set to idolatry and rebellion.

And yet we still try to use God's gifts to make beauty, truth, and sense of life apart from God. This is the essence of idolatry. No wonder the culture we make is messed up! Combine the Cultural Mandate with fallen hearts, and you replicate the fall's effects into every part of our culture-making (even the respectable parts like family and church). Popular culture is corrupted like everything else because every man or woman is born an idolater who (secretly or openly) despises God's rule over their lives.

Sin's corruption means that some of our parental suspicions of Hollywood and video games make a lot of sense! However, we've already seen how closely Scripture links culture and humanity itself. We could no more withdraw from culture than we could withdraw from other humans. In fact, the apostle Paul says we can't avoid associating with worldly sinners because "then you would need to go out of the world" (1 Corinthians 5:10).

Fortunately, although sin stains all of us, God in his mercy has not abandoned humans or our cultures. This brings us to the next part in the Bible's epic narrative: redemption.

As Jesus Redeems Us, So He Can Redeem Popular Culture

Had God left us to our own devices, the Cultural Mandate would have collapsed in on itself. We would have taken God's call to imitate him in our creative works and corrupted it so much that it consumed us all in hellish decay and infighting. But it hasn't because culture is not only fallen. God's grace continues to flow through us into the culture we make, and Scripture shows how God kept working in our cultures despite our fall into sin.

William Edgar points out that God used one of the darkest moments after the fall, the tower of Babel, to further the Cultural Mandate. By confusing language, he caused people to spread out and carry on their task of filling the earth with themselves and their works.[9] God does this repeatedly throughout the Bible. He reaffirms his determination that people (especially his people) be fruitful and multiply throughout the earth so that culturally developed creation will sing more intensely of his glory.[10]

Part of God's common grace is that it preserves some moral sense in human hearts (Romans 2:14–15). This allows even non-Christians to follow some moral code, however flawed. And it lets them create novels, television shows, music, plays, films, games, and beyond, which all reflect beauty and truth or expose the ugliness, lies, and evil of the fallen world for what they are.

In many cases, both Christian and non-Christian creators have made popular cultural works that explicitly reference the gospel of Jesus Christ. They include themes of heroism, redemptive sacrifice, love for friends, compassion for enemies, even resurrection (such as many fantasy or superhero stories). Popular culture can also emphasize other redemptive virtues, such as romantic love, forgiveness, restored family relationships, and maturity and wisdom through pain and defeat.

Of course, these aren't completely accurate copies of biblical redemption, but they are reflections. These can be stunningly direct in post-Christian cultures likes ours because our societies have long been saturated with biblical stories. But even in cultures with different histories, we find analogues and resonances with biblical categories such as sin, idolatry, sacrificial love, redemption of the guilty, and life beyond death. God has "put eternity into man's heart" (Ecclesiastes 3:11) so that light shines in culture's most unlikely corners. These images of redemption are reflected in popular culture because the people who create popular culture long for redemption, as we do. The fact that they are not Christians doesn't make their longing any less intense, even though we know only Jesus can fulfill this longing.

Ultimately, these common-grace gifts in culture point to God and the redemption he offers in Christ. Yes, sin stains all human culture, but in thousands of ways, popular culture directly or indirectly points to the gospel.

God May Let Us Enjoy Culture in the New Creation

What's next, eternally speaking? Many Christians assume that because popular culture contains some sinful elements it will be completely burned up in judgment. However, given what we see about culture's place in our God-given humanity, it would be odd if God simply ended such a gift when he comes to judge and renew the creation. The Bible gives us several hints that indicate popular culture will indeed be part of the new created order in some way.

First, the Word of God will last forever, and the Bible itself includes some popular-culture quotes—so those will stick around. Second, the theme of Christ's return is that the world will be restored, not destroyed. Evil *people* will be judged, but Romans 8:21 says "creation itself will be liberated from its bondage to decay" (NIV). Culture will thrive, not die. And third, the Bible's vivid pictures of life in the new creation are filled with continuations of our current culture. Isaiah 60 describes kings bringing cultural treasures into the New Jerusalem, and chapter 65 pictures us building homes, working with our hands, growing vineyards, making wine, feasting, and singing—familiar culture. (For an expanded discussion of the biblical evidence, see appendix A.)

This realization that parts of our present popular culture may well last, and will be included in the new-creation culture, changes everything. It means we're not just dabbling in something disposable or trivial. It means that when we deal with culture we must do so with both care and a sacred longing, for we are handling a gift of God that may extend into eternity.

Maybe you've spent time with family members or Christians who discuss popular culture—such as movies, games, or television stories—and then someone will laugh and say, "Well, enough of that, let's talk about the real world." Such phrases are understandable. But let us also realize that in the actual real world, real people enjoy popular culture. In fact, popular culture shapes the real world and helps us see reality better. These human stories and songs *are* the real world. In this reality, we as Christian parents are called to enjoy and imitate God, training our children for our mission of working and resting as families and as the church, and engaging our neighbors as ambassadors for the eternal kingdom, where our stories will continue and our songs will ring on.

Chapter 3
Gospel-Centered Parenting

Now that we've grasped popular culture's meaning in biblical perspective, let's talk about kids and parents in light of the gospel. How do we best parent our children in a world shaped by popular culture? Unless we understand God's good news and what it means for children and parents, any advice we give about engaging popular culture will likely be misunderstood. We will remain focused on the delusion that we can keep sin away from our kids rather than on teaching them to repent of their sin, come to Jesus, be transformed by him, and engage the world for him. So bear with us; this stuff is important.

Ted's story: Everything is about the gospel

When we lived stateside, some of our local church's small-group leaders wanted to teach a certain parenting curriculum. Our children's pastor thought the curriculum was unbiblical and dangerous, but some families in the church supported it. So the head pastor formed a study group. Four couples would go through the curriculum together: two couples in favor of it and two against.

We all knew and genuinely liked each other, but we found deep differences. My wife and I took the anticurriculum side in what turned out to be a fun but intense teaching exercise.

My greatest concern was that the curriculum taught parents how to control their children's behavior, as if this were the most important aspect of child-rearing. The authors promised that if we followed their step-by-step method and rules, we would doubtless raise solid Christian kids who respect authority.

The curriculum barely mentioned the gospel, or even grace. So one of my refrains became, "OK, but how does this square with the gospel?" After I said this for the umpteenth time, one of the procurriculum husbands blurted with exasperation, "The gospel! The gospel! Why does *everything* have to be about the gospel?"

I was dumbstruck. I think I said something like, "Ummmm, because it is?"

I still believe that is true. Everything *is* about the gospel. Many Christian parents with the best of intentions make parenting choices as if the gospel doesn't really matter. But if your parenting method edits out the gospel, it's not worth its salt. The gospel changes *everything*. And if parents don't get that—they might be decent, moral parents and maybe even "successful" parents—they won't be truly Christian parents.

THE GOSPEL TRUTH

People may understand the gospel differently, so let's make it plain what we mean.

We are God's creatures. We owe him everything—our lives, our obedience, our deepest love. But our lives are bent toward self, rebelling against God. Our rebellious hearts mess up everything—our relationship with God, with one another, with the very planet we live on. God could have watched us destroy ourselves, but he intervened by sending his Son, the God-man Jesus, to die and take the punishment we deserve. And God raised him by the power of the Spirit to a new life we are now allowed to share in. Once we were rejects, but if we are connected to Jesus by faith, we now have the status of God's beloved children, and nothing can change that. Though we still mess up, God is patient, and his Spirit is at work in us to change us. Eventually, Jesus will return and bring lasting glory not only to God's beloved children but to the whole cosmos—a new creation.

That is what we mean by *the gospel*. This salvation is by grace from beginning to end: forgiveness of sins by God's detail-shaping and history-ruling grace and change in our lives by that same ruling grace. The gospel is not simply, "Jesus died and was raised so my sins can be forgiven." This truth might be the core of the gospel, but it radiates outward. And that changes everything, including the way we understand kids and parents.

THE GOSPEL PURPOSE OF CHILDREN

When we accept this biblical good news, it undoes some myths parents may hold about their kids. One myth is the *myth of innocence*. The Bible states that sin is hardwired into kids from the start. Experience teaches us the same, as any honest parent will tell you. Kids don't need to learn selfishness; it's human nature.

Children do not need us to venerate them as models of innocence. They don't need a steady diet of self-esteem training. They need us to guide and love them wisely, knowing full well they are sinners. After all, this is how God loves us.

Here's a second myth: the *myth of ownership*. Some parents may see children as extensions of the self or a means of achieving their personal goals. We can invest our hopes and dreams so strongly into our children that we feel the right to bend them to our will. Treating a child this way will exasperate the child and can lead to childhood depression. But worse, it is a damaging attack on the created dignity of the child.

Parents don't own their child; God does. He has given each child an identity quite distinct from (though related to) the parents' identity. Wise parents keep their eyes and ears open to the particular gifts, strengths, and weaknesses of their children to steer them toward what God wants, not just what they want.

So, the myth of innocence venerates children as innocent treasures who can do no wrong, while the myth of ownership treats them as property. What, then, is God's actual purpose for children? Here are some truths we can affirm.

1. Children are made in God's image and bear his dignity.

Children are human beings, and we humans are called to a great purpose. One Christian creed says that our primary purpose is "to glorify God and enjoy him forever."[1] Children share this purpose!

Imagine walking down the street, and a man bumps into you, knocking you to the ground. You're riled, and so you shout something nasty to him, dust yourself off, and go on your way. But the man's friend follows after you. He taps you on the shoulder and says, "We are sorry for bumping you. But the man you insulted is the Chinese ambassador. You really should apologize." And you do because it wasn't just some random guy. He's a dignitary, a man who represents a large and powerful nation.

The same applies to each and every child, with this difference: they all represent and bear the image of God, a being far more powerful than the Chinese government.

But we must say more because children have a particular nature that makes them more vulnerable than adults to harm and manipulation. Jesus issues a blood-chilling warning to adults, letting them know that God is watching carefully over these children, *his* little ones: "Whoever receives one such child in my name receives me, but whoever causes one of these little ones who believe in me to sin, it would be better for him to have a great millstone fastened around his neck and to be drowned in the depth of the sea" (Matthew 18:5–6).

If Jesus says forced drowning would be the *easier* option, you know you're in trouble. Why is his warning so severe? Because God watches out for powerless people who bear his image, and children are among the most vulnerable. Yet they enjoy an exalted position in God's economy: "See that you do not despise one of these little ones. For I tell you that in heaven their angels always see the face of my Father who is in heaven" (Matthew 18:10).

Parents need to be careful to respect the dignity of children by being open to the way God has made them glorify and enjoy him. In a sense, parenting a child is a dialogue between the parent and the person God has created the child to be. Have your antennae tuned to how God has made your child. Know that even when you make mistakes, grace and forgiveness is available to parents, but let's strive to respect the person God is in the process of forming. This respect means that we will also respect a child's popular culture favorites enough to try to understand them.

2. Children are weak and fallen, so they need our protection.

Some parents may hang onto leftover beliefs from the myth of innocence and think, *I should just let my child grow however he will, like a flower. I need only nurture him.* But these flowers actually have poison flowing inside! In their hearts "folly is bound up" (Proverbs 22:15). Left to themselves, they will choose self-destructive paths.

Your child is a vulnerable creature, prone to wander from God just as he or she might wander away from you and quickly be in danger. The child needs you. God has placed this child in your care to raise up "in the discipline and instruction of the Lord" (Ephesians 6:4). You have a God-derived authority to guide this sinful human into wisdom and grace. Your child, a sinner, needs the gospel daily—needs to be reminded of the truth of God's holiness, power, and unstoppable kindness to the broken. This is all the more necessary for us to understand because we live in a confusing world formed by popular culture.

3. Children are God's gift to break up our self-centered living.

Parents are not only gifts to kids. Kids are gifts to parents. They intrude into our otherwise self-centered lives.

In becoming our Savior, Christ "emptied himself, by taking the form of a servant" (Philippians 2:7). In doing so he not only paid for our sins but laid down a path for us to follow. This is where kids come in. For parents, it is often the kids who take us out of ourselves and into Christlike self-emptying.

As parents, we are called to sacrifice for our children, and this includes giving them much time and attention. This point is important because, if we are unwilling to make that sacrifice, the effort required to be a pop culture parent will feel like a bother. We must learn instead that it is an honor to serve and to empty ourselves. It is God's will, in giving us kids, for them to make demands on us—including the demand that we enter their world. And so the gift of self-giving comes to us as we set aside our time, our preferences, and most of all our pride, to watch *One Piece* with our kids. And when we fail to give of ourselves and our selfish hearts are exposed—and they will be—we will be driven to the cross. Self-giving parenting is formed only through repeated repentance.

4. Children are our younger brothers and sisters in the Lord.

God has included in our children's identity the role of disciples, or potential disciples. That means they, like we, are called to be missionaries—not necessarily to foreign lands but to their own culture. Scripture assumes this calling in several passages, such as when Paul says our words should "always be gracious, seasoned with salt, so that you may know how you ought to answer each person" (Colossians 4:6). Peter also says we must set apart Christ in our hearts, so we are prepared to give an answer to anyone who asks about the hope within us (1 Peter 3:15–16) because we are called to shine in a dark world (1 Peter 2:9).

Because we are called on mission for the King, our homes should be missionary training grounds. Here our children will learn how to live in love for others, live in hope for eternal values, speak words of grace, and act for healing and peace—to be lights in the dark, messed-up world.

We see a hint of this when Paul commends Timothy, "I am reminded of your sincere faith, a faith that dwelt first in your grandmother Lois and your mother Eunice and now, I am sure, dwells in you as well" (2 Timothy 1:5). The gift of faith was passed down from generation to generation to produce Timothy, a missionary-pastor. Something right happened in Lois's parenting of Eunice and Eunice's parenting of Timothy. May we likewise raise up missionaries-in-training who will have a profound impact on our world for good.

THE PURPOSE OF GOSPEL-CENTERED PARENTING

When we take these truths about our kids' identity seriously, it radically changes our parenting. The gospel rewrites our motives for parenting and our view of popular culture. If the gospel is true, our job as parents is not primarily about sheltering or protecting our children (though we do some of that). Rather, it is primarily focused on equipping and nourishing our children to bring them into a mature, living faith. If the gospel is true, we must let go of our fears and attempts merely to control our children's behavior. We will be satisfied with nothing less than renewed hearts.

Of course, we naturally want our children to behave well and avoid the stain of worldly temptations. But if children are fallen and sinful, it's hopeless for us to try to protect them from the world and keep them innocent. Their sin-stained hearts already work against us.

Consider a child whose parents have carefully made several rules about popular culture. These may include rational restrictions, such as no smartphone use before a particular age or no TV after 8:00 p.m. It's good for a child to be obedient and keep these rules, but this does not necessarily mean he is spiritually mature. In fact, if the child feels that keeping rules makes him acceptable to God, this may indicate that his hard heart has wandered far from Jesus. True spiritual growth comes from an increasing appreciation of God's grace through Christ's death and resurrection and an honest relationship with Jesus that transforms the child's whole life over time. The calling of the gospel-centered parent (or any adult invested into the lives of children and teens) is discipleship. We are called to equip and encourage younger brothers and sisters by pointing them to the life-changing reality of the gospel.

In pursuit of this mission, we present five hallmarks of gospel-centered parenting.

1. Gospel-centered parents aim for heart desires and motivations instead of behavioral conformity.[2]

All intentional, engaged parenting aims either for the child's heart or for her behavior. Gospel-centered parenting aims for the heart. Gospel-centered parents want to engage their child's affections and desires, not simply manage how well they follow the rules.

This is quite a serious difference in parenting approaches. At some point, every Christian parent must choose which goal is more important to them. Do we want our child to develop a soft heart toward God or good behavior that may be merely for show? Do we prize a child whose heart responds to the gospel or a child who has his act together and does all the right things?

Imagine you have the power to control the future, within limits. You have two, and only two, options for how your infant daughter will turn out as she grows:

1. You raise a daughter who struggles, falls sexually, and perhaps becomes pregnant outside of marriage. But her experience humbles her so that she ends up with a genuine grasp of how much God loves her in the gospel. She repents and learns to live life depending day by day on Jesus for grace.
2. You raise a daughter who doesn't struggle that way. In fact, she doesn't struggle with any scandalous behavior at all. She always follows the rules and makes it to her marriage day a virgin. She even marries a young man who is also a virgin. But she has a cold heart toward God and never really grasps the gospel because she feels she has never really needed much forgiveness anyway.

Which path would you choose? We would choose the first option. Every time. Why? Because if you take an eternal perspective, you want your daughter to be humbled and understand God's love more than for her to behave based on a sense of lifeless duty. The self-righteous attitude that follows is often far deadlier than sexual sin because it's socially acceptable among Christians. It seeps like poison into the soul of a person who seems to be doing OK.

In Jesus's parable of the lost son (Luke 15:11–32), the wayward younger son is actually in a better spiritual condition than the older son. He at least *knows* he's a screwup, outrageously loved by the father, and he's humbled by that knowledge. He is under no illusions about his own holiness. He knows he is home only by virtue of his father's great mercy. By contrast, the older brother lives under an illusion.

He thinks that because he performs well he has the right to treat the father with contempt, refusing to join the celebration. His holiness is a sham because it is a cover for a hard, unrepentant, unloving, and unlovely heart. It masks spiritual poison that will eventually destroy him if left untreated.

Of course, all parents would prefer raising a child who doesn't struggle with messy sins *and* has a gospel-softened heart for God and a generous heart toward others. We don't want to pose a false dichotomy between gospel-heartedness and obedience. But we imagined this hard choice because you must be clear about priorities. Then you will be ready to show grace to your children when they mess up and struggle.

And they *will* struggle. Different children will struggle differently, but they are all sinners and they all struggle somehow. If we as parents are ready to embrace strugglers with gospel grace, we will be less controlled by fear—even in the scary world of popular culture.

2. Gospel-centered parenting allows freedom to fail.

Gospel-centered parenting also allows room for children *and* parents to fail. As our hard-choice illustration shows, being a parent rooted in the gospel means we are available for our children no matter what. We know firsthand God's redeeming grace. We know we are God's adopted children, and he will hold on to us. How then can we do anything but extend that same grace and faithfulness to our children?

This is easier said than done. Too often, we pay lip service to gospel grace, but our words and actions betray quite another attitude.

Ted's story: "You want me to be perfect!"

My oldest daughter was seventeen, and she had done something dumb, dangerous, and rebellious. She felt terrible guilt—but she only came to us to talk about it weeks later.

When I asked her why she had waited so long, she said with tears, "Because I was afraid of what you'd say. I was afraid of what you'd think of me. You want me to be *perfect*!" She seriously believed that we wanted perfect behavior from her and that if she couldn't deliver we would prefer the *appearance* of perfection. She was afraid that if she showed us the real her, she'd be rejected.

I responded, "When did we *ever* say that?! We know you're a sinner. We're *all* sinners who need grace. How many times have we told you the gospel? We don't expect perfection. You *know* this!"

But as I thought about it, I realized how often I had let critical comments slip out. I recalled how I tended to vent my frustration by making cutting, sarcastic remarks. I *said* I believed in gospel grace, but I lived quite a different message: that she'd better shape up or she was not worthy of my love.

I ended up having to seek my daughter's forgiveness, just as she had to seek ours. I told her I was sorry for being an idiot, for criticizing her rather than encouraging her, and that she shouldn't let my knuckleheaded comments obscure the fact that we did in fact love her, warts and all. A huge part of gospel-centered parenting is having the freedom as a parent to repent and ask your children for forgiveness.

My wife and I also told my daughter that we adored her and would not let her go, no matter what. No matter what stunt she pulled, no matter what sins she struggled with, we were there for her and loved her. We weren't going anywhere.

That is what the gospel looks like in a parent-child relationship. It doesn't mean we never discipline for disobedience, but love shapes whatever discipline we must enforce. We discipline *only* out of love, never out of annoyance or anger, and never in a manner that would make her doubt our love for her. We want only her best, to see her conformed to the love of Christ.

The gospel gives so much freedom and security for both children and parents. Children needn't fear rejection by parents, so they can show their true faces. Parents needn't fear that their mistakes will irredeemably scar and embitter their children, so they also can show their true faces. Parents and children can be real, forgiven sinners with each other.

Ted's story: The culturally sheltered son who rejected the gospel

Some years ago, I taught a Sunday school class about engaging popular culture, and someone asked how to engage popular culture with children. As we started discussing, one mother broke down in tears. I stopped the class and asked her what was wrong. She confessed she had been overprotective of her son. With the best intentions, she had shielded him from popular culture, forbidding him from seeing certain movies. Years later, her son left home to study film, and he discovered how many cultural riches had been denied him. He developed bitterness toward his mother and later rejected the faith in which he was raised. For him, Christianity became a killjoy religion of narrow-minded do-gooders who "protect" their children from good movies. He wanted no part of it.

On that Sunday, this mother asked me with tears how she could mend those bridges. I told her repentance was the key; she must ask her son's forgiveness and seek to rebuild those bridges. It would be a slow, painful process. But God has the power to restore the years the locusts have eaten (Joel 2:25). He can heal the damage we ourselves inflict.

For my part, I've sometimes needed to ask forgiveness of my children for the exact opposite failure: letting them see too much. Sometimes we're watching a movie or television show, and I am too slow with the remote control. I have to hit stop and say, "I am sorry for letting you watch that scene. This wasn't the best for you. I messed up as a parent. I should have protected you better. Would you forgive me?"

And they do. So far, none of my children has turned out to be an ax-wielding prostitute. But more importantly, all of them understand the gospel. They get how Jesus's death demonstrates to messed-up sinners that God loves them always. His love is like a river that never runs dry. He pours his love upon them and us with ridiculous generosity.

****

An important side note: understanding the gospel is *not* a guarantee that your child will continue the faith into adulthood. Some walk away *despite* understanding the gospel. But even when a child does wander away, being grounded in the gospel is key to maintaining a good relationship with that child.

God's unfailingly faithful and generous love is the context for a parent-child relationship to grow. Nothing can harm us while we're under God's protecting grace. He alone is our north star, guiding us home.

3. Gospel-centered parenting woos the child's heart with the gospel's beauty.

This context of God's wildly undeserved love transforms us into people who *do* long to keep God's laws as Jesus did because we long to be like him. Paul puts it this way: "For the grace of God has appeared that offers salvation to all people. It teaches us to say 'No' to ungodliness and worldly passions, and to live self-controlled, upright and godly lives in this present age, while we wait for the blessed hope—the appearing of the glory of our great God and Savior, Jesus Christ, who gave himself for us to redeem us from all wickedness and to purify for himself a people that are his very own, eager to do what is good" (Titus 2:11–14 NIV).

Paul affirms that mere commitment to Christian duty is not why we are able to obey God. Rather, we are powerfully motivated by grace. God transforms us through the power of his undeserved love for messy, screwed-up rebels like us (and our children).

How does that work?

The great nineteenth-century Scottish pastor-theologian Thomas Chalmers might help us figure out how grace changes us. In his sermon "The Expulsive Power of a New Affection," Chalmers asserts that behavior is controlled by our hearts' affections; we do what we want to do.[3] It's all about desire. So, if our heart desires an idol—a false god that promises life to the full—we will chase after it. The solution? Change the desires of the heart.

But heart desires are notoriously difficult to change and cannot be overcome by mere willpower or moral effort. A desire that has been installed on our heart's throne, to rule our wants, will remain king until a more beautiful and powerful ruler topples it and woos our hearts away from idols. Parental focus on behavior modification misses the point, for it effectively does an end run around the child's inner desires. The deeper, more significant battle is for the affections of the heart, and that is not won by scowling at the world so much as it is by showing your child the beauty of the gospel.

As the heart changes its base loyalties and affections, behavior will also change. But these changes don't work in reverse. If we force conforming obedience on a child, we will produce only resentment that will later bear a bitter harvest. Your mission is the heart—to ferret out the distorted desires, hopes, and fears that lurk within your child and to woo your child's heart to a better affection: the beauty and majesty of Jesus.

How would this work in everyday life? Obviously, the family must be learning the Bible together because that is where the gospel is found. Make your home a Scripture-soaked place through family devotions, Bible story times, private quiet times, catechism, any means you can use to familiarize yourselves and your children with biblical truth. Pray for and with your kids, that the gospel will enter their hearts.

You will also apply the gospel to real-life situations. If you have a young son who hit his kid sister, you may need to discipline him, but you also need to make a case in an age-appropriate way regarding the heart issue at the core of his behavior. You need to woo his heart back to gospel love—even love for annoying little sisters. When he understands that he has done wrong and feels the wrongness (the guilt), he comes to understand and appreciate God's love for him more deeply *because* of his sin. When guilt gives way to gratitude, God once again is installed as the rightful king of your son's heart.

Over time, however, the gospel itself can seem cliché. All three authors of this book grew up in the church and can attest to how hearing the same phrases over and over, singing the same songs, can breed an overfamiliarity. The gospel no longer seems strange and wonderful. It is here that engaging with popular culture can help reignite kids' imaginations. Popular culture is a key part of showing the beauty of the gospel *especially for kids who have grown up in the church* and are tired of the typical phrases and clichés we use to describe it.

Popular culture can woo imaginations both through contrast and reflection. By *contrast*, we mean the gospel shines brighter when we see the emptiness of the false gospels in popular culture. When the hero saves the world through violence, you can talk about how violence often *doesn't* save the world and how God actually saved the world by allowing his Son to become a victim of violence, absorbing its ugliness. By *reflection*, we mean that popular culture sometimes gives hints and echoes of the beauty and power of the gospel. When we see a character learn to forgive a friend who has betrayed her trust, we hear an echo of the gospel—of God's forgiveness of our betrayal. As counterintuitive as it sounds, with adult guidance, popular culture can actually place the gospel into new imaginative contexts for children, helping them see its power and beauty anew.

4. Gospel-centered parenting is incarnational.

A time-tested proverb declares, "90 percent of parenting is just showing up." This is no doubt true. Being there for events big and small—Little League games, elementary school performances, graduations, a college rejection letter—means a lot to a kid. But showing up is not enough; *how* you show up is decisive. Some kinds of parental involvement make the gospel attractive. Others do not, as we see in these examples.

Ted's story: "Repent, or devil smash you in hell!"

Several years ago, I took my wife and daughters to a fan convention called Dragon*Con. People of all colors, shapes, sizes, and backgrounds came together to participate in panel discussions, watch and discuss their favorite shows, catch sight of their favorite celebrities, and dress up in bizarre costumes (the more bizarre the better). One of the highlights of the convention is the parade. Costumed fans converge and march through downtown Atlanta. We watched row upon row of Darth Vaders, hobbits, Marios, superheroes, zombies, and other characters pass before our eyes. Wonderful stuff.

Right after the last float passed, the street preachers descended with their bullhorns, blaring out their messages of judgment and repentance. One preacher was followed by a man holding a huge sign on a pole. On it was a picture of the Incredible Hulk. Its text read, "Hulk say, REPENT, OR DEVIL SMASH YOU IN HELL!!!"

Fans drifted away, muttering resentfully. My eldest daughter overheard one fan say, "We don't go into their churches, so why do they invade ours?"

Please notice: in his mind, this street preacher probably believed he was being culturally relevant because his sign had a picture of the Hulk. In reality, he was anything but. He was judging the fans from the outside and doing more harm than good for the cause of the gospel.

On the other hand, I met a number of Christian fans. They too dressed in odd costumes and contributed to the discussions. Dragon*Con even gave the group a room for a Sunday worship service. The sermon was delivered by a pastor dressed up as King Fergus, Merida's father from the film *Brave*. These Christians hung out with the fans in the fans' own territory. They didn't judge fans from the outside. They even dressed in "native garb" (cosplay).

Guess which method comes closer to Jesus's own method for reaching sinners. Which approach looks more like Jesus hanging out with the deeply unpopular tax collectors and sinners? Hint: it's not the guy with the bullhorn. And guess which method has a greater impact? If we want to draw people to the gospel, we must be incarnational and relational, entering into their worlds. Parents are often tempted to parent from above, from a position of detached authority looking down on the child's world, judging and dismissing it, safely ensconced in the parent's comfort zone. But we only effectively woo our children's hearts to the beauty of the gospel when we mimic Jesus by being incarnational. That is, just as Jesus entered our world, we *enter* the worlds of our children, including the culture they enjoy.

Children long to share the things they love with their parents. They long for our approval. They want us to enjoy their culture with them. This longing is an opportunity: we can step into their worlds or else reject them. One path leads to more engagement with your child's cultural choices. The other leads to less.

Ted's story: How not to enter your child's favorite world

When my brother and I attended middle school, our local public television station ran the British comedy program *Monty Python's Flying Circus* late on Saturday nights. We loved the bizarre, slightly naughty humor, even when we didn't get the jokes. After some years, the television station decided to end the show. But before they did, they ran a *Python* marathon to give their viewers one last giant dose of absurd British humor. It was during this marathon that my father, after years of ignoring it, finally decided to come down to the basement to watch the show with us.

It was awful. He just sat there and said, "That's not funny. . . . That's not funny. . . . Why do you boys find this funny?" My brother and I could not wait for him to leave. Through his attitude, he effectively abdicated the right to speak meaningfully into our cultural choices. He hadn't cared about the show before, and he obviously didn't get it now. So what right did he have to criticize our show? He had rejected what we held dear without even trying to understand. In a sense, we felt as if he had rejected us. *That* is parenting from above, parenting from the outside.

Compare that to my decision to join my kids in watching *One Piece*, a show I was tempted to dismiss. By repenting of my above-it-all attitude and jumping in with them, I was in a position to woo their hearts with the gospel and show them how beautifully the gospel shines when compared to what the world offers.

Similarly, when I helped pastor a church with Korean kids, I engaged in their favorite pop music. This opened so many avenues for discussion about deep subjects: sex, work, play, faith, reality. This provided me golden opportunities for getting into important issues with adolescents in a nonthreatening way. But many others had overlooked these opportunities. I remember one high school student coming up and saying, "It's just so weird, having you, an adult, treating this music as if it *means* something." In other words, they only knew parents who habitually dismissed their music as frivolous and not worth discussing or were ready to judge it as too sinful to be worth talking about. How much these parents were missing! They were passing up a golden opportunity to live in their children's worlds and speak encouragement and wisdom into their lives at a delicate time in their development.

****

Of course, sometimes you must say no when your child has gotten involved with a show, game, or music that is age inappropriate, too dark, or too much for them to handle. But *why* you say no and the *way* you say no—these make all the difference.

We will discuss this more in later chapters. For now, suffice it to say that the normal, go-to pattern for incarnational parenting is involvement over judgment. Play the games your kids play. Watch the shows your kids watch. Listen to the songs your kids listen to. And talk about what you find. Enter their world rather than dismissing or judging their cultural choices out of hand. Being involved in this way deepens relationship and helps you to understand your child's heart. And then, when you need to say no, you can talk with your child about the heart issues involved and how to make wise choices given their strengths and weaknesses.

The guiding principle for incarnational parenting is this: we must be present in our children's popular-culture worlds in some significant way. The important word is *significant*. This means we do more than occasionally pop our head into their rooms to see what they are watching on YouTube (though that's advisable). It means finding time to watch stuff, play stuff, listen to stuff *with* your kids and to talk with them about it. If we don't, we're letting our kids build their own little worlds in which popular culture alone, and not the gospel, is wooing their hearts.

5. Gospel-centered parenting raises culturally savvy people lovers.

Let us suppose your child's heart is wooed by the beauty of the gospel, and her imagination begins to be captured by the depth and breadth of God's love for her. Now what should you expect?

One way it will inevitably show is in relationship. The apostle John says repeatedly that if someone really understands what God has graciously done in Christ, it will show in how he loves other people (1 John 3:16–18, 23–24; 4:7–12). This is the truest and most reliable indication that God's transforming grace has gotten ahold of the heart and wooed the affections. People who understand God's crazy love for them will have a hard time suppressing a crazy love for other people. That's why they will also want to share that good news about this grace with others. They will have a natural enthusiasm for sharing, like a fan who has just seen an awesome trailer for a coming movie. There's too much awesome not to share.

But how do you share in a way that people can hear? In our post-Christian culture, most people are dismissive toward Christianity. So do you hoist your Hulk placard and dust off the bullhorn? Or do you step into their world and try to speak their language? This is what culturally engaged gospel-centered parenting prepares your children to do: share the awesome in a language their peers can comprehend.

Of course, sometimes parents should be concerned about the influence of non-Christian friends. Bad company can surely corrupt good character. Parents should be involved with their children's non-Christian friends, as they should be involved with their non-Christian popular culture. But if we truly believe in the gospel's beauty and power to change lives, we will naturally want to follow in Jesus's footsteps and get involved with people who are far from God. That's true for us and for our children.

Yes, children need solid Christian friends, but they also need non-Christian friends. They need to "shine as lights in the world; holding forth the word of life" (Philippians

2:15–16 KJV). *This* is the chief end of gospel-centered parenting: to raise up and equip the next generation of children who worship Jesus and shine like stars to the non-Christians around them as they hold out the word of life.

This is an exciting and weighty calling. Parents shouldn't be preoccupied with only surviving until Jesus returns. We have a job to do: train young apprentices in the art of soul diplomacy. Someday, God willing, student will surpass teacher. Our children will have learned the gospel as lifestyle, walking the path God has put them on with gospel-wooed hearts as they woo others. This is what the Christian parent longs for, our reward for years of engagement with kids and their cultural worlds.

One last thought: no one does this perfectly. Every parent makes mistakes, has regrets, wishes they could find a do-over button. Parenting is messy. Our children are messes, and so are we. But we are messes who have been saved by the blood of the Lamb, in whom the Spirit is working, slowly, patiently. The same gospel to which you are trying to woo your children prevails also for you and your parenting. It's all woven through with grace and divine power.

Chapter 4
The Problem with Hands-Off Parenting

So far, we have seen why we must engage popular culture with our kids, only after we begin to view both popular culture and our parenting in light of the gospel. But no matter how firmly we agree with the gospel, it's easy for us to lose sight of these purposes.

Parents who love the gospel rarely decide, "Gee, today I think I will respond to popular culture in unbiblical ways. Ha, ha!" Instead we lapse into false beliefs from poor teaching on the topic. Or we give in to empty promises of safety for our kids. Or we default to whatever is convenient. Some parents become overprotective—which we will look at in chapter 5. But other parents take a hands-off approach to popular culture. That's what we'll explore in this chapter.

WHAT WE MEAN BY *HANDS-OFF* PARENT

Imagine that popular culture is like another environment you know well: your own home. Every home has items and places that are unsafe for all children. In the garage we keep tools with sharp blades or buckets full of screws and nails. In the kitchen we store cleaning chemicals. Usually adults know how to use all these items safely, but children must learn the differences between things like bleach and water. Naturally, we teach children who are young or immature to avoid certain things. We might also set up rules and install childproof devices such as locks or baby gates. Then as children grow, we begin to teach them to walk up staircases, garden with sharp tools, cook with the stove, and later to drive heavy vehicles. After parental guidance and training, things that were unsafe for little ones become safe for older kids.

Giving a three-year-old keys to the house to explore as she sees fit would not end well. Yet parents sometimes drift into a hands-off parenting approach, ignoring the need to help children understand and engage our culture. Or we intentionally avoid speaking into their experience of popular culture because we want to avoid the legalism we were taught.

In this book we won't be alarmist, but we must speak the truth in love. Popular culture can be like a bleach jug, a steep staircase, or gasoline. We must take caution before we expose a child to any of this because popular culture impacts our kids' spiritual and emotional lives. Kids need parental guidance and engagement, or they might get hurt—maybe not hurt physically but hurt spiritually.

Let's explore some false beliefs that can lead to a hands-off parenting approach to popular culture. We will ask questions that parents may have about intentionality engaging in popular culture with our kids, and we will suggest a biblical answer to those assumptions.

Question: Isn't popular culture just a trivial distraction?

Popular culture seems trivial because popular cultural works are often fleeting. Plenty of people can get along in school and work without watching movies, listening to songs, or playing video games. Others mostly use popular culture to escape from reality or distract themselves. Wouldn't our time be better spent teaching biblical doctrine or morality?

Answer: Popular culture shapes a child's reality.

The fact remains that popular cultural works are actually deeply meaningful in themselves, even when they *seem* trivial to us. When someone says, "Oh, that's *just* a song"—or game, show, movie, book—they forget that it's a product of human creativity, which is part of God's plan for us.

Popular cultural works can indeed distract us, but that does not mean they are *simply* distractions. They also can be deeply meaningful. Some influence our world for generations. All of them influence *somebody's* world for a time. Popular culture offers imaginary worlds for our children to inhabit, and that alone has power to form and transform the inner worlds of our children (and ourselves). These works help shape our beliefs about what is right and wrong, noble and villainous, cool and passé.

In a sense, popular culture isn't an escape from the "real world." This gift *creates* our real worlds. We cannot simply dismiss it as trivial.

Question: Isn't it legalistic and intrusive to guide our children's cultural pursuits so carefully?

Some Christian parents recall the strict rules their own parents imposed on them when they were kids. Or they've heard that legalism is bad, and they don't want to become *that parent*. As a result, they may take a hands-off approach and offer only loose guidelines to their kids about movies and shows and such, in order to avoid legalism.

Legalism *is* a real problem. Legalists look to their own ability to fulfill a rigid list of dos and don'ts rather than trusting in Christ's finished work on their behalf. Such an approach completely overlooks the bankrupt state of our hearts and tends to replace grace with religious rules that separate us and our children from Christ's love. Legalism is an affront to grace. Jesus and Paul both warned against it (Luke 11:37–54; Colossians 2:20–23).

Nevertheless, some Christians favor legalism as a go-to strategy for popular culture. Parents fear popular culture's impact on their kids and seek security in rules rather than in God himself. You don't want to do that, you may argue. You don't want to be like the joyless Pharisees who replaced God's actual commands with human tradition (Mark 7:9).

Answer: God's grace must make us eager to be more discerning.

We agree; it is good to avoid legalism, but a desire to avoid legalism should not cause us to be careless about popular culture.

Parents who worry only about the virus of legalism may develop an infection called "cheap grace."[1] Its symptoms? We treat sin casually, believing that because God saves us, perhaps we need not work out our own salvation. We may also believe that because God has allowed people to make good things in the world, we can accept anything and criticize little in popular culture. This is the opposite of mature and discerning engagement of popular culture!

If we accept cheap grace, we find our hearts hardened to God's mercy. For example, when the nineteenth-century German poet Heinrich Heine lay dying, at the end of his scandalous life, his priest asked if Heine believed God would forgive him. Heine purportedly snapped, "Of course he will—that's his job." This is reckless presumption. By contrast, Paul asked, "Are we to continue in sin that grace may abound?" and firmly answered, "By no means! How can we who died to sin still live in it?" (Romans 6:1–2).

Christ's amazing grace does relieve our burden of duty-driven rule keeping. But this grace is *transforming* grace that frees us to become more like him, reflecting his glory in how we discern and enjoy everything in life. In a mysterious way, we and God actively work together to pursue holiness in Christ: "Therefore, my beloved, as you have always obeyed, so now, not only as in my presence but much more in my absence, work out your own salvation with fear and trembling, for it is God who works in you, both to will and to work for his good pleasure" (Philippians 2:12–13).

We know God enacts his own good will for our kids, transforming them into Christ's image, so we can explore popular culture with our children—or learn where we should abstain—with a healthy "fear and trembling." If we strive to know our children's hearts and draw alongside them into their worlds, we can enjoy popular culture and teach children wise discernment rather than cheap grace.

Question: Haven't we done our job, and kept our kids safe enough, if we simply limit them to "family-friendly" entertainment?

Rather than spending time to engage popular culture with our kids, we may simply choose a category of popular culture that we consider safe and leave them to their own devices. As long as it's *old* TV shows or movies, we assume our children are relatively safe, and we needn't bother being involved. So we make choices based on things like

- **Word of mouth and recommendations.** We depend on the opinions of friends or trusted websites to assure us that a particular show, song, or story is safe.
- **Positive associations.** We trust names of known actors, artists, companies, or directors.
- **Nostalgia.** We fondly remember songs and stories that seem harmless because we recall that they posed no personal temptation for us. For example, many parents smile on classic Disney films such as *Peter*

Pan or *101 Dalmatians* or classic TV series such
as *The Andy Griffith Show* and *Little House on the
Prairie*. One fan of a Christian media service's social
media page said directly, "We need for television
shows to be as they were in 1950."[2]

What happens next? Christian parents may presume
their job is done and their children will fare well if they only
supply them with "wholesome" popular culture. Then we
may assume that if growing children want to enjoy anything
else, that's at best a risky exception. Parents may also decide
that if a story or song contains nothing objectionable (such
as violence or sex), or if the product was made by Christians,
then parents have no need to engage these stories with their
children. After all, aren't these stories safe?

Answer: "Safe" isn't always spiritually safe. Idols often hide under *safe* or *family-friendly* labels.

Sure, older stories or songs, which have stayed popular
for generations, may have fewer easily-spotted objectionable
elements such as swearing, violence, or overt subversion of
biblical sexual morality. Familiar or intentionally wholesome
stories may also seem more age appropriate for younger or
less mature children when parents can't be around.

However, family-friendly/safe/wholesome does not mean
"free of the distorting power of sin and idolatry." For example, even some beloved classic TV shows, without bad words
or innuendo, still present messy themes that parents must help
their children discern.

- In the *I Love Lucy* episode "The Séance," Lucy starts
  getting into horoscopes and numerology and even (as
  the title gives away) attempts to contact the dead.[3]
- *The Andy Griffith Show* episode "Three Wishes
  for Opie" finds Barney Fyfe, Floyd Lawson, and

Goober Pyle also trying a séance. This time, Barney uses occult items designed to put him in touch with a ghost, who does actually grant wishes.[4]

- *Little House on the Prairie* frequently reflects pictures of idyllic 1800s culture in a version of the American frontier that includes local church life, prayer, or even miracles attributed to God. However, the series shows a Christianity-derived religion that has little to do with the biblical gospel of repentance and faith in Jesus Christ. Many of these stories often show faith as a means to family values, rather than vice versa.

We could go into other potential hazards of "safe" stories and songs, such as greed, materialism, or instances of racism and sexism that classic television stories may play for laughs— or pretend didn't exist. For example, we don't see any black people living in Mayberry. If parents do not explore these messy stories with their children, these stories could tempt some children (and parents!) to idolatry, based on their hearts' temptations and their assumptions about how the world works.

Even some Christian popular culture can appear to endorse idols in disguise, such as

- Honoring the nuclear family over other members of the church, such as unmarried Christians or couples who cannot have children, encouraging families to become insular and leaving singles lonely and excluded in the Christian community.
- Echoing moral self-righteousness, which makes the gospel irrelevant and turns people cold, hard, and unforgiving.
- Teaching the health-and-wealth or prosperity gospel, which twists God into a genie who rewards faith with success and ignores the gospel that includes suffering.

Creators of Christian entertainment may not intend to offer idols in disguise. But because they are sinners living in a fallen world, they cannot help promoting idols that are often invisible to those creators themselves. We are all still learning to discern and fight our own idols. If we overlook the idols in family-friendly culture, how will our children learn to recognize them? How will they avoid the seduction of family-friendly idols?

What if we simply tried to improve on our family-friendly culture to make sure we keep it free of idols? For instance, some parents may want Christian storytellers to create characters who act only in basically good ways or who are taught clear moral lessons so that children will also be taught moral behavior. If a Christian-authored book shows a hero who makes a bad choice, parents may assume the work itself is bad—as if portraying characters realistically, as fallible and sinful, leads children into sin.

For example, one Christian-published book recounts the semiautobiographical story of a girl growing up in her Swedish Christian family and includes chapters about her disobedience as a child. One reviewer wrote, "I feel that my children will come away from this book thinking that some sins are justifiable, like . . . name calling, lying, stealing, etc."[5] This parent assumes that the only legitimate function of a story is to give children moral instruction, but Scripture itself would not pass this standard. She ignores how stories glorify God in other ways, such as showing "whatever is true" about the real world—in which children do in fact sin!

In fact, sometimes the stories that seem safest and most full of light are actually spiritually dangerous. Paul warns us to beware of "angels of light" (2 Corinthians 11:14) that appear good and shiny but are really emissaries of the Evil One. Often, we assume this verse is meant for *other* people who are susceptible to being tricked by evil in disguise but that we are somehow immune. Paul's point, however, is that evil can look good *to us personally*. Evil can appear as *our* angel of light, as an idol crafted to appeal to *our* hearts.

Just because a piece of popular culture claims to be Christian does not mean it is idol-free. It often means its idols will likely be *more difficult* to spot because they are the idols of our Christian subculture. For example, if we idolatrously believe that life and meaning can be found ultimately in a perfect church or family, some stories and songs (including those made by Christians) will offer us that graven image. And if we fear for our children's safety, we will idolize some Christian cultural works that *promise* to keep our children safe—regardless of whether they reflect our only true security, the gospel.

Yes, a person's desire for safe entertainment for children can itself become an idol, like an acceptable white magic that Christian grown-ups trust to transform their children's hearts instead of trusting the Spirit of Christ. However, good stories that might not look so "good" can glorify God by encouraging our empathy for sinful, fallible people. Good stories and other popular cultural works also help guide us into love and repentance by exposing the motives of the bad guy, especially when his sin causes us to examine our own hearts. In fact, the Bible itself already does this.

Stephen's story: Christians don't dance?

Well-intended Christian stories may weaken or even contradict biblical truth, especially in the eyes of a child who isn't yet skilled at seeing all things in light of the gospel.

As a child, I read plenty of books from Christian publishers. In one semiautobiographical children's chapter book, a stern schoolmaster warns children to stop pretend dancing. In another book, a father teaches as gospel truth the notion that children can never pretend to be bad guys. Neither story questioned the grown-ups' teachings. In fact, the stern father's legalistic lecture was the lesson of that story! As a result, for years I actually assumed these rules reflected authentic Christianity (and my parents may have never known).

Christian writer Alan Noble recalls a similar childhood response to a bit of Christian popular culture, the children's VHS series *McGee and Me*. In "The Big Lie," a kid named Nick tells a tale about his scary neighbor. In a side story, his cartoon sidekick McGee breaks a window, blames a little boy, and watches as the boy is dragged off by cops. Noble writes, "The 'biblical' lesson is that no matter how trivial a lie might be, once spoken, it begins a web of destruction and evil, consuming innocent people, cutting us off from God, and making an already-crucified Christ cry. Oh, wretched man that Nick is! Who or what will rescue him from this body of death? . . . Nick is overwhelmed with guilt and fear, and his father's response is to further explain the incomprehensible evil which he has committed, and then to tell him to just go figure it out."[6]

Children might correctly interpret this and similar stories if they know the surrounding context of Christ's gospel of redemption (to which the McGee story subtly alludes). But if children are just beginning to understand the gospel, the story might instead lead them to confusion or despair. Some kids may even interpret the story as teaching legalism, and as a result they may resist the gospel when they encounter it. We must understand all stories in light of the gospel, and who will give children that gospel context if not us?

"Family-Friendly" Stories Can Leave Children Unprepared for the World Outside Their Homes

Some parents may use Christian or family-friendly entertainment as a buffer against the world outside their own family. They may feel that the best way to keep kids safe in that dark world is to present their children with sanitized versions of reality.

Because of this expectation, even mildly edgier Christian-made culture makes some believers nervous. For example, the creators of a 2014 remake of *Left Behind* (the one with Nicolas Cage) promoted the movie to Christians. But some Christians, based on their social-media comments, responded with alarm because even a mild movie apocalypse wasn't safe or family-friendly enough. Their reaction ignores the purpose of human stories and songs. At its best, popular culture reflects both the real and the ideal—the way the world is and the way we long for the world to be. When we want to show kids only a "safe" world, without dark or disturbing themes, we may demonstrate that we prefer wishful thinking to the truth. Such popular culture will leave children unprepared for the complexities and nuances of reality beyond the home.

If family-friendly stories are poorly made, this actually presents another subtle hazard to children and adults. It teaches us that creative excellence is somehow secondary as long as the message is "wholesome." That's a lie that has done much damage to the church, which should glorify God with cultural excellence before a watching world.

For all these reasons, we carefully conclude that family-friendly popular culture contains problems parents often don't see. Notice that we do not cry in moral panic, *"Safe" stories and songs are always dangerous, and "wholesome, family-friendly" entertainment is a lie!* Rather, we say, let's quit giving this culture a free pass. Let us grow out of assumptions that family-friendly or "Christian" stories are the only beneficial stories. Instead, let us take the same precautions with these stories as we would with any culture. *Any* story and song will include ugliness and untruth to some degree. After all, we still live in this dark age and await the dawning of Christ's new creation. We and our kids need to give family-friendly culture the same intentional engagement as any form of popular culture.

Question: Can't Christian resources do the job for us?

Christian parents have many resources to help us understand popular culture, such as books, movie-review websites, and recommendations from family and friends. Some of these resources can be quite helpful. Can we outsource our discernment by using these resources in place of personal involvement with our kids' favorite entertainments?

Answer: Some resources may reflect the gospel but still have poor Bible teaching or ignore the biblical purposes of culture.

God bless many Christian leaders for trying to help parents exercise discernment in the world. After all, we are the body of Christ, and some of us are gifted with more talent for analyzing popular culture than others. Such Christian leaders, ministries, and reviewers can certainly advise parents in their job. (After all, that is what we seek to do in this book.)

However, if we outsource our own jobs and depend solely on trusted leaders to tell us what to think about popular culture, we bypass real engagement with our children. We risk abandoning our own responsibility to be guides and mentors. We abdicate our God-given responsibility to raise our children.

Some of these resources also vary in quality and could be based on faulty theology or traditional assumptions rather than God's Word. Even Christian or culturally conservative leaders who profess faith in the gospel can have flawed approaches to popular culture. Parents should exercise biblical discernment not only about popular culture but also about the Christian resources they wish to consult about popular culture. We suggest parents ask these questions of any cultural discernment resource:

- How do the beliefs and words of the Christian reviewers compare with the gospel and gospel truths? How well does their behavior align with gracious actions?

- Do the reviewers try to view popular culture's purpose according to Scripture? Or do they simply assume popular culture is neutral, sinful, or a distraction? Do they oversimplify or settle for shallow assessments, such as simply assuming that family-friendly stories are always the best kind?
- Does the reviewer have anything to gain from working audiences into moral outrage—such as ratings, political clout, or selling their own programs?
- Does the reviewer bother understanding the work of popular culture before launching into criticism? Or is he a leader with an ax to grind?

No one can offer a one-size-fits-all resource because each child has different spiritual strengths and weaknesses. Cultural discernment resources from ministry leaders, pastors, or authors can help you, but they can never replace you. Be discerning about the discerners and separate their wheat from the chaff. And always understand that your mission of child-rearing starts with you, the parent.

Question: I feel overwhelmed engaging with my kids and popular culture! Do I have to deal with this alone?

Some of us are thinking, *This is too much to follow.* Or, *It's too academic.* Or, most likely, *You ask the impossible! There's no way I can keep up with all those new shows, games, memes, apps, and artists!* These are not small concerns.

Answer: If you belong to a church, you have help around you!

Christian parents do not raise their children alone, trapped within the walls of a home. They join other believers in a church, a local body of Christ. Even in small churches, other Christian parents have raised godly children. They have a combined total of hundreds of years of experience. Let's learn from them! After all, we are not the first generation seeking to raise discerning children in a world full of popular culture.

Of course, we must test all the parenting wisdom we hear against Scripture, but you mustn't go it alone. Ask your church leaders if your church offers some sort of support network for parents raising kids in a popular cultural world. If they do not, then you may have to take initiative. Meet over coffee, send an invitation to dinner or dessert, or watch a movie together with other parents and talk about it. If it's hard to get a group of parents together, take your children's or youth's minister out to dinner. Find a couple in your church who are kindred spirits, but older and wiser than you, and plan to spend time together. In the body of Christ, there is no reason for any parent to feel overwhelmed and isolated. Take heart and find help!

Question: What if I don't have time to engage popular culture with my children?

Even if we know our children's entertainments matter, we also know life is crazy. Already we spend so much effort feeding and clothing the little tykes. Sometimes busy parents are tired, and we just need to start a movie or send our child to a game in the next room, so they will stay quiet and entertained while we try to recover. How can we find even more time for all this engagement?

Answer: This is an amazing opportunity that gets easier with practice and need not be a burden.

Busy parents may suspect they can't do this without a three-inch Christian curriculum notebook with a Scripture-supported worldview-analysis program in 122 easy steps. For a topic that is vital to our God-given identity and mission in the world, a training course would indeed help. But we don't need a course to begin rebooting our assumptions about popular culture and our calling as parents. We began this book with that reboot, so you're already better equipped to explore popular culture with your children.

With practice, the whole process gradually comes to feel more natural. We no longer struggle through a foreign language. We realize that popular culture has always been our language, the language of humanity, this whole time.

We (the authors) have often "caught" this from others who *lived out* joyful Christian cultural engagement every day in small and big ways. Real-life practice with real people can be more helpful than formal lessons. So if you choose to use cultural worldview studies about popular culture, please use them as ways to listen to your children's actual questions and enjoy open conversations with them. All the parenting programs in the world will not give parents ears to hear their children. Kids need parents with hearts and minds willing to listen, engage, and guide.

This doesn't have to feel burdensome if you go about it wisely. For example, if you have young or pre-teen children, you could introduce them to the popular culture you enjoyed as a child. Children love to get to know another facet of your personality. And it's a great way to start because you are already familiar with these works. It's super effective!

However, parents cannot expect their children, who are growing up in an ever-changing world, to only enjoy the popular culture of yesteryear. As children get older, they begin to care less about their parents' old entertainments and more about their friends' current entertainments. For example, Jared says he will always enjoy Dallas Cowboys football and the television shows *MacGyver* and *Tom and Jerry* because he and his dad watched them together for hours, but he also developed new cultural tastes.

As children become less interested in their parents' choices, parents who are serious about engagement *will* need to invest more time. That's why we do encourage parents to schedule time for popular culture "homework." But aside from the work to which we're called, engagement should also be restful. It is tremendous *fun* to spend time with children and enjoy together the popular culture that fascinates them. For example, in the Turnau household, Ted and his family have clocked many hours reading fantasy novels aloud, playing video games, and watching movies and television shows (especially anime) with their children. It has brought them closer and led to many vital discussions.

This does require intentional time-budgeting. For example, parents whose children can't get enough of a seemingly mindless television cartoon may need to sit down with their children and view a few episodes to think about the stories and discuss them. Who knows? There might be more there than they first thought.

Popular culture does not come at us lecture style. Instead, it brings story, image, rhythm, and sound to spark little moments of revelation in our hearts. Parents can use these when children ask a question or repeat a popular culture quote. Such moments can shape a child's life more than any formal curriculum could.

What if we simply found time—perhaps even the time we already make for our own entertainment—to love our children by showing them that we take their popular culture seriously? What if we simply enjoyed what they enjoy without first launching into criticism? This alone would mean the world to children, with or without a formal curriculum. Our children would see their favorite grown-ups approach popular culture not with boredom or carelessness, or as entertaining diversions, but with joy and intentionality. This alone would make a huge impact on how the children themselves approach popular culture.

Stephen's story: The power of a parent's casual observation

When my parents bought a new van for our family, it came with an amazing, incredible, fantastic technology: a small television set with VHS player right there in the van. You could watch videos. On the road! In 1992, of all times! So we did. So many videos. They included a tape my mom picked up at the store called *Yogi's Great Escape*, which featured Hanna-Barbera's smarter-than-average bear on the run from Ranger Smith and company.

I wasn't the biggest fan of this cartoon, but my younger siblings watched it repeatedly. My parents may have never seen it, but from the front seat, they heard it plenty. And at one point, Ranger Smith is car-chasing Yogi and Boo-Boo. He orders them to pull over. Yogi, of course, doesn't conform, opting instead for various picnic basket-based hijinks.

Then my mom or dad remarked, "Doesn't seem like Yogi has much respect for authority."

To this day I remember even this brief, casual engagement with the story. My parents took the story seriously, having understood the story's context, and offered a moment of gentle challenge. It was perfect for a child of nine or ten. Their remark got my mind spinning. Was Yogi Bear right to try to escape? How much authority did Ranger Smith have, even outside Jellystone Park? Can we laugh at such cartoon acts of rebellion, and if so, how come?

PRACTICAL TIPS FOR FINDING TIME TO ENGAGE

First, if you feel overwhelmed, Ted's family once heard this golden advice from their church's children's pastor: "Deliberately set up schedules to make it easy on you." In this case, you could determine the hours you have at home with your children then set a pattern. For example, you could find an hour or ninety minutes after supper and cleanup, time that doesn't interfere with homework and family Bible devotions, for enjoying popular culture with your kids. During this time you can watch a show together, play a game, and read a book aloud.

Second, remind yourself of seasons of life. Smaller children will need more immediate time and attention. Older children are more independent and will need less. When you are in a pattern that seems burdensome despite your best time-management efforts, remind yourself that this is not permanent. It is a season of life, and it will change as your child changes. Learn to savor each season for what it is. This will help you enjoy the process of raising children rather than seeing it as a prison.

Third, engaging in popular culture with your child does not mean that you have to watch everything your child watches or listen to every song or play every video game. If your child is really, really into Lightning McQueen, watching a *Cars* movie fifty times will drive you bonkers. But you do need to watch a *Cars* movie at least once or twice (more if you too are really into Lightning McQueen). Be knowledgeable enough about what your child enjoys that you can have meaningful conversations about certain key shows, movies, games, and songs. And let your children know that participating in their entertainment is not a burden for you but a joy—even if you can only take that certain cartoon in limited doses.

MOVING PAST HANDS-OFF PARENTING

This is indeed a daunting responsibility, with a lot to learn and many risks. You are not alone in this mission. We wrote this book to encourage you! However, Christians know a far better "resource guide" for this task of parenting in popular culture. The Father sent his Son as a shepherd. He draws alongside us by his Spirit to encourage and advise us (John 14:16–18, 26; 16:7–15).

Moreover, you are part of the family of God. You have brothers and sisters who are wiser than you. They have raised children to love Jesus, and they have much experience to share. Ask them! You may also know brothers and sisters who are gifted in doctrine or cultural savvy. Let them love you and your family. Write a list of questions and invite them for coffee. Ask them to pray for you and advise you how to go about this. This is how the church ought to work. It doesn't mean they are infallible—the final decision rests with you, not with their advice. But we all need the help, so be encouraged!

Finally, browse our resource list at the back of this book. It includes several specific ministries—including ours—and other places you can use to find reviews and more to help get you started.

As grown-ups entrusted with the raising and teaching of children, we must recall that we aren't at the top of the parenting chain. The Father is. No one is so mature that we cannot step back, evaluate our own hearts and temptations, and humbly concede, "Yes, I'm tempted by the hands-off approach to popular culture. I'm tempted to be lax about teaching my children how to handle popular culture."

To switch metaphors, parenting means running—not running *from* the world of popular culture but running *to* the safety and wisdom of our Savior. We resist the temptation to be lax in our own shepherding because we want to follow the Good Shepherd. He intentionally guides his flock—including you, his child—beside still waters and restores your soul. He laid down his life for his sheep. He is trustworthy. So put on your robe and sandals, grab your staff, and pursue your child-shepherding call with confidence in the gospel and the wisdom God gives needy parents. The Good Shepherd has your back.

Chapter 5

The Problem with Endless Childproofing

We have explored how Christian parents can forsake gospel-centered parenting by taking a hands-off approach to their children's popular culture enjoyments. But what happens when parents go to the opposite extreme? What if parents make "avoid and suspect" their default response to human stories and songs? Is it possible to be overly cautious? What problems come with always saying no, or not yet, to popular culture?

What Do We Mean by "Endless Childproofing"?

To illustrate, let's return to our image of household dangers. Wise parents lock a home's bathroom cabinets, barricade hallway steps, and keep young or immature children away from items they cannot (yet) use safely for good purposes. But it is possible to take caution too far. What if parents forget to remove locks? What if they actively *refuse* to remove the locks? Imagine warning a ten-year-old to avoid the staircase or forbidding a sixteen-year-old teen from heating noodles on the stove. Parents who do this are not acting out of discernment, wisdom, or conviction but out of fear.

Some parents know popular culture can be dangerous to young children, so they childproof by locking away culture without any planned end date. For example, columnist Rod Dreher, who is known for his "Benedict Option" response to culture, remarks,

> As longtime readers know, we homeschool our kids, so they are not exposed to the usual American pop culture trends. We do not fully shelter them from the culture, not at all, but we curate what they are allowed to see. We have zero participation in American television culture, except for old things we choose to watch with Netflix and Amazon Prime. Point is, we are blissfully unaware of how the cult spreads through the culture. . . . We are going to have to take radical steps to withdraw from this popular culture if we are going to spare our kids its madness.[1]

We certainly see wisdom in curating what immature or young children are allowed to see. However, Dreher recommends zero participation with any newer TV shows. Parents who do the same may not have given any thought about popular culture's original purpose from a biblical perspective. Perhaps they haven't considered any plan for how and when to withdraw these childproofing measures so that children can mature and wisely engage the world around them.

Endless childproofing can cause children to grow up believing they only glorify God individually in "spiritual" ways but not in cultural ways, as God has told us to do. They can begin to equate holiness with "blessed ignorance" and isolation. They become cut off from their neighbors.

In extreme cases, Christian teenagers can be left as naïve as young children about the world around them. For example, Stephen has encountered children so unfamiliar with simple things of culture that seeing televisions in public left them confused and enthralled. In another case, a sixteen-year-old young adult was forbidden to view G-rated Pixar films unless the parents saw them first (which they often never got around to actually doing).

Such an approach replaces Scripture's perspectives on popular culture with human fears or traditions. Anytime we say, "This is what the Bible says," when in fact the idea comes only from a Christian friend or leader, we must reevaluate our beliefs. Despite our best intentions, such rules and traditions have the potential to create at least four different relational barriers: between our children and the world they are called to engage as Christ's ambassadors, between our children and the church, between our children and ourselves as parents, and, most seriously, between our children and God himself.

In this chapter, we will again use a question-and-answer format to compare false assumptions with Scripture and take care to discern the bad ideas and good motives. But we'll also recognize legitimate concerns about how and when to guard—not only guide—our children in popular culture.

Question: If popular culture is corrupt, shouldn't we avoid exposing our children to this toxic influence?

Let's not downplay the truth: our cultural entertainments reflect God-given human creativity, but they're also tainted by sinful motives and ideas. So if popular culture can be used to corrupt young, impressionable minds, why should we participate? Shouldn't responsible parents avoid the whole sinful mess in the name of preserving children's innocence?

Answer: Isolation won't keep corruption away nor lead children to be convicted of their sin.

Remember that children are not innocent but, in fact, are born with a sinful nature and need to be saved. Still, sometimes we can't help but believe our children are *relatively* innocent. We are partly correct because the world does have plenty of nastiness young children don't know about: internet porn, photos of terrorist violence, casual blasphemies by comedians. It's also true that children, especially small children, imitate behavior of characters they like and think are cool. Even we adults can find in popular culture enticements to lust or anger or covetousness. So the idea that it might "corrupt the youth" seems to make sense, but more needs to be said.

One suspense film explores what happens when humans try to stay pure by avoiding the surrounding culture, when they protect their families from an outside world of sin through isolation and rules. In *The Village* (2004), director M. Night Shyamalan shares the story of an 1897-era community where residents have no contact with other villages. The village's elders urge people to live in harmony and follow rules. Rule 1: avoid objects with the wrong color, red. Rule 2: do not stray into the village's surrounding woods, for there dwells a race of frightening creatures in dark robes. The villagers call them, "Those We Do Not Speak Of."

One young man, Lucius, grows restless and asks the village elders if he can go to the towns. His mother says no. Towns are "wicked places where wicked people live," she says. Lucius tries to be content. It helps that he and a young blind woman, Ivy, are pursuing a chaste, parent-supervised courtship and then marriage. All seems to be going well.

But sin is crouching at the village's door. Noah, a jealous young man whose mental disorder gives him the mind of an "innocent" child, attacks Lucius and stabs him. The community is paralyzed, and the elders lock Noah away. Should they let Lucius die or try something? The elders appoint Ivy to find medication in the wicked towns. They say the evil forest creatures will not attack an innocent, blind woman. However, we soon learn the elders have built their entire society on multiple deceits. They started with the great lie that laws and cultural seclusion could guard them from evil. But that evil already lives among them, not only in the heart of the young man Noah but in their own hearts.

Jesus knows human hearts. He knows we prefer to blame our sin on anything besides ourselves. That's why he challenged the Pharisees' attempts to scapegoat things in the world rather than confronting their own heart problems. Jesus never taught people to make up rules (the Pharisees' tradition of the elders in Mark 7:3) to protect them from the supposed worst corruptions "out there." Instead, he proclaimed the kingdom and called people to repent of their inward corruption.

If salvation primarily meant conformity to acceptable behavior, then parents would sensibly expose their children only to popular culture that features acceptable behavior. But true salvation engages the heart in a deep-love relationship with God that makes us grateful, eager to please our Father, and confident of forgiveness after we fail. If salvation is God's work and goes deeper than our obedience or disobedience, then nothing can separate your child from his love! *Nothing* means nothing, not "height nor depth, nor anything else in all creation" (Romans 8:39). This includes popular culture.

As pastor/author/music producer/parent Mike Cosper says, "While our stories [from TV and movies] are indeed shaping our hearts and imaginations, they cannot do any permanent damage to those who are in Christ. In other words, you're not going to watch a movie that will steal your soul; the world can't really hurt you. Instead, you can take comfort in knowing that you're forever secure in the hands of Jesus."[2]

The gospel's rock-solid stability allows us to train our children how to live wisely in a world where we find all sorts of bad models, false and dangerous ideas, and tempting paths. But such training is necessary if we plan to follow Jesus where he has placed us, rather than trying to recreate our own narrowly enclosed world, like the residents of *The Village*.

Remember, in parenting, we must prioritize our child's heart desires. A child who stumbles into sin is not a mark of shame for the parent. Rather, it is an opportunity to apply the grace of the gospel to a softened, repentant heart. It is an honest, teachable moment wherein the gospel can shine. Popular culture, even in its depiction of sin and idolatry, can likewise be an excellent way of bringing about teachable moments, exposing the motives of the heart so that gospel truth might be applied. If children will grow into mature Christians, they must be able to live in the world, relying on God's grace rather than remaining sequestered from it, fooling themselves that they don't need grace. Parents also need reminders: this world is not a scary, unpredictable world where anything can happen. It is a world governed by a loving God who cares deeply for your children and in whose arms they are eternally secure. It is a world we can approach with confidence as we look for opportunities to engage the heart.

Question: Why bother with popular culture when our children can learn all they need to know from the Bible?

Many Christian preachers have ignored their call to teach the Bible. Instead, they may have sermon series with titles based on popular TV series. Or they might string together a series of personal anecdotes and moral lessons rather than bringing to their congregations what the Word of God has to say in a particular text. In response to this error, we might say, "We don't want to be like those guys. So let's only teach our children the Bible."

Answer: If we obey the Bible itself, we must follow both of God's great commands, to make disciples and to share in culture.

One sixteenth-century Reformation slogan was *sola scriptura!*, that is, "Scripture alone!" We believe in this principle. The Bible alone is our final authority on Christian faith and practice—the means God has appointed to help us grow to be more like Jesus in the world.

However, if we respect the truth of *sola scriptura*, we must surely obey the Bible's Cultural Mandate and Jesus's Great Commission, so we can bring people to Jesus. This means knowing the popular myths and narratives they know. In this case, if we respect the Bible's authoritative command for us to make disciples, this means we cannot limit ourselves to just the Bible. The Bible alone is our authority, but it is not our only source of information about the world or those we are called to love.

The great theologian Karl Barth is famously reported to have said preachers should have a Bible in one hand and a newspaper in the other, yet "interpret newspapers from your Bible."[3] We would add: any effective Christian ambassador should also subscribe to a streaming service or two. We should have a few movie ticket stubs in our back pocket, a best-selling novel in our backpacks, or a good pop album on our music players.

The Bible's definition of *spiritual* is wider than we imagine and includes the gift of popular culture. Christians can unwittingly erect boundaries between so-called "spiritual" pursuits, like prayer and Bible reading, versus "material" pursuits. This is called dualism, and it clashes with the Bible's teaching that God created us to glorify him in material, creaturely ways.

When Christians receive with thanksgiving the good things God has given us—such as nature, sex, and even politics and sports—they help recover a biblical vision of spirituality. All of these things are spiritual *if* we enjoy them in a way that conforms to the Spirit's will for us—that is, with thanksgiving and not as substitute gods. However, many Christians still look at popular culture with dualistic assumptions. For example, we may assume that physical sports can be redemptive and build character but video games are a waste of time and "unspiritual." Or we may assume that Christians can engage in politics for good purposes but shouldn't waste time reading comic books.

Parents who teach kids to enjoy popular culture in a God-honoring way are performing an intensely spiritual task: they teach children to see culture through Bible-enlightened eyes.

Question: Don't certain Bible verses clearly teach us that we stay godly by avoiding the world's influence?

When Christians warn about popular culture's risks, they often refer to specific Bible verses, such as Psalm 101:3; Ephesians 5:11–13; Philippians 4:8; and 1 Thessalonians 5:22.

Answer: We must read these verses in their original contexts.

When many Christian leaders speak of popular culture at all, they emphasize warning about the dangers of popular culture or the hazards of cultural engagement. They do not also explore the Bible's positive presentation of human culture sharing. Still, let's look closer at Bible verses often used to support a warning-only view of popular culture. (For pastors and leaders, we'll delve into a little Hebrew and Greek to understand these texts.)

Psalm 101:3

I will not set before my eyes
    anything that is worthless.
I hate the work of those who fall away;
    it shall not cling to me.

Many Christians believe David's words support modern cautions against watching movies and television or playing video games. If any entertainment contains something "worthless" (older translations used the words *vile* or *wicked*), then we should not set it before our eyes.

However, that seemingly obvious interpretation of Psalm 101:3 misunderstands the Hebrew verb *shiyth*, "to set before." In this context of this psalm, to set before one's eyes does not merely mean "to have in one's field of vision." It means something more like "to set one's mind to, to set as a course of action." This is why, in the verse's second half, David talks about his hatred of those who fall away—that is, those who deviate from righteousness by pursuing worthless idols. It's not about the vision of the eyes as much as the vision of the heart and will. Psalm 101:3 warns us against pursuing idolatry, not only watching certain things on TV.

Christians who rely on Christ's righteousness can engage cultures with ungodly values if we do not let false gods entice our hearts. We can train our children to do the same.

Ephesians 5:11–13

> Take no part in the unfruitful works of darkness, but instead expose them. For it is shameful even to speak of the things that they do in secret. But when anything is exposed by the light, it becomes visible.

For many Christians, this meaning seems simple enough: withdraw from darkness. Popular culture sometimes portrays "unfruitful works of darkness," such as murders and sexual sin. So we should refrain from participating by abstaining from watching, listening, or playing a cultural work that edges too close to that territory, right?

But this passage does not say to fear the world; it says to intentionally shine light into darkness. The meaning of this passage turns on two important words.

1. The word *sunkoinōneite* ("take part") in verse 11 means "to join in fellowship with." You can even see *koinōnía*, "fellowship," in the middle of the word.

Christians are not to join in with non-Christians in clearly sinful activities.[4] Non-Christians perform deeds of darkness that Christians must not participate in. Presumably Paul is referring to the list of sins he mentions earlier in this same chapter (see vv. 3–7), such as sexual immorality and greed, as well as obscene and vulgar talk. Paul clearly forbids Christians from joining with non-Christians in an evil common cause. But for Paul, participation does not mean merely "witnessing evil behavior." It means "joining forces with people who commit evil behavior."

2. The word *elénchete* ("expose") in verse 13 means to convict someone by bringing something hidden to the light, out in the open. The late biblical scholar John Stott pointed out that, in the context of the whole passage, Paul is probably saying this occurs quite naturally simply by living as children of light.[5] Living as Christians will inevitably expose evil and bring conviction to those alienated from God, as surely as a flashlight reveals something hidden in darkness. The idea that the light exposes the darkness presupposes that the light shines *in the darkness* rather than remaining sheltered (say, under a bushel basket, as in Matthew 5:15–16). Letting the light shine to expose the deeds of darkness only happens when we dwell near those alienated from God *and* their culture.

What about verse 12? Paul seems to warn against even speaking about what evildoers do in secret. But Paul himself speaks about secret evils in Romans 1:24–32; 1 Corinthians 6:9–10; 1 Timothy 1:8–11, and elsewhere. The Bible also reveals some secret evils (see Genesis 19:30–38 or Judges 19, for example). Is Paul a hypocrite? Is the Bible off base here?

No, Paul is underlining the shamefulness of the secret deeds of darkness and warning the Ephesians not to dwell on them. We must read verse 12 with verse 13: "But when anything is exposed by the light, it becomes visible." As we live out our faith, our light will naturally reveal shameful truths about the lives of non-Christians.

To be sure, if Christians are tempted to *dwell on* some evil ideas, images, or emotions in cultural works, it is best to avoid these works. But to use this passage to avoid *all* contact with non-Christian popular culture misses the point.

Philippians 4:8

> Finally, brothers, whatever is true, whatever is honorable, whatever is just, whatever is pure, whatever is lovely, whatever is commendable, if there is any excellence, if there is anything worthy of praise, think about these things.

Many Christians use this passage as a checklist to discern a cultural work's suitability for children of any age. Is a cultural work true, honorable, just, pure, lovely, commendable, excellent, and praiseworthy? Then it's OK. Or does the cultural work include anything that does not fit on this list? If so, then it fails the checklist, regardless of the Christian's maturity level.

This interpretation misses Paul's points in this passage and in his letter to the Philippians. *Honorable, lovely, commendable, excellent,* and *praiseworthy* are unusual words not found elsewhere in his letters. Most commentators agree that these terms originated not in the Old Testament but from pagan Greek moral philosophers of the time.[6] In other words, to make this list, Paul actually drew upon the non-Christian culture around him! In effect, Paul borrowed from the culture around him to help us see good and true things in that culture. As Bible commentator Gordon Fee puts it,

For many who were raised in evangelical traditions, verse 8 ought to be a breath of fresh air. Contrary to what is often taught, implicitly if not explicitly, there is a place in Christian life for taking into serious account the best of the world in which we live, even though it may not be (perish the thought!) overtly Christian. Or to put it another way, it is decidedly not Paul's view that only what is explicitly Christian (be it literature, art, music, movies or whatever) is worth seeing or hearing. Truth and beauty are where you find them. But at all times the gospel is the ultimate paradigm for what is true, noble or admirable.[7]

This verse is far from a checklist mentality for popular culture. Instead, Paul propels us to look for whatever good is to be found in our world.

1 Thessalonians 5:22

Abstain from all appearance of evil (KJV).

Some Christians believe we must not only avoid committing actual sins but also avoid anything that could *appear* evil to someone else. However, a quick study of the full chapter in 1 Thessalonians shows that the term *eidos* ("appearance" in the King James Version) has nothing to do with someone's opinion of how something looks.

Paul tells Christians to respect teachers but also test them, no doubt by comparing their teachings with Scripture and the gospel. They must avoid false teaching—not what *appears* to be false but what is actually false. The King James Version's "appearance" is better translated into current-day English as "form" or "kind" of evil.[8] In fact, no modern Bible translation uses "appearance" here, and original readers of the KJV probably took *appearance of evil* to mean actual evil.[9]

Indeed, to misread it as meaning "anything that might look evil" leads to an absurd standard no one could keep, not even Jesus. He ate with sinners and talked with prostitutes, and the Pharisees thought his actions appeared to be evil. Jesus claimed to be the great I Am, and the Pharisees picked up stones because it appeared that Jesus had committed blasphemy.

Christians must not let a misreading of this verse restrict our freedom to enjoy certain things with thanksgiving to God. Moreover, if we misuse this verse, we may be fueling hypocrisy, teaching our children that we value outward appearances more than the truth.

Question: If my child is exposed to popular culture's images of sin, won't this cause my child to sin?

Some Christians believe—or act as if they believe—that people who see a picture of sin or have been exposed to knowledge of a sin are actually sinning. We might not find this belief articulated in Christian sermons or commentaries, which are often disinterested in the topic of applying the gospel to popular culture. However, this belief has been common among everyday Christians, possibly filling our void of teaching about biblical discernment and popular culture.

For example, Ted taught a series of workshops on engaging popular culture in a church in the midwestern United States. He planned to show the movie *Pacific Rim* (2013) to the church's youth group. It is rated PG-13, has no sexual content, some violence (against monsters), and fairly mild language. One influential church member looked up the movie on a Christian website, which mentioned that characters misuse the word *God* several times and utter the words *hell* and *damn*. This same member then spread the accusation that, by watching this movie, Ted would "cause the youth in the church to blaspheme." In other words, by hearing the Lord's name taken in vain, Ted would be "forcing" the youth to blaspheme. The church elders allowed Ted to proceed but only after they installed filtering technology, which completely butchered the movie.

Some Christians also seem to assume an even more direct relationship between watching depictions of sin and sin itself. For example, some Christian leaders have condemned any enjoyment of a popular fantasy novel and film series. They enable the idea that any depiction of imaginary acts labeled "magic" is automatically sinful for us. One Christian media host labels "fiction that contains witchcraft, divination, sorcery" as simply "the stuff that God hates."[10] In another broadcast, this host said, "It's a sin. Deuteronomy 18. God hates that stuff. I'm not going to ingest that stuff, nor am I going to let my kids [ingest it]."[11]

Answer: Scripture never claims that seeing sin is the same as sin or will always lead to someone committing sin.

Here we must be direct: People who believe this idea often mean well and are trying to follow a standard of holiness they believe is biblical. But this view of discernment, based on the notion that "seeing sin = committing sin," is not biblical, spiritual, or wise.

Hearing someone blaspheme does *not* cause a person to blaspheme. Sin requires actual motivation and desire. In Ted's case, if the youth of that church desired to swear and curse, motivated by anger or disrespect of God, they didn't need *Pacific Rim* to help motivate them. If they did not, the movie was not going to force them to. And for the fantasy series, if someone indulges in occult practices, they will have done this because of their own heart-level idolatry and not because the story made them do it. Such bogus beliefs about sin actually hinder Christians from dealing with the real problem: our heart desires.

To be sure, a weaker Christian who sees a picture of sin in a story *can* be tempted to sin. But in Romans 14 and

1 Corinthians 8–10, Paul does not apply a one-size-fits-all standard. He does not act as if all Christians have the same struggles. He never assumes we can anticipate every hypothetical situation that would make *anyone* stumble into sin. Instead, Paul encourages love for one another and the pursuit of wisdom in specific situations.

Further, we cannot logically accept that seeing, hearing, or reading sin is itself sin (or will cause us to sin) without also concluding that sin is impossible to avoid. For example, the same Christian media host, later in the same radio episode, praised the classic Jane Austen novel *Pride and Prejudice*. But that story also includes pictures of sin, right down to the two sins named in the title and practiced by Elizabeth Bennet and Fitzwilliam Darcy. If we consistently applied the same "seeing sin = committing sin" standard, we would need to abstain from reading *Pride and Prejudice*, just to be safe against pride and prejudice.

Most Christians (including this radio host) rightly avoid such a claim because they rightly understand that some stories can portray sin without automatically being sinful. They also rightly know that Scripture itself describes a whole host of sins such as idolatry, adultery, murder, blasphemy, and false teaching! To be consistent, we must take our expectations about these stories that show sin and apply these same expectations to *all* popular culture.

At this point, however, some of us might be tempted to think, *Yes, this is so convicting. Our rules are inconsistent. We can't restrict some contemporary novels but allow classic books because they're all full of sin. Therefore, maybe we should not only forbid* Harry Potter *but also* Jane Austen! If we suspect this, then we've gone out of the frying pan and into the fire. Rather, we must have more insight into the real problem: not the images or words out there but the sin that dwells within our own hearts.

Question: Doesn't God give us instincts to know what culture to avoid?

Caution! Your parent senses are tingling! Suddenly you lunge to the side and catch your toddler just before she hurls herself over the edge of a balcony. We thank God for these instinctive moments. These instincts can also help us recognize and guard our children from popular culture that they cannot understand because it's not age appropriate.

Some Christians believe we can use our instincts alone as a way to determine a story or song's acceptability. While parental feelings are important, are they enough? Are they always an accurate indication of God's will?

Answer: Our instincts can help us, but they can also lead us astray.

For example, some Christians have felt a personal revulsion to certain aspects of popular culture, such as Halloween decorations, creepy movie creatures, or even dinosaurs.

Stephen's story: The Bible says dragon pictures are bad?

In the 1990s, I attended a Christian seminar that taught "basic principles of morality" (but mostly the appearance of morality). In classes, I met an older kid named Stuart who liked to draw sketches of dragons. Never before had I imagined things like this, and I felt it best to warn Stuart his sketching was spiritually dangerous.

In this case, for me, what I assumed was my spiritual discernment was actually plain old human fear of the unknown. Unfortunately, this led to quite a real danger: I had claimed to say "the Bible says this" when God's Word said nothing of the sort.

Unfortunately, I think I ended up pressing Stuart under a false conviction. Here's hoping he later learned that one can portray fantasy creatures for God-exalting reasons. After all, the Bible itself describes a dragon as a picture of Satan (Revelation 12) but also describes a dragonlike creature who resembles Godzilla (Job 41) as a picture of God's power!

****

Although our instincts may help us discern our children's unique weaknesses and needs, we cannot rely primarily on instinct, impression, or something like inner nudges as if these are equal to biblical discernment. We need a better guide than that.

Sometimes evil is obvious and ugly. Sometimes we may also need to make sure we don't treat a cartoon picture of evil as if evil itself is a joke. But when Christians are bothered by a creepy-looking image, mask, or toy, it's tempting to explain this as a demonic presence rather than admit to our own (subjective) feelings. But let us not confuse the two. A devil mask is simply a popular image of devils. It has little to do with the true nature of demonic evil itself as the Bible describes it. Never does God's Word reveal what demons or Satan look like, other than saying Satan can appear as an angel of light (2 Corinthians 11:14). Things that give us good vibes might be evil, such as that smiling televangelist in a suit who claims to give the gospel but instead wants to fleece his flock. Things that give us bad impressions might be good, such as the biblical teaching about hell and God's wrath. Only by comparing these ideas to God's Word can we know. It's a far more trustworthy resource for discerning evil.

Question: What if there are younger kids in the house? Shouldn't we keep them sheltered as long as possible?

It feels safer to teach only what's true and avoid showing evil. Why expose our children to specific details about the lies people believe or the sins they commit?

Answer: Children need to see examples of error; it's one way they grow.

Of course, parents should take precautions about what their young or immature children are exposed to when those children cannot discern between truth and error. But as children grow older and more curious, we can actually deepen children's appreciation of the truth by exposing them to error. In fact, if we don't show them unbiblical errors, such as a popular story's presentation of idols, we cannot really train them to discern true from false, like a grown-up. Do we really want our children to stay childlike? Don't we want them to become mature?

John MacArthur notes, "Naiveté is not a trait to be cultivated in our children. Prudishness is foolish immaturity. It leaves our children gullible and vulnerable. The naïve are the easiest targets for the seductive wiles of temptation. Throughout the book of Proverbs, the naïve (*simple* in many translations) are held up as negative examples. It is a grave mistake to think of our children as little angels who need to be handled delicately so they don't get corrupted. Rather, they are corrupt little sinners who need to be led to righteousness."[12]

Suppose your thirteen-year-old girl has been hearing about new television shows, songs, and movies from her older friends. She is eager to go exploring, but should you let her do this when your eight-year-old son can't also come along? You might be tempted to find something that is appropriate for the youngest child and require your older daughter to stick with that story or song so you can all enjoy it together as a family.

But this will frustrate the thirteen-year-old. She wants to grow up. You wouldn't avoid teaching her about deeper biblical subjects (such as the purpose of intimacy in marriage) just because the eight-year-old isn't ready for them. In the same way, you need to let her practice discernment by allowing her to experience more mature cultural works, with the parent serving as guide and "practice partner."

You might adjust family bedtimes and wait until younger children are asleep before staying up with the older kids to enjoy and explore a story that's closer to her interests. Or you may explain to younger siblings that their older brother or sister will soon join high school, then begin driving, so now it's time for more freedom (which the younger kids will eventually enjoy when they reach this age).

Ted's story: Exploring the graces and idols of *Malcolm X*

Our daughter Ruth was still fifteen or sixteen when my wife and I joined her to watch director Spike Lee's film *Malcolm X* (1992). Malcolm X was and remains a controversial figure. This film reflects many of his controversial ideas, including much of the teaching of 1960s Nation of Islam leader Elijah Muhammad. It also shows a man searching for meaning. Malcolm X starts as a manipulative criminal and gains moral integrity. Toward the film's end, he's even repentant and moving in a positive direction. The film also shows America's heritage of racial discrimination.

We must have stopped the film twenty times so Ruth could ask questions: Was there still racism in the United States? (She grew up overseas, so she knew little of America's continuing struggle with racism.) What would have happened if Malcolm had met a compassionate and intelligent Christian in jail (instead of the narrow-minded priest he did meet)? Was Malcolm X right about white people, that they are all "devils"? Why would black people be tempted to believe that? Why did the Nation of Islam kill him at the end? Would he have changed even more had he survived? What would American society have looked like if Martin Luther King and Malcolm X had joined forces?

So many questions and all of them good questions. We got to shine the light of biblical truth on a difficult era and a difficult man. We got to sort out truth from error, wisdom from deception. The gospel shone the brighter because of it. And Ruth took another step toward becoming a grown-up.

MOVING PAST ENDLESS CHILDPROOFING

It makes sense that parents may fear the influence of popular culture on the hearts of their children. But endless childproofing pins our hopes on the wrong savior. Let's trust in God's saving grace, which alone makes us holy. And let's heed his call to us and our children to move out into the world and love it wisely. Equipping kids, rather than perpetually sheltering them, is the way parents move forward in faith and obedience to that call.

Here this book takes a turn. We're done showing you *why* you need to be a pop culture parent. In the following chapters, we'll show you *how* to enter your children's cultural worlds and share gospel wisdom with them.

Chapter 6

Five Simple Steps to Engage Popular Culture with Your Children

Let's remember: it is OK to enjoy popular culture only for the sake of enjoyment. Popular culture is often awesome. Why? Because it is made by those who bear the image of an awesomely creative God.

For example, Ted remembers seeing *The Avengers* (2012) in the movie theater. Four or five times during the movie, he prayed a quick prayer of thanks: "Thank you, God, for letting Joss Whedon write that line." Joss Whedon is an avowed and vocal atheist, but that needn't stop us from enjoying the excellence of his dialogue and storytelling. *That's* one proper way to understand Philippians 4:8. "Whatever is [awesome], . . . think about these things."

But in a fallen world, Christians cannot afford to simply suspend our critical faculties. Yes, give room to let the piece of popular culture speak. But if you just float on that enjoyment, you will have nothing to say to those dwelling in a dark and dying world besides, "Yeah, that was *epic*." Your enjoyment of popular culture should lead you to reflection and discussion with others. Those critical faculties, informed by the Spirit and the Word, need to kick into gear. The good news is that such critical engagement doesn't lessen but enriches our enjoyment of popular culture.

In this chapter, we explore how you can engage popular culture personally. This is a necessary discipline if you expect to be able to teach your children to do the same thing! First, we will present a framework of questions that we call *popologetics*. This will help you unpack and respond to a piece of popular culture. Second, we will explore some mistakes people often make in using popologetics. Third, we will consider how you can simplify these questions for the needs of children.

FIVE QUESTIONS TO ASK ABOUT ANY WORK OF POPULAR CULTURE

It's not difficult to engage critically in popular culture, but it does take some thought and practice. The key is asking the right questions about each story, song, game, or anything we find in human popular culture. (We adapt these from Ted's first book, *Popologetics*.[1])

1. What is the story?

Most popular culture has a story form, and getting that story straight is the basis for everything else. So make sure you understand the story's characters, plot points, conflict, and so on. Do the story justice, at least in your own mind.

2. What is the moral and imaginary world?

The next step is to think about what kind of imaginary world the story has drawn you into. Think about the style of this particular world. Think about how the producers have created this specific style in this specific medium. Ask questions about the moral and spiritual assumptions that exist in this world. Over time you will build up a pretty good feel for the imaginary landscape of this particular popular cultural work.

3. What is good, true, and beautiful in this world (common grace)?

Remember in earlier chapters when we explored *common grace*? Theologians use this phrase to refer to God's good gifts that he gives to all, such as rain and sunshine and the ability for even sinful people to keep reflecting God's image. All popular culture is made by God's image-bearers, so goodness and truth are still woven into our culture. What aspects of this work of popular culture resonate with goodness and truth? What aspects of this world and story is your heart drawn to? What is awesome here, and why? How does the goodness, truth, and awesomeness in this popular cultural work point to the goodness, truth, and awesomeness of God? How does its story connect with God's story?

4. What is false and idolatrous in this world?

A popular cultural work doesn't only shine with goodness. The work also twists that goodness away from its proper role (glorifying God) and into the service of an idol, a God substitute. To critically engage popular culture, you must accurately diagnose that idolatry and show it to be a forgery—a false god.

5. How is Jesus the true answer to this story's hopes?

In this last step, we show how the gospel actually fulfills whatever good hopes, dreams, and promises the idol cannot give us. What promises did the story or song present that its idols cannot actually fulfill? How does the gospel meet our desires for good things in ways the idol cannot match—in ways that show the idol to be a fraud?

Ask and reflect on these five questions, and you begin to explore a Christian view of that popular culture work. This can lead to interesting conversations in which the gospel arises naturally, not shoehorned into a conversation.

MISTAKES PARENTS CAN MAKE WHEN EXPLORING POP CULTURE

In teaching this method to both kids and adults, we often see some misunderstandings.

1. We can forget to respect the style and excellence of human art.

Christians tend to be so focused on content and worldview that they underestimate the significance of form and style. We are used to reading words in the Bible, and we simply don't register other structures as meaningful. Or perhaps Christians lack the vocabulary to describe the look or feel of a piece of popular culture. We have even heard Christians disparage style as proof a cultural work isn't worth engaging. They say, "Oh, that's just about style, not substance."

But style *is* substantial because it *forms and informs* the content of a cultural work. Style gives the imaginary world its own unique spin, and this will shape the meanings and messages that emerge from that world.

So, as engaged parents, spend the time and effort to learn the stylistic vocabularies, tricks, and tropes of different media. For example, if you seriously want to learn about film style, go spend some time watching videos on Vimeo's channel Cinemacuteo (and the dozens of other channels that cover similar territory). It's fun stuff, and you'll learn lots. The videos tend to be short and accessible. And watch lots of well-made films that are worth talking and thinking about (it's a wider category than you might imagine), and consider how and why the director chose *that* particular shot, angle, lighting, and so on.

For example, if you're into music, you might read *Pitchfork* or *Paste* online and listen to songs on the website Bandcamp or even YouTube. If you enjoy video games, search for the particular game followed by the word *playthrough* to get a feel for it.

Stylistic gestures in popular culture *mean* something. Don't underestimate the power of style.

2. We can assume an overly narrow view of God's common grace.

Sometimes when Christians try to find what is good, true, or beautiful in a popular cultural work (question 3), they prefer to identify nice or moral elements. They forget that the Bible doesn't always present niceness and moral decency to us, and yet even these parts are full of grace. If we truly see sin for what it is—ugly and destructive—*that* is evidence of grace. But if we glamorize sin, we may take part in a deadly deception.

Let's remember that it can be deeply disturbing to confront God-given truth. Recall that the Bible itself presents grotesque narratives—such as in Judges 19, which shows the violence of a rebellious Israel, or in Revelation 19, which shows Jesus's violent dispatch of his enemies.

Similarly, when a manmade story's hero (such as Batman or Luke Skywalker) learns about how deeply evil penetrates society and even his own heart, it is God's common grace that he gave the storyteller insight to see that evil *as* evil. It tells the truth about human reality. Of course, this does not mean that bleaker and darker examples of common grace are all appropriate for younger children. They might be too much for a child until she reaches her teens. However, we must know that common grace doesn't always match the ideal of a "family-friendly" story or show. Remember that such stories might actually undermine God-given truth by distorting idolatry into respectable, candy-coated poison.

Common grace comes in all sorts of surprising forms. Be ready to be surprised.

3. We can mistake the fictional character for the world itself.

In discussing a story's idolatry (question 4), Christians may respond like this: "Well, that character killed someone/lied/committed adultery, and so that's where the idol is."

That's not always the best answer. When we attempt to track idolatry, we are not concerned with the actions and motives of individual characters *unless those characters represent the story's or culture creator's positive viewpoint*. In other words, if we see villains presented as vile persons, that is the voice of writers or directors telling us they *don't* approve of them. You will almost never find the idol there. Instead you need to find where the voice of the culture creator endorses actions and motives that contradict Scripture. Then you need to unveil that idol's ugly ineffectiveness—how it spins a web of lies that ultimately leaves us empty.

Look at the moral and spiritual shape of the imaginary world as a whole, not just this or that part. Don't get so hung up on the morality of the trees that you miss the spiritual condition of the forest.

4. We reduce the gospel to justification by the cross.

When thinking through the last question, about how Jesus is the true answer to the story's hopes, it is easy to confine the grace of God to the forgiveness of sins. That is, indeed, the center of the gospel message, but this means we miss the awesome breadth of the salvation God offers.

Sometimes we reduce the word *gospel* to the process of an individual getting saved. But we may miss the many other facets of the new life that comprise the good news. In 2 Corinthians 5:17, Paul tells us that once we are connected to Christ, we enter into a new mode of existence called the new creation. Or, as Jesus says in Revelation 21:5, "Behold, I am making all things new." Not some things. Not only your personal guilt and shame. *All* things—the Son of God makes new every aspect of creation distorted by the fall.

This job will be completed when Jesus returns. Until then, we must show this newness in how we live and treat one another and this world. The new creation is about hope. It is woven into every strand of the Christian's life tapestry, present and future. And the best part of any critical engagement with popular culture is that you get to ruminate on, and sometimes share, the hope offered by life in God. Don't make it narrow—it's incredibly huge and diverse.

The common thread that ties all of these missteps together is that each narrows the focus of analysis too much. We don't mean that your analysis should be vague. Be as detailed as you like. But keep in mind that your real target is the imaginary world as a whole, for it is the overall resonance of these imaginary worlds that shape cultures and attitudes. And keep in mind the magnificent breadth of God's grace that answers the idolatrous challenges of these imaginary worlds. Keep the big picture in view.

MAKING THESE QUESTIONS ACCESSIBLE TO KIDS

We have used these five questions in conversations with middle and high school students. But for younger children, here are some tips for scaling down the discussion.

First, keep it short. The younger the child, the shorter amount of information he or she will be able to absorb and sit still for. Lengthy lectures don't work. Give bits and pieces as they are able to listen. Pro tip: if they squirm, that's their body telling you they are too full of information. Time to move on.

Ted once led discussion on the film *Wreck-It Ralph* for children between ages four and six. We found lots to talk about, such as by asking: Who were the good guys? Who were the bad guys? The film doesn't make this easy; Ralph is a video game "bad guy" who's lonely and tired of being bad. We even explored how we can tell a good act (Jesus would like it) from a bad act (Jesus would *not* like it). Unlike college students who can go for a couple hours, these kids lasted maybe fifteen minutes. Don't worry if you don't have a "complete" conversation. Kids that young can only absorb so much. Use your few minutes well.

Second, encourage them to ask questions. Younger kids loooooove asking questions. Make sure they understand that it's OK for them to interrupt a movie or television show to indulge their curiosity (within reason). If the initiative comes from them, you will have more of their attention. And the discussions will be much more fun for both of you.

Third, ask *them* questions. Don't just throw statements their way. Make them think. "Why do you think Iron Man did that even though he knew he might never come back? Why do kids like making stuff in *Minecraft*? Why do you think 'Old Town Road' is as popular as it is? Princess Vanellope was all alone for so long. How do you think that made her feel? Have you felt like that, too? The bad guy did a really bad thing. Why do you think he did it? Why was it bad? How do you know it was bad?" It is when they have thought about it and come up empty that they'll really want to know. Drawing them in to active participation will also help discussions last a bit longer.

Fourth, make the discussion age appropriate. For older kids, you can expect a degree of sophistication (more for later teens than early teens and tweens). Older kids can handle abstract concepts like worldviews and moral assumptions. Elementary-age kids are still developing the ability to think that way. They have a hard time grasping abstract concepts. Instead, you have to make the discussion concrete: "Who was the good guy? Who was the bad guy? What made the good guy good? What did he do that was good? What did the bad guy do that made him bad? What do you think God wants the bad guy to do?" By sticking close to concrete things, events, and persons, you can help young minds sort through pretty complicated moral and spiritual concerns.

For teeny-tiny children, age five and younger, make these questions even clearer. Young children are quite empathetic. Very small children have been known to cry when they see another child fall or get hit because they feel their pain. They don't distinguish between self and others as automatically as older children. Use that. "How would you feel if you had a power like Elsa's that could hurt your sister? Would you maybe avoid her too? Do you think she felt lonely?" Even though they lack systemic thinking, their levels of empathy can be much higher, and that allows them to attune themselves to the emotional weight of a character. The work you do here will be more about feeling the security of God's love, the rightness of walking his path, and the warmth of loving others the way Jesus has loved us.

All of this assumes you've already done a popologetics analysis yourself and you're ready to talk to your child about it. By using these four tips, you can help break it into understandable chunks that won't make your child choke.

WATCH, LISTEN, PLAY WITH YOUR CHILD—AND ENGAGE!

Popular culture is a fertile field ripe for exploration if you want to engage it with your child. The key to effective engagement is to learn to love (or at least like) what your children adore and are amazed by in popular culture. Watch, listen, and play with them, talking about what you're doing. Look for teaching moments, and, above all, *listen* to their heart.

How can you know what is healthy and appropriate for your child to engage and what you should avoid? There are no hard-and-fast rules that can substitute for nuance and wisdom. Instead, learn to trust the wisdom God gives through his Word, through wise counsel, and through your own parenting instincts. Consider what is age appropriate as well as the unique strengths and weaknesses of your child's heart. The next chapters explore how you can know the heart of your child and the various developmental stages.

Chapter 7
Discerning Your Child's Hidden Heart

Understanding movies, music, and games is only one part of being a pop culture parent. You also need to read your child. It's important to know what's going on in your child's heart.

Obviously, parents should check out popular cultural works before their children participate in them. Check ratings and reviews. If you are unsure about a show, watch it beforehand. The chapters on different stages of your child's growth will also help by giving guidelines for what stories, songs, and games are generally appropriate for different age-groups. However, no child is "general." Each child is unique and may need special protections or guidance. In our experience, that uniqueness often surfaces after engaging a particular popular cultural work. Popular culture has a way of exposing the hidden heart.

Several clues can give you insight to your child's emotions and temperament: patterns of words and actions, preoccupations, dreams, and creative expression. These can help you figure out where your children are developmentally and what entertainments they are ready for. And, of course, simply talking to your children is a great way of learning how they are processing popular culture.

Let's explore these clues, while knowing they work differently for kids of different ages.

1. WATCH FOR MOOD SWINGS.

Ted's Czech pastor offered some wisdom in a sermon about Ephesians 4:26, "Be angry and do not sin; do not let the sun go down on your anger." He said emotion is a gift, a gateway between us and others. Do not be afraid of your child's emotions; they are a window on their heart. Healthy children have pronounced emotional reactions to things, including stories, songs, images, and games they encounter. So watch for how they react.

This is easy to do with the very young. Little kids tend to be unguarded in their reactions. Their eyes light up and they squeal with delight, or their eyes darken and they scream with rage, or they hide their eyes and they whimper with fear. The older kids get, the more they learn from the adults around them, and their reactions tend to be subtler. But if you know a child, you can pick up even on subtle emotional cues: posture, tone of voice, eye contact (or lack of it), and so on. If you are unsure if a child is ready for a specific piece of popular culture, watch, listen, read, or play it with them, and take note of their reactions. If they seem to be comfortable, having a good time with it, then it may not be a problem. Or it may. But to determine that, you'll need to see other indications.

Sometimes mood is not so easy to read. Perhaps your child fits on the autism spectrum. Those reactions can be exaggerated or so subtle they are difficult to see. But even parents of autistic children can learn to read emotional cues. If you have a nonspectrum child who seems to be flatlining emotionally, and there is no obvious reason (such as exhaustion), this could indicate depression. Don't mess around with depression: seek medical attention and counseling for the child.

For a child who expresses emotions normally, an adverse emotional reaction or change of temperament can indicate this child isn't ready for this particular popular cultural work. Even if you think he is, perhaps the child is extra sensitive in this area and cannot process it. In the future you should probably tread carefully when dealing with this type of movie, show, song, or game. However, an emotional reaction of pleasure or comfort may show he or she is ready for this kind of entertainment.

2. Watch for Patterns of Words and Actions.

Another clue to the effect of popular cultural works is how your child "acts out" and speaks out. Attentive parents get an early feel for how their child acts and talks. When Brian is hungry, he'll act out. When he's sleepy, he might say angry words. And so on.

This may sound rigid and mechanical, but we can say children have *scripts*, patterns they follow through normal life. When children deviate from these scripts, a wise parent will know something's up. Perhaps it is simply a bad day at school. Perhaps it is something more serious, like bullying or a developing addiction. Teachers and counselors are trained to watch for deviations from scripts as signs that a child might have suffered abuse or trauma and may need counseling. If you notice changes in behavior and speech patterns, talk to your child and rule out the more serious possible causes, as well as the smaller stuff (such as simple bad days). Your child must understand that you are an ally in the gospel. She can find grace for any sins she may feel guilty about. Ask her gentle but penetrating questions to explore if something serious is going on. It might also be something less worrisome, such as hormones or an unexpected growth spurt.

If you have ruled out other causes, you may want to look into potential issues with popular culture. This is especially true with younger children who are exposed to fictional violence they cannot handle. Some children are wired for more action/adventure and take it in stride. Others react with more aggressive behavior, at least in the short term.[1]

Children also tend to imitate things they've seen. If they receive sexual content beyond their maturity level, they can also act out in ways that can be unhealthy and dangerous. Even for tweens and teens, media can provide orientation and models to follow. As Christian media scholar William Romanowski notes, "Cultural texts—soap operas, the lives of celebrities, films—serve up ready-made 'scripts' that provide templates for everything from the perfect relationship and the perfect kiss to the perfect crime."[2]

We won't often find only one cause for a change in a child's actions and words. But if you do notice a change, talk to your child and see what part, if any, their popular cultural diet might play.

Wise parents will not only watch for changes in behavior and speech. They'll watch for ways that popular culture mixes with established patterns. We know children are sinners from birth, and their default behavior is a messy mixture of sinful coping mechanisms (idolatry) and the Spirit's influence in their lives. So pay attention to the normal inclinations of your child, and use some common sense about what to engage and what to pass by. If the story or song feeds your child's idol at a vulnerable spot, move on.

An obvious example of common-sense parenting: Don't engage in material with sexually suggestive scenes with your preteen or early-teenage children (let alone a younger child!). Even for older teens, be ready with the fast-forward button!

This approach also calls for some tricky questions, such as: Is my daughter's obsession with Disney princesses the beginning of a consumer-driven idolatry? Are such films forming within her a warped and unbiblical understanding of womanhood? Or is this just childhood fun and whimsical fantasy? Should I watch these films with her and talk about what contentment and womanhood mean for a Christian, or should we avoid them for now?

These are not easy questions, and parents must carefully search out the answers. But they are worth asking and worth talking over with your child, especially if you see evidence in words or behavior of emerging patterns of sin that need to be dealt with.

We definitely favor critical engagement with popular culture wherever possible, but you may find times to avoid engaging. Ask yourself: Is my child ready for this in terms of maturity and disposition? Would this help train my child or set him or her up for damage? As we have seen, endless childproofing is not in your child's best long-term interest. But neither is presenting more challenges than the child can bear presently. You know your child best, so as you look to the future, pray and reflect on what is best and what God desires in your child's life at this particular moment.

3. BEWARE A CHILD'S OBSESSIONS, DREAMS, AND WEIRDNESS.

This last group of clues to your child's inner world includes all the stuff that doesn't fit into mood swings or behavior patterns. These clues are more like attitudes or postures toward popular culture. They are more difficult to define, but they definitely play a part.

Ted's story: A drift to the dark side

When my oldest daughter, Claire, was very young, she was drawn to dark cultural works. She loved the movie *Anastasia* (1997), a Don Bluth animated feature, supposedly for children, that strays into grotesque themes. The villain, Raskolnikov, dies early and then returns as an undead warlock who routinely pulls out his eye to look around. We honestly didn't pay close attention, thinking this was just another goofy children's movie.

It's worth pointing out that even in a grace-filled environment kids can clam up if they don't want parents to forbid them their beloved entertainment. The reason we didn't catch the darkness of *Anastasia* is because, even at age four, Claire was determined not to let us know because she really, really loved the movie. And she knew that we would not let her watch it if we knew it distressed her. (She kind of liked being distressed in that way.)

Later, when her big brother began playing *Baldur's Gate*, a turn-based fantasy adventure game where the hero slays monsters, Claire began drawing. She habitually drew, so that didn't bother us—until we noticed she was drawing decapitated knights with blood spraying everywhere. Then she told us about the creepy imagery seeping into her dreams.

So we suggested she avoid the room when Roger played his game. But even after this, Claire remained fascinated with dark imagery in popular culture. In her teen years she started struggling with depression, and suddenly her cultural obsessions made sense.

You could argue that Claire's cultural choices caused her to be attracted to dark themes and images. You could also argue that she was wired that way and expressed that temperament through her cultural choices. Or it could have been some combination of the two. Whichever it was, it was not a healthy dynamic, and it indicated deeper troubles under the surface. We tried to steer her toward less dark material, but she found a lot of it vapid and superficial (and she was often right). People who struggle with depression often seek out cultural works that express what they are feeling inside and want to know they aren't alone. For us, this was an indication that she needed help in her struggle, and we listened.

Consider everything about your child, even things not easily categorized, when thinking through your choice of whether to engage a cultural work. Even seemingly extraneous information can often provide vital clues to the interior landscape of your child's heart.

4. TALK WITH YOUR CHILD.

Up to now, we have only dealt in clues and signals. But of course, you can best learn about your child's heart by simply asking your child, "What's going on inside you? How are you doing? How is your heart?" In a normal, loving, grace-filled relationship, your child will feel safe revealing to you what's happening inside. But he will clam up if he feels this openness invites your wrath or disappointment. Only the gospel gives a child freedom to open up about his heart without judgment, and that can lead to good discussions about how popular culture interacts with a child's inner landscape.

This does not mean we should always accept a child's statement at face value. Kids can be quite protective of their chosen entertainments. So you have to be patient, ask good questions, and trust that your child will, eventually, choose to be honest with you.

Of course, even an honest child can have a hard time revealing her heart. If she is small, she may also not have the vocabulary or maturity to share about her temptations and idols, at least not without your help and guidance. Try using vivid, concrete language. "What makes you happy these days? What makes you sad or scared?" Ask your child what sort of animal they feel like and what that animal might be thinking. If she is not into animals, try dolls, trucks, or whatever interests her. Use your imagination and wisdom to draw her out.

For older kids, temptations and false worship can be confusing and disturbing. You will need to be patient and look for opportunities, windows when the teen is willing to talk seriously. Then ask open-ended, nonjudgmental questions that can help shine a light into that web of feelings and yearnings: "What is it that you want out of life? What's that one thing that would make you satisfied? What do you find yourself thinking about most these days?" And be ready for a long conversation if the child decides to answer honestly.

An older child's self-deception or deception of others can run deep, and often he will not reveal the truth without some gentle but insistent probing (always in the context of love and drawing alongside of rather than judgment). Sometimes, the truth may be that a piece of popular culture is drawing your child's heart in directions that are not healthy nor God honoring. When that happens, rather than just banning the popular cultural work, talk about better alternatives and come to an agreement with your child. In this way, talking over heart issues becomes a way of building trust.

Despite the difficulty and confusion kids face, your child is *still* the best source for revealing his inner landscape and secret idols. Be proactive in engaging the child while you decide about how and where to engage the culture. Be gentle and supportive, but ask good, age-appropriate questions. (Note that the more complex, introspective questions are aimed at older pre-teens and teenagers. For smaller children, we must adapt them into simpler, more concrete terms.)

1. Ask about the popular cultural work's impact on our *beliefs*. "Did this song confuse you about right versus wrong? Does God seem farther away or harder to believe after reading this book?"

2. Ask about the story's impact on *emotions*. "Do you feel too scared after watching that? Does this game stoke your anger inside more than you feel you can handle?" The parent's assessment may not completely match the child's, but getting input from the child is crucial in opening up honest communication about popular culture.

3. Ask about the entertainment's impact on *desires*. "What did that show's episode make you wish you could have or be? Are you drawn to things after that film that you feel are out of line with God's desires

for you? Maybe more than you could handle? Did this game make you hunger for revenge?"

These questions simply will not work unless you've cultivated a relationship with your child where asking heart questions is normal *before* you've attempted to engage with them over popular culture. So ask questions about what they learned in Sunday school or from that week's sermon and what it meant for them. Ask them about their relationships with siblings or friends at school. Ask them what scares them, encourages them, their dreams and fears. And always ask in a way that makes it clear that you love them and are for them. *Then*, on that basis, you are ready to ask hard questions, heart questions, concerning popular culture.

Asking wise questions can help you know where to apply gospel grace and encouragement, help with healing, assuage fears, and sound warnings. Such discussion helps you discern what cultural works your child is ready to engage and which ones to delay or avoid altogether.

Discipling Your Child's Heart with Popular Culture

As you talk and listen, looking for clues of your child's maturity or weaknesses, remember the overall goal: discipleship. The gospel-centered parent's goal is not to protect but to pass on wisdom; not to set up rules but to train the next generation of gospel-grounded, culturally savvy lovers of God and people. In the end, your mission comes down to you, the quality of relationship you have with your child, and the wisdom the Spirit gives.

During this whole process of discerning popular culture that's appropriate for your child, we must keep in frequent prayer. Pray at all times for your child and with your child. All of this heart-seeking discernment depends not on clever questions but on the Spirit.

Ted's story: When the show must not go on

One night the Turnaus were watching television together. I decided we should try the first episode of a television series one of my students recommended, called *Mr. Robot*. Its main character, Elliot, works for a computer security firm. He also has crippling social anxiety and a deep cynicism about other human beings. He believes the worst about people and then hacks into their online lives and confirms his worst suspicions. He likes his therapist (he's hacked her accounts, too), but during their sessions he sits there, stonewalling her, lying about his emotional responses. And he's paranoid that he's being followed by men in black. It's cloak-and-dagger stuff with an interesting, emotionally broken protagonist.

About halfway through the episode, my seventeen-year-old daughter, Ruth—who struggles with social anxiety and has trouble opening up to her counselor, *just like Elliot*—said, "You know, I'm not so sure that he's a great role model. This show might be a temptation for me. I guess it depends on where his character ends up."

Right then, I stopped the program, and we had a family discussion.

Roger, my twenty-five-year-old son, said he also didn't like the show because it simplified computer science (his college major) for dramatic purposes. I could tell that he was really uncomfortable with our hero's social awkwardness. Part of me wanted to plow ahead because I liked the show, but part of me was concerned for my daughter.

My wife, Carolyn, took advantage of the pause to do some cleaning in the kitchen, and I asked her to join us so she could give her advice. She agreed with Ruth that this program would be better for Carolyn and me to watch together. I saw her wisdom, and we talked about the themes of the show. Then we switched to a favorite anime that everyone wanted to watch.

Notice what went right. First, I wanted to engage an excellent work of popular culture with the whole family. No shame there. That's what you do if you want to train up your kids to be culturally savvy and spend time with them doing something you all enjoy.

Second, our relationship with Ruth is open and honest. She knows we have her best interests at heart, so she's learned not to hide stuff. *She* took the initiative and told us what was going on inside her heart.

Third, sensing my own inner indecision, I asked my wife for advice. She has a good feel for what our kids can handle and what they can't. But before this brief consultation, Carolyn and I have enjoyed hours of discussion about popular culture, so that we are pretty much on the same page. In the area of our kids and popular culture, we trust each other.

Mr. Robot became the parents' viewing choice when the kids were doing something else, like playing a video game. (And bonus points for Carolyn: she sensed that I was really getting into the show, so rather than banning it entirely, she made it our program. She gets me.) In the end, Carolyn and I protected our daughter where she is vulnerable. We also deepened our patterns of honest communication and loving relationship with her and with each other. Ruth showed we can trust her by being honest with us. And Ruth has another example of her parents listening to her, knowing her, and caring for her.

This is the way family discussions about popular cultural engagement should go. There's no real recipe except developing trust and communication over the years of discerning what to engage and what not to engage in popular culture.

Chapter 8

Introducing Popular Culture to Young Children

It's child's play! No, we don't mean that discipling children is so easy a child can do it. What we mean is that your children will play. And if you wish to be a pop culture parent, you *must* play with them. To disciple your children, you must live in their world, and the world of young children is full of dolls, LEGO bricks, sports, video games, board games, TV shows, movies, music—and parents. Young children want their parents in their world. They love you, they love movies and TV, and they love to play. So love them back by capitalizing on all of their loves.

When you keep in mind young children's stages in life, you will be aware of their potential idols. You will better relate to them and guide them into healthy choices and understand their external and internal struggles and how God might be working in them. In other words, understanding your young children's development will help you better disciple them in a world full of popular stories, songs, and beyond.

What are young children like—physically, mentally, and socially—in these years?[1]

PHYSICAL GROWTH AND BOY-GIRL DIFFERENCES

Young children have bodies that are quickly growing. They are gaining muscle coordination and becoming faster and stronger. The difference between boys and girls also starts to matter more once kids hit school age. Young boys begin to identify with their fathers and girls with their mothers.

Let's look at some guidelines that may help parents disciple their children through these changes with biblical wisdom and grace. Keep these in mind as you navigate the often-bewildering world of popular culture with your young children.

Guideline 1: Celebrate human value and bodies.

We should celebrate human value. Because young children's bodies will change rapidly, they not only notice their own body's changes but also compare themselves to their peers. They will be tempted to value themselves and others based on who is bigger, faster, stronger, smarter, or better at making things. They could even make fun of others who lag behind, or they may be tempted to devalue themselves if they are slower or faster than their peers. Counteract these temptations by celebrating all humanity—all image-bearers, no matter their stage of physical or mental growth.

For example, when your children see other children on TV or in movies make fun of one another, discuss this sin with your children. It's wrong to make fun of others. But you must also teach them *why* the act is sinful—because it devalues God as Designer and Maker of human beings and devalues humanity as God's image-bearers. Always be ready to affirm human beings' immense value in God's eyes. Be ready to affirm your child's immense value in God's sight as well, especially when he or she feels worthless. A child who knows his or her worth before the King will then understand why we must value others.

This is not only a matter of self-interest, valuing others so we ourselves will be valued. We shouldn't merely ask our children, "Do you like to be made fun of?" as if how we want to be treated is the sole basis of our treatment of others. If we follow Jesus's Golden Rule—do to others what you would like them to do to you—we will get pragmatic results. However, his command offers more than practical value. It is rooted in the very character of God, a loving Father who loves undeserving people. Jesus says that if we love others "your reward will be great, and you will be sons of the Most High, for he is kind to the ungrateful and the evil" (Luke 6:35). We should imitate our Father. That's our identity: a people who show their love for God by unconditionally loving others.

Guideline 2: Celebrate differences between men and women.

Young children are beginning to understand the differences between boys and girls in today's world. So parents should encourage their children to celebrate God-given human gender distinctions and their own genders, whether male or female.

Parents should encourage their children to be like mommy or daddy based on their gender. Celebrate gender distinctions as you see them rightly reflected in popular culture, such as a loving father who provides, protects, leads, and loves his household (Genesis 2:5–9, 18–25; Ephesians 5:22–33) or a warrior mother who fights for her household through working with her hands, nurturing her children, submitting to her husband, and loving her household (Proverbs 31:10–31; Ephesians 5:22–33). When popular culture blurs gender lines, you should point it out so that you may celebrate God giving your children specific genders, male or female, for the purpose of relating to him and others.

Image-bearing is a human endeavor, but it is also a gender endeavor, because

> God created man in his own image,
>> in the image of God he created him;
>> male and female he created them. (Genesis 1:27)

Help your children understand the givens of created natures, including specific genders. Boys were created by God to relate to him and others forever as boys, and girls were created to relate to God and others forever as girls. Gender and its distinctions are good.

But heed this warning: it is dangerous to treat gender *stereotypes* as if they too come from God. If you add human-made stereotypes to the Bible's description of males and females, you will embitter your children. By putting too much pressure on your children to fit human-made stereotypes, you may unintentionally encourage them to identify more with the opposite sex than their created sex. Parents should correct the blurring of gender lines in popular culture but without reinforcing gender stereotypes.

Gender stereotyping can also have other unintended consequences, such as bullying. If a boy doesn't fit the hunt/fish/sports/cars stereotype and likes dancing and arts instead, he can be bullied ruthlessly. If a girl tends to be a tomboy, she can find herself cruelly teased. This should not be; God has not made all men or all women to enjoy all the same things. But he *has* made males and females with specific roles within marriage and the church, which also means something about their roles in society.

Of course, Christians debate many gender-role questions: Should women fight alongside men in military front lines? Should men spar with women in combat sports? We must let Scripture alone define these roles. For instance, when we watch a movie that seems to blur gender lines, our criticism must be based on real biblical issues and not gender stereotypes. A boy who does not like sports is not necessarily feminine, and a boy who likes sports is not necessarily masculine. It just means he does or doesn't like sports.

Even with good modeling and teaching, a small minority of young children may experience *gender dysphoria*, an intense discomfort that comes from feeling mismatched with their biological gender. This is part of living in fallen flesh in a fallen world. For the grace-centered parent, it is important not to ignore the child's pain or add to his or her pain by shaming the child. The gospel must be good news for these children as well. Make sure your child knows that your love for him or her will not evaporate in the face of such struggle. Look for resources to understand him or her better.[2] Find help, and never let the child forget the grace available in Christ to strugglers.

Guideline 3: Celebrate godly opposite-sex attraction.

Parents should also celebrate godly attraction between husbands and wives. Of course, we must do this in age-appropriate ways. Start by making sure you do not make sex a taboo subject in your home, for young children need guidance. But also recall that young children will not need many details. They need to know God loves us and protects us with his law that limits sex to a lifelong, male-female relationship.

In popular culture and society, sexual attractions that are contrary to nature (Romans 1:18–27) are celebrated and treated as equivalent to opposite-sex attraction. When parents see our world celebrating these unnatural attractions, they should seize the opportunity to reinforce God's design for males and females through good biblical discussion of sexuality. Husbands and wives should be attracted to one another (Genesis 2:18–25) instead of being attracted to others of the opposite sex or to their same sex.

Nevertheless, because of our original sin and guilt in Adam (Romans 5:12–14), we are all born sinners. All of us are broken in different ways because of mankind's fall into sin. And all sexual attraction is broken to varying degrees. But heterosexual attraction is the only God-designed attraction with a God-designed outlet—marriage between one man and one woman in covenant together for life (see Mark 10:2–9).

When your children see examples of sinful attractions in popular culture, remind them that God still loves these people. Jesus will receive anyone who comes to him in repentance and faith, regardless of his sexual orientation. If your kid also struggles with such attraction, love him and remind him that grace is offered to us all. Encourage your children to see the value of all persons as God's image-bearers, that we are human beings as they are. Reinforce the reality that all of us are sinners in need of a Savior.

Parents should also be concerned with ungodly lust for members of the opposite sex because most children will struggle with this sin when they get older. They will battle with sinful inclinations, thoughts, and actions. The best way for parents to celebrate godly opposite-sex attraction is to exercise it in their marriage in front of their children through valuing each other equally and showing affection to each other (in a way that's appropriate for kids). Your children should know that you are attracted to one another, but you don't have to gross them out!

Parents should also be ready to talk about any sexually intimate relationships they observe in popular culture—like happy marriages, cohabitating couples, heavy kissing of couples, or gay relationships. This way, we can point out the positive, chip away at the culture's idols, and reinforce God's design for males and females in marriage or singleness.

Parents should also tell their children about "the birds and the bees." At the very least, parents should tell them that God created sex for marriage, meant for husbands and wives to become one flesh. Husbands place a seed inside their wives, and that is how babies are made. Parents may tell their kids that their bodies will change within a few years, and they will be able to get married and have babies as a result. Or, possibly, they will stay single for the glory of God. As you engage pop culture, you should be ready for questions and be ready to respond in a biblical, gentle, age-appropriate manner. Your response will say a lot to your children about how trustworthy the Bible's approach to romance and sex really is.

A final note: parents should not expose their young children to explicit or strongly implied sexual content in popular culture.

GROWTH IN MENTAL PROCESSING

In these years, children are mostly concrete thinkers. They love pictures, songs, and stories. They understand rules, consequences, and rewards for doing good.

But young children struggle with the reasons behind rules, consequences, and rewards because reasons require abstract thinking. When they reach school age, they slowly begin to move from concrete thinking (that is, "punching my sister is bad regardless how I feel") to abstract thinking ("I know *why* punching my sister is bad"). Their minds develop so they can consider their actions and see cause-and-effect patterns—motives and reasons why they acted in certain ways.

During the later elementary years, children begin to see the value of creativity and work. They begin to set goals and try to meet them. They understand that work brings rewards and money has power to get them things they want, such as toys and games, which encourages them to value money.

With these changes in mental processing in mind, here are some guidelines that may help parents debunk some idols and disciple children to holiness, even in a world filled with confusing messages from popular culture.

Guideline 1: Teach kids to use concrete and abstract thinking.

Because young children are primarily concrete thinkers, emphasize rules and stories as you participate in popular culture with them. This includes the commands of Scripture, the gospel message, the short stories of Scripture, and the grand story of what God did for them in Christ. For example, it might be easy to say, "Be kind to people." But the Bible speaks to a child's concrete imagination when it says, "There was this guy who went down a lonely road when robbers attacked and left him for dead! Two religious people passed him by, but a Samaritan, a guy the good religious people hated, stopped to help him." Children will internalize rules and develop empathy from the images and rhythms of the story.

Popular culture does the same thing, which is why parents must break down these stories, songs, and games to explore them on a level kids can understand. They will struggle figuring out how to apply what they learn to their everyday lives, but don't be discouraged. By bringing the Bible to bear on popular culture, you are helping to lay a foundation your children will build on for the rest of their lives. With your guidance, they can know God's Word and practice applying it to their entertainments and will learn how to think about it more abstractly as they grow. These years are crucial; teach them God's Word, and teach them how to respond with Scripture to popular culture as you participate with them.

When you see good and bad elements in popular culture, ask your children, "What does the Bible say?" Then, share biblical wisdom while pointing to God as the source of good (kindness is good because humans mirror God as his image-bearers) and pointing to Christ as the only cure for the disease of sin. Make sure you lean into both the short stories of Scripture and the grand story because children understand stories more easily than isolated propositions.

But also stay mindful of children's developing power of abstract thinking. Answer their questions with more probing questions that explore motives and reasons *behind* an action. Help them consider God's rule and God's stories and how God's motives are grounded in his identity and purpose. Ask *why* certain elements in popular culture are good or evil. Help them identify a story's problem and ask if the story provides a true answer. Ask why the story's solution is true or false, in light of what the Bible says. In this way, you train your children to think systemically, which is vital for forming a biblical worldview. You may be surprised at how deeply young minds can think when given the chance.

Guideline 2: Make a game out of engaging popular culture.

Young children have short attention spans, and they may struggle to stay thoughtful throughout an entire television show or movie. So as you enjoy popular culture together, be prepared to stop the show to talk about what they think and feel. These pauses will also help with those short attention spans. Ask questions such as: "What does the character want? What does the character live for? What is the character's problem? What does the character think will fix the problem? What's the point of the story?"

But you shouldn't be the only one asking questions.

Prompt your children to ask their own questions. Children love to ask questions, after all. The younger the children, the more they inquire about their world. So capitalize on this curiosity instead of silencing it. This will take some patience! You *want* your children to ask questions about everything. Don't get annoyed if they ask the same questions over and over. Answer them with patient wisdom each time, for you are training them to be discerning adults. You can even answer their questions with questions. It will stretch their developing brains. If they're stumped and hungry for the answer, only *then* provide it. By making time for questions when enjoying popular culture, you turn it into something they can actively participate in rather than passively consume.

For example, when you watch a Disney movie, you can help your child to see what is clearly good and clearly evil.

Ask her: "What is the *source* of evil in the story? What is the *answer* to evil?" The Disney movie will not say, "Sin is the problem, and Christ is the answer." It will present some sub-biblical source and solution. You need to guide your children to dig deeper for the truth. Try not just to give them the correct answers. Instead, help them connect the dots by thinking biblically. Remember the goal: we want our children to be able to engage popular culture by themselves as they mature, eventually without our guidance.

In light of these tips, how do we make a game of engaging a story or song with children? We suggest these gamelike approaches to the five popologetics questions we explored earlier. (You can always find those at the front of this book.)

Play "Tell Me a Story"

Make sure your children understand the story by having them repeat it in their own words. In the retelling, you can chime in and help them see what the story is about. This helps clarify any confusion or details that might have gone over their heads. Help them see the main and supporting points of the story. This is not as hard as it sounds. Kids are geared for stories! They learn what makes a story tick from an early age.

Play "Show Me the World"

Help your children see the storyteller's clues to discover this imaginary world. Ask your children: (1) "Is the world of [name of movie/show/game] the same as our world or different? *How* is it different?" (2) "Who is the good guy? Who is the bad guy? What makes the good guy good? What makes the bad guy bad?" (3) "What are the rules of this world? Do you think things work in this world the way Jesus would want them to? Why or why not?" (4) "What does the story need to get a happy ending? What made this a happy ending? What would a sad ending be like in this world?"

Play "Find Common Grace"

Ask your children to point out truth, "things Jesus would like" or things that agree with what the Bible tells us. When a character does something good and praiseworthy, pause the movie and point it out—if your children don't beat you to the punch! Then ask your children, "Why would Jesus like it?" Get them thinking in line with biblical, gospel truth.

Play "Spot the Hooey"

Your children can find two kinds of hooey: sin and idols (that is, false gospels).

Sin is disobedience to God's Word. Encourage your children to point sin out when they see it in popular culture. Such exercises will help you discern your child's heart and level of understanding of sin and will help you to teach your children that sin is ultimately against God's wisdom and will for us. When a character does something sinful, discuss this with your children. Ask: "Did the character do something bad? Do you think the storyteller thinks it's bad, or is he OK with what the character did? Do you think Jesus would think what the character did was bad? Why would Jesus not like what the character did?" Discuss how your children sin and how we must repent and confess that sin to God, who loves us.

Then go on an idol hunt with your kids. What does this story/show/game say is worthy of celebrating? What sort of false gospel does it present? False gospels are anyone or anything other than the gospel of Jesus Christ that claims to offer salvation from life's ultimate problems. If your children know the basic gospel of Christ, they can find the various false gospels that don't match this standard.

This will be harder for young children because this often requires abstract thinking. So parents will need to use concrete terms. Remember, the gospel means more than Jesus died for my sins. It also means: Jesus made me a child of God, so I don't have to fear anything or anyone. (This gives us ultimate security.) Jesus knows me and has given me some things I'm good at, and he's given me a job to do, a part to play in his big story. I know why I am alive! (This gives us ultimate meaning/identity/significance.) And so on.

Try to find the idols that offer these, and try to show how they don't really measure up. For example, help your children see the false gospel of moralism—being good for goodness's sake. If a person seeks moral worth apart from Christ, he will end up self-righteous. This will alienate him from God rather than saving him (just as it did with the Pharisees). God responds to humbled, repentant hearts, not hearts convinced they really need no saving. Likewise, family is a great gift but cannot really save us. Friends are wonderful but cannot make us right with God.

Help your young children to recognize these and other false gospels in popular culture and to understand why the true gospel is so much better for us. We were never meant to find ultimate happiness, ultimate security, ultimate comfort, or ultimate significance apart from God. Only God can give us these things. And since our fall into sin, we need a Savior to bring us into right relationship with God. Praise God, he has provided this Savior. "For while we were still weak, at the right time Christ died for the ungodly" (Romans 5:6).

If you want help identifying cultural idols and false saviors, worldview apologetics can help. A list of good resources for critiquing non-Christian worldviews can be found in appendix B in the back of this book.

Play "Find the Real Gospel"

Young children may not *deeply* understand the good news of Christ and repentance and faith in him. But they can know what the gospel is because it's essentially a story: Christ died for our sins, and he rose from the dead to forgive us our sins, according to the Scriptures. If we repent of our sins and believe he died and rose from the dead for us, he will cleanse us of our sins and bring us into right relationship with God. He will help us live for him and love others well. He will give us a family, an inheritance, resurrection, the defeat of evil, and a new-made world.

Teach your children to look for these gospel threads in other stories. Popular culture often defines evil and shows an escape from it. Yet, we know that the only way to escape God's wrath and "the present evil age" is Jesus Christ (Galatians 1:3–5). Out of this relationship in Christ flows comfort (no matter how bad my day is, God is there and has me), security (no matter how scary it is, God is there and loves me), and significance (no matter how futile it feels, God is the ultimate Author of my story, and it all means something).

By using a story or song as a foil, you can extend your children's understanding of the gospel beyond just *Jesus died for my sins*. You can help them say, "*Because* Jesus died for my sins, these other things are true about me and my relationship to the world. I can live in a way that pleases God." You'll be saying this in a way kids can comprehend because it sets their lives in the big story God is writing. Because a popular cultural work rarely points to Christ as the good news, you can seize the story or song's salvation-oriented themes as chances to point to Christ—showing how the gospel outshines the idols of our culture.

For example, think about how popular culture values superheroes who save others from evil. Also consider how popular culture often highly values a hero dying for someone else, showing their value in their selfless, self-sacrificing love (for example, the many Christ-figure motifs in superhero stories). There is no greater real example of self-sacrificing love than God the Son incarnate laying down his life for sinners.

Guideline 3: In a consumer culture, encourage contentment.

Parents should encourage their children to practice contentment in God over greed.

In today's culture, this is not easy. The love of things or money is a temptation for all age groups, but it starts in the young years. Children feel they need the next toy, computer game, or movie. Consumer culture pours gas on these flames. Ads encourage children to ask their parents to buy more stuff, and few shows or movies celebrate contentedness. Instead, we see many rags-to-riches stories because, in consumer culture, who is content with rags?

These pitfalls aren't limited to TV and movies. Our birthdays and Christmas celebrations can encourage children to ask for and get more stuff. This is not inherently sinful, but a person who craves contentment in stuff *is* practicing sin—a type of idol worship.

For example, popular culture can exacerbate feelings of discontent through constant stimulation over mobile devices. A growing number of studies suggest that children who spend too much time on mobile devices have stunted emotional intelligence and behavior problems.[3] Without guidance, a mobile device itself can become an idol. It helps if kids do not have their own mobile device until they are more mature. Even a parent's device can undermine a child's contentment. However, if you've chosen to allow your children limited device time, stay involved with your child in setting limits (such as device-free bedtimes and mealtimes) and helping your child find good content. Finding a good balance leads to contentment in the right places.

Let's encourage our young children to be like the apostle Paul. For him, Jesus was enough. Paul wrote from prison, "I know how to be brought low, and I know how to abound. In any and every circumstance, I have learned the secret of facing plenty and hunger, abundance and need. I can do all things through him who strengthens me" (Philippians 4:12–13). The apostle Paul's contentment was based not on temporary events or his accumulation of stuff. Paul could see the bigger picture given by life in Christ. In Christ, we have everything we need, eternally secured for us (Ephesians 2:4–7; 2 Peter 1:3–4). We're royal sons and daughters awaiting our inheritance (Galatians 4:1–7). From that perspective, being in prison with Christ was better for Paul than being free without Christ.

When you see discontented people in popular culture, ask your children why the people are not content and if they should be. Some kids are driven to succeed at whatever they attempt and detest failure. Remind your children that they should work hard, using their gifts for God's glory, but that they shouldn't base their contentment on "success." Success always gets redefined and always eludes. We're never successful *enough*. We always ask ourselves, "What have I accomplished lately?" rather than resting in Christ's accomplished work.

Other kids experience discontentment because they expect life to be an unending flow of fun experiences. Interrupt that flow (with homework or chores) and discontent quickly surfaces. Popular culture resonates with that message: it's all about entertainment, about you having fun! But that is not how God designed us to live. There are rhythms, and rest and entertainment are part of that. But young kids need to consider Jesus who came not to be entertained but to love others, save them, and gather a family of God's people to himself. Even when life is difficult (as it often was for Jesus), teach children that God can help us get through the hard and boring parts. Children need to know that they belong to God and he calls them to a lifetime of good works, including their everyday tasks. When they learn this rhythm, it helps build contentment as they walk through life with God.

The world's view of success—whether accomplishment or endless entertainment—does not save us. If our children have Christ, they are successful according to the only definition that ultimately matters. Remind them of the never-ending value of eternal life with Christ, "happily ever after."

GROWTH IN IDENTITY AND RELATIONSHIPS

Young children are often clingy, showing their dependence on their parents. But toward later elementary-age years, children grow more independent. This impulse is God designed and is inherently good. But because of sin, this independence often comes with backtalk and rebellion against parents. So parents need to step back to give children more independence but also encourage children to continue respecting parental authority even when they don't agree with it.

As children become more independent, they develop increasingly close friendships with children outside of their families. They gain the ability to empathize. They begin to value the opinions of others. They also become increasingly self-conscious, worrying about their hair, clothes, or being treated like babies by their parents (like public hugs and kisses, wiping faces, cutting food for them).

Children learn that they do not always get their way. They learn how to react selfishly or selflessly. They realize they cannot control others and learn how to control themselves and their emotions. Children also tend to be competitive, so winning and doing a good job become very important to them. They learn to practice for the sake of winning and to deal with losing. These are opportunities for the gospel to shine. Whether kids win or lose, they can rest in God because of Christ's finished work. He has already won the battle for them—the only battle that really matters!

Based on this time of growth, here are some guidelines to help you disciple your children, dethrone potential idols, and lead them to the gospel of grace.

Guideline 1: Help your child celebrate God-given community.

Young children need their parents and often want to spend time with parents. While they're still little, they care what we think, so celebrate this. Intentionally invest in your children with quality time (including enjoying their popular culture with them). Be careful with critical comments, making sure you are building up your children in the instruction and discipline of the Lord instead of tearing them down (Ephesians 6:4).

Teach your children about community. For Christians, God is not alone. God is one but also is a community—Father, Son, and Holy Spirit—loving, adoring, and interpenetrating (*perichoresis*)[4] one another from eternity past to eternity future. Our need for community is the result of our being created in God's image because he is a divine community, one God who is three Persons and three Persons who are one God. We are not made to be alone. In this way, the church itself bears the image of God communally as it displays Christ to the watching world.

When you see community in popular culture, celebrate that. Show your children how characters reveal their needs for family and friends. Show characters who seem to need no one and yet reveal that they really do—a frequent theme in many popular stories (such as *Home Alone*, *Elf*, and *The Grinch*). Discuss the truth that mankind is ever dependent on God and his Word but also made to be in relationship with other people.

But also point out how friends and family can become idols, things we come to believe have the power ultimately to tell us who we are. Family cannot actually provide this need, and neither can our friends. If we believe they can, we become people pleasers, or even codependent. Celebrate God's good gift of community—expressed in family, friendships, and the church—without turning these into idols.

Guideline 2: Help your child celebrate godly independence.

The Christian faith values both community *and* independence. All Christians function as Christ's temple together (Ephesians 2:22), but each Christian is also individually the temple of God (1 Corinthians 6:19–20). So also pass on to your child the need to value an intimate, individual relationship with Christ.

Instead of stifling your children's growing independence, celebrate and support it. Remember, your goal is to raise God-fearing, mature adults and work yourself out of a job.

As you engage popular culture with your children, point out when characters exercise a healthy independence. Celebrate when characters fulfill tasks on their own, create art, make excellent plays in sports, compose music, or sing. As we depend on God for all things, he also made us both to need others and to stand on our own two feet. We "bear one another's burdens" (Galatians 6:2), but also "each will have to bear his own load" (v. 5).

This independence is not an invitation to self-centeredness. We now live life *in Christ*; our individuality is tied to his (Galatians 2:20). For Christians, being an individual never means being alone. But kids must learn to function independently if they will ever use their talents for the benefit of others and God's glory. Encourage them to form a personal relationship with Christ on their own, to use all their individuality in union with him.

Enjoying individuality is great; however, some caution is warranted: popular culture creators sometimes overcelebrate independence and turn it into an idol. Consider the many cool "rebel" characters, such as Bart Simpson from *The Simpsons* or John McClane from *Die Hard* or sitcom kids who rebel against out-of-touch, stereotypically foolish dads. Americans often assume rebellion is good and authority is usually bad or stupid (after all, our nation started that way, right?). But independence from wise advice, or from family and friends, can also lead to idolatry and self-destruction. Teach your children how to tell the difference between healthy independence and idolatrous independence. The dividing line is love and respect: Can a child exercise individuality and (limited) independence while still loving and respecting others around him—especially those God has placed in authority over him? That is God's norm. Even Jesus, that most remarkable of all individuals, loved others and submitted himself to the Father's authority.

Guideline 3: Help your children celebrate their gifts in God's world.

Instead of focusing on winning and losing, teach your children to celebrate all abilities as ways to honor God, not ways for us to boast about being better than others. We must encourage our children to maximize their God-given gifts instead of stifling, diminishing, or ignoring these gifts. If our children are athletic, let's encourage them to use their athleticism for God's glory. If they are budding intellectuals, let's encourage them to maximize their intellectual gifts for God's glory. If they are imaginative and creative, encourage them to explore and hone those gifts. Encourage children to celebrate who God, in his sovereignty, made them to be, even if they are not the best, smartest, or most creative. Help your children to be the best God-created original them they can be.

But here is the sobering truth: not every child gets to be number one. Children also need to learn how to resist jealously and instead celebrate the gifts God has also given *others*.

As you engage popular culture with your children, help them recognize unique qualities of characters in games, stories, and songs. Who excels doing what? Who maximizes the use of their God-given abilities? Who squanders these abilities? Help your children recognize their own gifts and help them celebrate everything about them that is God designed. They are fearfully and wonderfully made. God doesn't make junk!

Also teach your children to be content with their God-given set of gifts. Not every child can be the star athlete. Not every child will be the wiz kid at school. Not every child is destined to be the greatest dancer, musician, or painter. Popular culture, especially culture aimed at young children, often teaches that every child is special and extraordinary. This is partly true, for each child is made in God's image. But in God's providence, he has not made every child extraordinary. Help teach your children to value ordinary, everyday faithfulness and to be humble when they come in second or struggle with homework that doesn't come easy. God has wisely given what he believes each child needs. Help them to understand and find contentment there.

Now that we've discussed some guidelines for engaging popular culture with our maturing elementary-age children, let's move to our practice session using some age-appropriate popular culture.

Chapter 9

Practice Session for Young Children: *Frozen*

We've examined how elementary-age children develop. We've offered guidelines to help disciple them and to help recognize areas of struggle and potential idols. Now, we'll interact with one popular cultural work that is appropriate for this age group: the movie *Frozen*.

Before we dive in, let us be clear about the purpose of these case studies. We don't at all recommend you try asking your children all these questions or discuss every detail of *Frozen* because this case study is *not* meant to directly equip your children. It is meant to equip you, the parent. That's why this and the case studies in coming chapters will be detailed—so that when your child asks questions, you will have a detailed resource to help guide your answers. More importantly, we want to provide a model of *how to do this for yourselves*. That means you'll want to become familiar with the kinds of questions to ask about any cultural work, how to ask those questions, and what issues you might encounter. So be patient and get ready to explore.

Any parent of young daughters knows *Frozen* (2013). The song "Let It Go" reverberates in your subconscious. *Frozen* broke many records and became one of the most financially successful animated releases ever, grossing $1.2

billion at the box office (and that's *before* adding in merchandizing and video sales).[1] Jennifer Lee's loose adaptation of a Hans Christian Andersen fairy tale is smartly written and challenges tried and true Disney themes, to the delight of children and parents everywhere. What made it so special? How should Christian parents talk with their kids about this magical, musical blockbuster?

Let us walk through a quick apologetical analysis of *Frozen*. After each step in analysis, we will give brief suggestions about questions you could ask. But do be aware: the discussion must be kept brief and probably won't follow the five steps exactly. Be ready to be flexible and responsive to your child's questions and interests.

STEP 1: WHAT IS THE STORY?

The story revolves around two royal sisters, Elsa and Anna, in the fictional kingdom of Arendelle. Elsa has ice powers, and during playtime she accidentally strikes her younger sister in the head with an ice beam. Kindly rock trolls save Anna from death and advise young Elsa that she must learn to control her powers. The incident leaves Elsa terrified of her powers, and her parents keep her isolated to hide them. The parents then die at sea.

The sisters grow up and grow apart. Anna doesn't understand the isolation and separation.

At last the day arrives for Elsa to be crowned queen of Arendelle. To Elsa's relief, the coronation proceeds without incident until afterward. Anna, who has instantly fallen for the visiting Prince Hans, believes she has found true love. They decide to marry, and Anna asks for Elsa's blessing. Elsa refuses, becomes upset, and reveals her power by accidentally creating a wall of icy spikes separating her and Anna.

Elsa flees into the courtyard, again accidentally using her ice powers and frightening her celebrating subjects. Branded a monster by the greedy Duke Weselton (often mispronounced "Weasel-Town"), she flees into the mountains. Alone there, Elsa finds freedom. Safe from hurting others, she creates a stunning ice palace, singing the iconic "Let It Go" to celebrate not having to be the "perfect girl." Now she can be who she truly is. But she doesn't know her powers have brought eternal winter to her beloved Arendelle.

Meanwhile Anna goes to find and bring back Elsa, leaving Prince Hans in charge of the kingdom. She meets a kindly ice cutter named Kristoff who leads her to the mountain. There they meet the obligatory Disney comic-relief character, Olaf, a friendly snowman Elsa inadvertently created. At the palace, Anna confronts Elsa and pleads for her to come back and undo the winter she brought. Elsa, upset that she doesn't know how to undo her magic and will never be free, accidentally blasts Anna with ice—this time in the heart.

The rock trolls advise Kristoff that Anna's heart will freeze and she will die unless someone performs an "act of true love." Thinking immediately of love's first kiss (because, hey, it's a Disney movie), Kristoff takes Anna back to Arendelle so Hans can kiss her. Meanwhile, Hans and his men have tracked Elsa, take her back to Arendelle, and imprison her. Using her ice powers, Elsa escapes into a blinding blizzard.

Hans finds Anna waiting for him in the castle. But on the verge of delivering true love's kiss, Hans reveals himself to be the true villain. After a good villainous monologue, he locks Anna in a room to expire and goes into the blizzard to find and kill Elsa. Olaf the snowman finds Anna, tells her what true love really is—"putting someone else's needs before yours"—revealing that it's been Kristoff all along who loves her. He helps her escape. Dying but determined, Anna goes into the blizzard as well to find him.

These characters all come together on a frozen fjord at the film's climactic moment: Anna sees Hans raising his sword to kill Elsa. She chooses to run away from Kristoff and toward Elsa, to put herself in the way of the blade meant for her sister. At the very instant the sword falls, Anna freezes solid with a wisp of steam escaping her mouth (in a moment reminiscent of the Beast's "death" in *Beauty and the Beast*). The sword shatters and a powerful explosion hurls Hans away (the power of love, of course). Elsa, weeping, embraces her frozen sister who then returns to life. Anna escaped death by performing the act of true love—not a romantic kiss but self-sacrifice for her sister.

Suddenly, Elsa discovers how to stop the winter. Love. She returns summer to Arendelle, takes her rightful place as queen, and expels the villains. Anna and Kristoff share a kiss, implying a future relationship, but she's learned to take it slow. The sisters reconcile, and Elsa uses her now-controlled powers to make a skating rink in the courtyard of the now-opened castle of Arendelle. And they all live happily ever after.

Throughout the film, both sisters grow in important ways, and the ways they grow give us clues about the questions the film means to ask and answer. Anna learns what true love really is. Olaf the snowman, while slowly melting from a fire he made to keep Anna alive a bit longer, defines true love for her as "putting someone else's needs before yours." Elsa learns what true freedom means. After singing "Let It Go," the movie's most powerful statement about freedom, Elsa returns to take responsibility for the damage she's done. We could say that the film's true motivating question is: How can love and freedom possibly dwell together? How can we be free to be ourselves without hurting those we love—without bringing winter to Arendelle? Like all fairy tales, the story seems simple but conceals hidden depths.

Playing "Tell Me a Story"

This game helps the child understand important details of the story that he or she might have missed. Kids excel at relating to concrete situations, actions, conditions, and characters. So stay as concrete as you can.

Start by making sure they tracked with the story. Did something happen that didn't make sense? Sometimes their attention lapses or something just doesn't compute. Use questions to talk it over, explaining the whys and wherefores until you feel they understand the story. Some examples of clarifying questions (feel free to add your own):

- Why did the rock troll king tell Elsa she must learn to control her ice powers? Did her parents do a good job doing that? (Not really.)
- Why did Anna follow Elsa into the mountains, when Elsa just wanted to be left alone? (She cared for her sister, and the kingdom was hurting.)
- What did Olaf say about true love? (That it's about putting other's needs before your own, a hard thing!)
- Why do you think Anna *didn't* die when she froze? (Because she performed an act of true love just in time.)
- What stopped the snow and ice and saved Arendelle? (Love that replaced fear in Anna's heart).

Step 2: What Is the Moral and Imaginary World?

Next, you can spend time sharing with your child the imaginary world of *Frozen*. Ask what it would be like to live there, what makes it similar or different from other movies, how it makes your child feel. All of these have to do with the style of the film. You will also want to describe the rules that govern this world, what counts as good or bad, what makes things work or fail.

Like all recent Disney animated films, *Frozen* is visually stunning. The rich blues and whites of winter eventually give way to the warmth of summer greens, oranges, and yellows. The movement is lifelike, and the characters' design is classic in-between-realistic-and-cartoony. Animating snow was a specific challenge for this film, and the *Frozen* team had to create new software for it (but you won't notice because it looks so natural).[2] The overall effect of this mastery is a movie that holds the eye because it is gorgeous to look at.

The sound that accompanies the visuals is just as arresting, especially the music and voice talent. The standout is Idina Menzel, a Broadway actress who has impressive range and can belt out a tune with the best of them. As we all know, her Elsa is responsible for the most memorable song in the film. Josh Gad's Olaf is whimsical but grounded and sympathetic enough to be the voice of wisdom for Anna. He won an Annie Award from the International Animated Film Association for his performance.

Essentially, this is a hyper-real world of eye-popping winter beauty, magic, wonder, and talking snowmen. It is also a place where people are prone to burst into song at any moment. Who wouldn't want to live there?

Despite the fantasy elements, these characters inhabit a world strikingly like our own. In Arendelle, people make boneheaded romantic mistakes and feel oppressive pressure to conform to social expectations. In this land, siblings grow up and grow apart, and people fumble over how best to express their true selves.

This last concern of expressing the true self touches on a theme within most Disney animated films: authenticity. Authenticity asks the question, "Who am I, really? Not just who do people say I am, but who am I deep down?"[3] Then once you find yourself, in the words of *Aladdin*'s genie, "Beeeeeee yourself!"[4]

This theme resonates most powerfully in "Let It Go." Elsa declares herself free to be herself and free from others' expectations. In earlier drafts of the script, Elsa was written as a straight-up villain (more like Hans Christian Andersen's original story *The Snow Queen*) who deliberately targets her sister Anna on her wedding day. It was Robert Lopez and wife/collaborator Kristen Anderson-Lopez's song that forced screenwriter/director Jennifer Lee to reevaluate and rewrite Elsa's character not as evil but as fearful, suppressed, and yearning to express herself.[5] As a result, some fans saw parallels between Elsa's hunger for freedom and the coming out of closeted LGBTQ+ people.[6] And since Elsa has no romantic partner, fans at once began a campaign to #GiveElsaAGirlfriend.[7] (Then, of course, an evangelical Christian counter-campaign suggested a #CharmingPrinceForElsa.)[8]

All of this is rather ironic, given that *the whole point of the movie* was to undermine our overexaltation of romantic love in the first place. But fan response also underscores how deeply people resonate with the theme of expressing one's authentic identity, either by building ice palaces or through sexuality. One might even say that, in this imaginary world, the issue of expressing the self takes on an almost religious weight, along with the other question that drives the film: What is true love?

Playing "Show Me a World"

You likely won't spend a lot of time talking about the style of the film, but you can explore the moral and spiritual assumptions by delving into the characters. Kids this age empathize with how others feel. So ask them questions about characters' emotions and motivations. These may be kind of open ended, so be prepared for the discussion to wander about a bit.

- What do you think Elsa was feeling when she made her ice palace? (Relief, happiness.)

- How do you think she felt when she found out that her kingdom was hurting because of the cold? (Regret, deep sadness.)
- Do you think Anna was being smart when she wanted to marry Prince Hans? What do you think she wanted? (No, she was being foolish. She was in love with the idea of being in love, rather than what true love is all about.)
- Why did Olaf start a fire even though he might melt? (Because he truly loved Anna.)
- Why do you think Anna went into the cold to look for Elsa even though she knew she might die? (Because she learned what true love was really about; Olaf showed her.)

A lot of the meaning of the film can be made explicit in this way.

Step 3: What Is Good, True, and Beautiful in this World (Common Grace)?

Next, let's examine how the film answers these key questions. Before we critique *Frozen*, we should acknowledge what *Frozen* gets obviously right from a Christian perspective, the common grace woven into the story and style of the film.

First, the story's emphasis on self-expression has biblical roots.

It flows naturally from the fact that God created beings in his image, each of whom has unique gifts, character, and ways of living in the world. When we meet another human being, we are standing before a treasure. We must not lightly bury the particular gifts and quirks of others unless we wish to do violence to God-given human individuality.

Frozen nicely captures the frustration of a child whose unique gifts are suppressed and hidden by parents who fear what others might think. To sacrifice a child's individuality for the sake of social conformity is, frankly, a sin against God and devastating for the child (it's the "myth of ownership" we discussed in chapter 2). A child's special gifts, like Elsa's, can be magnificent if they are allowed to shine. How much heartache could Elsa's parents have avoided if, instead of locking her away, they found an expert who could train and hone Elsa's gift? Because they didn't, Elsa suppressed her own gift, hid from her sister, and wallowed in shame and fear, until her emotions exploded and hurt the ones she loved.

Frozen understands the violence that can be done to a child's soul when parents place pressure to conform over loving support. Parents, find your child's gift and "let it grow!" In this way, parents can honor the uniqueness of what God has created your child to be.

Second, *Frozen* captures Anna's agony at being separated from her sister.

Anna doesn't even know why Elsa has been locked away, and the film understands the destructive power of secrets, fear of exposure, and isolation. Elsa isn't the only victim here; Anna also suffers slow alienation from her only other family member, and that pain festers and turns into a desperate need to connect with someone—*anyone*—else. No wonder she naïvely runs into the arms of the first handsome prince she stumbles across. Of course she misunderstands true love; she'd never encountered the real thing before. And what Anna had been denied, she will take for herself.

Frozen has some real insight into the consequences of sin in family relationships—how secrets, fears, and loneliness have the potential to destroy. The winter that imprisons Arendelle and the cold that is seeping into Anna's heart to kill her are perfect metaphors for that bitter legacy of secrecy and fear.

Third, *Frozen* broke with the Disney tradition that romance always saves the day.

In a pantheon of passive princesses longing for a prince to show up and deliver love's first kiss to save them, Anna and Elsa stand out. Anna's big mistake is that she hopes a head-over-heels romance and a quick marriage will redeem her from isolation, loneliness, and powerlessness. She rushes into the arms of a villain, while her romantically unattached sister has a cooler, wiser head. (Seriously, how many quick divorces can be laid at the feet of Disney-fied romantic expectations?) In portraying Anna's actions as foolish, the storytellers proclaim an important truth: loverman won't save you—saving love must be sought elsewhere. Romantic love is wonderful, a beautiful gift from God. But *Frozen* rightly pops the inflated expectations that we and Hollywood often bring to it. *Frozen* gives the ideology of romance a needed icy blast.

Fourth, the film knows what true love is.

The wisest line in the whole movie is given to a melting, talking, comic snowman: true love means putting another's needs before your own. At the climax of the film, Anna is faced with the choice of running into the comforting arms of Kristoff, who loves her, or running into harm's way to save her beloved sister. She chooses the path of true love. Love is not an "open door." It's not about the comfort of romance. It's not about the tingly feelings of falling in love. It's about sacrificing one's self for another.

The parallels with Jesus are stunningly direct: Anna becomes a Christ figure, saving her sister at the cost of her own life, and her act of true love is rewarded with resurrection. This is gospel love: "There is no fear in love, but perfect love casts out fear" (1 John 4:18). Anna's sacrificial love for her sister jolts Elsa out of fear so she can at last see clearly how to rescue Arendelle—through love. The sacrificial love of Anna melts the icy grip of winter on the land and allows the life-giving summer to enter. This love opens the door to resurrection life.

Playing "Find Common Grace"

In this game, you can move the conversation into deeper territory by bringing in Jesus as *a character*. The film may exclude Jesus, but that doesn't mean he's not a character who is watching every story all the time. And, being Lord of creation, his opinion about things is pretty important. The grace and truth within the story only stands out as grace and truth when they are compared with Jesus's words and actions. So ask questions like

- What do you think Jesus would tell Elsa to do when she's so afraid she can't let Anna into her room? (Jesus would want Elsa to love her sister by controlling her gift, rather than being lonely and afraid; but that's hard, isn't it?)
- Do you think Jesus agrees with what Olaf said about true love? (Hint: He does.)
- What do you think Jesus thought about Anna's decision to run away from Kristoff so she could save her sister? (He would be glad that Anna loved her sister more than she loved being in love.)

In this way, you can get them thinking about the good messages of the film as they are compared with Jesus, our only sure standard of goodness.

STEP 4: WHAT IS FALSE AND IDOLATROUS IN THIS WORLD?

A story's idols are often connected to its common grace. That is, we often take truly excellent parts of creation and, instead of enjoying these gifts with thanksgiving to their Giver, we twist them into functional new gods to save us.

Frozen's idols begin when the story emphasizes expressing your authentic identity in "Let It Go." This idol has been a staple of Disney movies over half a century (usually revealed by the line "Believe in yourself!"). This idol actually starts from the truth that God created each of us with unique gifts. But sinful humans isolate this truth from the Creator and make his gift of our uniqueness into an idol. In service of this false god, we establish a new higher law: thou shalt express and celebrate thine own uniqueness, no matter what.

It might be coincidence that Elsa sings "Here I stand" in each refrain, echoing the story about Reformer Martin Luther's steadfast loyalty to biblical doctrine at the Diet of Worms. But the defiant sentiment is the same: you can't move me because I am clear on my ultimate loyalty.

What's wrong with loyalty to expressing your authentic self? In a word, *selfishness*. It declares that the self and its desires must come first, regardless of what God wants or what is good for others. Taken to its logical conclusions, it will destroy relationships, families, careers, even lives in its mad scramble for attention (for what is self-expression without an audience?). Humility, caution, empathy—all these evaporate in an ongoing celebration of self.

And what is this authentic self? The problem with this concept is that self-identity proves a mere vapor without a bigger story to provide meaningful context. The self cannot be actor, director, and screenwriter of its own ultimately fulfilling story. That's the modern and postmodern lie. The truth is, the self needs an environment that not's only about the self. When life becomes all about self, we find that self becomes an unstable, evasive mirage. The search for self becomes an endless hall of mirrors. The self remains restless and malcontented. Recall church father Augustine's famous words: "You have made us for yourself, and our hearts are restless until they rest in you."[9] So looking within and "being true to yourself" is not the answer. The self needs a bigger drama to give it meaning.

Fortunately, the film gestures in this direction by spoiling Elsa's self-expression party with the news that her people were suffering *because* of her self-expression. She can't just let it go and stay in her ice palace. We all live in communities. We live in webs of relationships, people for whom we are responsible, people responsible for us. None of us lives to ourselves alone or dies to ourselves alone. In reality, there are always limits to self-expression. The authentic self cannot play god.

"Aha!" says the film in reply, "but that's the point! We balance our self-expression with love for others." So *that* becomes the actual chosen god. As if that balance were easy, or even possible, to maintain. As if one could live consistently for freedom of self *and* put others' needs before his or her own. There's the rub: it cannot be done.

In the film, these two idols (freedom of self and love for others) harmonize too conveniently. It's a *deus ex machina* moment. That phrase refers to Greek dramas where all seems hopelessly lost and Zeus comes down and saves the day. It now means any resolution that seems so convenient it strains credulity. In *Frozen*, this occurs when it suddenly dawns on Elsa, "Oh yeah, love," and the winter she created dissipates effortlessly into the sunny skies. Days or even weeks of winter—after *years* of fear, secrets, and alienation—are forgotten in a mouse's heartbeat.

When Ted saw this moment for the first time, he silently called out, "Shenanigans!" This is a game played by the Turnau family when watching television or a movie. When someone spots an inconsistency so blatant that it destroys the suspension of disbelief, the offended party will call,

"Shenanigans!" And they'll usually pause the movie or show to talk it over. It can be something as minor as a stuntman who doesn't quite look like the actor he's replacing or something as major as an inconsistency that violates the work thematically—like Elsa's "Storm-B-Gone" brainwave.

To reverse the kind of damage presented in *Frozen* and find a way for love to triumph takes patience, pain, and effort. We must die to self. It's not a matter of balancing self-expression and love but of carrying crosses. Nobody does that perfectly and consistently, without lapses into self-centeredness. Trying hard cannot save us from ourselves. What can? That leads us to the final issue: the relevance of the gospel.

Playing "Spot the Hooey"

Before we move on to the final step, here are a few questions you might try to help kids see the power—and ultimately the deep wrongness—of the idols the film promotes. Typically, you will find a lot of overlap with the common grace elements. That is, the best God-given things in life make the best idols. Again, you will want to bring Jesus into the conversation because he is the ultimate judge of the idols.

- Did you ever feel like Elsa when she built her ice castle? "I don't want to be good anymore. I want the freedom to do what I want to do!" Do you think having that attitude could hurt other people? Would it be worth it? What do you think Jesus would have to say about it? (Be ready to talk about the proper use and abuse of gifts, like Elsa's ice powers: we can be selfish with them, or love others with them).

- What's up with Elsa just suddenly realizing that the answer was love all along? Did that seem a bit fake to you? Do you think it would be so easy for Elsa in real life? (Of course it was too sudden. In any real person, overcoming that fear would take a long time and they would fall back into the old fear and habits many times. Idols are tough to overcome!)

STEP 5: HOW IS JESUS THE TRUE ANSWER TO THIS STORY'S HOPES?

Frozen might agree that "love covers a multitude of sins" (1 Peter 4:8), but it promises that this happens effortlessly. If we could just love selflessly, all the contradictions and pain of our lives would disappear, like the dissipating winter in Arendelle. Under the rule of love, self-expression won't hurt anyone—no icy blasts, only a skating rink in the town square. If we could love like this, all would be well. We just need to find out how to be good enough to truly love.

This "gospel according to *Frozen*" ignores the real Jesus. It suggests that if we try hard we can be Jesus for each other. Not a bad idea, actually. The world would be a better place if everyone acted like Jesus. But this makes our inner goodness our new savior, and the real, historical Jesus becomes unnecessary and extraneous. Dragging in Jesus feels awkward and humiliating.

So why do we need outside help? Why complicate things with this Jesus business?

To bring Jesus into the picture is to bring reality into focus. As our history and relationships show, we humans are incorrigibly self-centered. That's our default setting. *No one* is truly good enough to fulfill *Frozen*'s savior standard. Sure, we may meet really good and selfless people out there, but none are free from lapses into selfishness—being or doing as they like and forgetting about everyone else. And none are free from the abuse of others who themselves habitually lapse into selfishness.

We are also hopelessly optimistic about our own improvability. We assume that if we just follow some program, meditation regime, diet, or discipline, we'll become better people. Such self-improvement schemes are updated versions of Benjamin Franklin's list of virtues: if you overcome one, you'll stumble at another; if you overcome all but one, you'll still stumble at humility because you'd be taking pride in your moral achievement.[10] You see, we cannot by ourselves undo the damage we've done, and we have no real power to eradicate our own selfishness.

Only Jesus demonstrated perfect selflessness—God in the flesh who exemplified true love by putting others' needs before his own, going to the cross for the unworthy. We need him not just as a model, though that's important. We need what his death achieved: cleansing and power. In Christ we are cleansed from guilt, and by his Spirit we have power both to forgive and overcome our own selfishness (albeit imperfectly) in repentance.

If you belong to a community of people committed to forgiveness and repentance, then it is possible to slowly and patiently bring down the walls of isolating ice palaces. You can heal years of alienation, warm frozen fjords, and find ways of loving others more than yourself. In Arendelle, it never occurs to anyone that a truly loving person might have to *rein in* her self-expression. But in real community, love often demands it. Does that mean the unique gifts of the individual are swallowed up or suppressed by social conformity? Far from it.

Here's the gospel-based paradox *Frozen* glances at but ignores: in losing oneself, a person becomes most truly, authentically oneself. Only by dying to self and becoming centered on Christ can you be resurrected as the person each of us is meant to be. This is what Jesus meant in Mark 8:34–38:

> And calling the crowd to him with his disciples, he said to them, "If anyone would come after me, let him deny himself and take up his cross and follow me. For whoever would save his life will lose it, but

whoever loses his life for my sake and the gospel's will save it. For what does it profit a man to gain the whole world and forfeit his soul? For what can a man give in return for his soul? For whoever is ashamed of me and of my words in this adulterous and sinful generation, of him will the Son of Man also be ashamed when he comes in the glory of his Father with the holy angels.

Here, Jesus shows the urgency of his earthly mission. He is headed for the cross, and those being saved will follow. Those ashamed of him who try to save themselves will lose everything. This truth solves the riddle *Frozen* poses but cannot solve: How is it possible to be free and authentic *and* also to love in a way that puts others first? Insisting on your own rights to express yourself? No, that's a nonstarter. The only answer is to lose yourself utterly and place all your hopes on Christ, following him wherever he leads rather than your own path. This means we love others with true love—which puts others before self—as an act of service to Christ who laid down his life for us.

And here's where the magic happens, for by laying down your life you find that you receive it again, fuller and richer than before. Those unique gifts gain clarity and purpose because we don't use them only for self-expression but to love and serve others. By giving our lives to Jesus, we find them again, growing in glorious ways as God intended them to do. The true self only unfolds in commitment to love others, only in community.

Elsa needs Jesus to show her life through death to self. Anna needs Jesus to show her how to forgive, heal, and live out true love. Arendelle—and planet Earth—needs Jesus.

Playing "Find the Real Gospel"

Finally, move the conversation onto home turf. Connect what they learned about what Jesus likes or doesn't like in the movie to what's going on in their own stories. And be sure to remind them of the gospel when they've gone wrong. Remember, Jesus is not only their King who wants his people to be good; he is also their loving elder brother who extends grace at every turn.

- Have you ever felt bad like Elsa because you hurt someone? What do you think Jesus would say to you? (Answer: Jesus would forgive because he died for our sins. He understands our hurts and helps us ask forgiveness for our sins.)
- Did you ever want to run away like Elsa because you were afraid? (Answer: Jesus is there to protect you and help you where you are scared. He's always with you.)
- Did you ever do something silly like Anna just because you were lonely? (Answer: Probably, but remember that Jesus stays with us always.)
- Do you think it is easy to put other people's needs before yours? Do you do that every day with your siblings? (Answer: No, of course not! We sin, need forgiveness, and can find it *because* Jesus showed *us* true love by putting our needs before his. And now he wants us to be like him, even when it's hard.)

In this way, *Frozen* can be so much more than an occasion for kids to wonder at the snow and sing along with the songs for the umpteenth time. It can be a way for kids "to grasp how wide and long and high and deep is the love of Christ" (Ephesians 3:18 NIV).

Chapter 10

Exploring Popular Culture with Older Children and Preteens

Many parents are afraid of the middle school and early teen years. The mythology of the "terrible teens" is enough to send chills up our spines. One minute, you have a loving, adorable, dependent, cuddly little kid. The next minute, the adorable child is transformed into a snarling, spiteful, rebellious, sneaky, deceitful teen. And parents stand slack jawed, stammering, "W-w-who *are* you? And what have you DONE WITH TIMMY?!" The demon-teen chortles and grins an evil grin, the parents scream, and the screen fades to black (the color of nightmares).

The truth is far more complex and far more encouraging. Even though you may feel as if your preteen or early-teen (about ages eleven to fourteen) kid is slipping from your grasp, the truth is that he doesn't need you any less. In fact, he needs you even more. But he also needs you to parent differently. These years are a tremendous opportunity for speaking truth, wisdom, and gospel mercy into your child's life during a time of massive change.

Parents who withdraw from their children during this time and then later try to engage their worlds will find the children have become closed off. That's why we need to stay present in our children's worlds during these hard, confusing, and sometimes painful years of transition. In many ways, you establish the right to speak into your child's life later by being there now, during these crucial years. Don't let this period pass you by.

Let us review three areas of change your older children undergo in this stage of growth.[1] Then we'll explore how these changes relate to the decisions we make in how we explore popular cultural works with our older and preteen children.

GROWTH IN BODY AND SEXUAL DEVELOPMENT

The first and most noticeable change in your child is puberty. It can be confusing and sometimes frightening, especially to boys because they reach emotional maturity more slowly than girls.

Remember that your child is dealing with insecurity and awkwardness on multiple levels: his or her own body shape is changing or not changing fast enough. Girls are experiencing menstruation, often an upsetting process. Classmates' bodies are changing, too, but not necessarily at the same time. Girls are likely maturing ahead of boys, both physically and emotionally. And girls and boys are probably thinking about each other with different agendas—boys excited by visual stimulation and girls gravitating toward promises of relationship. It's a pretty bizarre time in the life of any child—when children form opinions about what it means to be a real man or a real woman. And popular culture has a *lot* to do with this.

All of this means that we need to tread the territory of sex in popular culture with great caution. And we're talking about a *huge* swath of territory, because much of popular culture is obsessed with sex and romance. So be on the lookout for the "sexy" pitfalls. Be willing to preview movies, television shows, and songs, so you can be sure what you're dealing with.

Guideline 1: Don't expose children to sexual content too early.

Early adolescence is a fragile time for children. If they are exposed to sexually explicit or even sexually suggestive material, this can traumatize them. In this age group especially, children simply don't have the mental and spiritual equipment for dealing with adult-oriented fare.

For some, sex is still the great unexplored country. But too many children get informal (and wildly inaccurate) exposure to sexual material at earlier ages. A recent study found that "half as many parents thought their fourteen- and eighteen-year-olds had seen porn as had in fact watched it."[2] So talk with your tweens and teens about pornography, limiting access to the internet where needed. Preteens and early teens exposed to sexual material can respond with terrified withdrawal, precocious sexual acting out, or other behavior changes. Be vigilant about what your child sees. Be willing to monitor or limit access to the internet or phone, for even the most innocent of image searches can result in sexually oriented pictures (and your child's searches may not all be innocent). You want to reduce the impact and allow for appropriate sexual development as best you can.

Guideline 2: Be ready to answer questions about sex.

Despite your best efforts, your child might see or hear something about sex that she doesn't understand. Be prepared for awkward questions about sexuality. Parents should be willing to address this early so that they become their kids' primary source of knowledge about sex, rather than peers or the internet. But even if you've already given them "the talk" about human intercourse, give them freedom to ask questions and expect honest answers. This means "the talk" should work more like an ongoing conversation with your child that occurs every time there's a need to discuss.

Some Christian parents may feel uncomfortable talking with their children about sex at this age. In fact, you probably ought to be ready even sooner than age eleven—kids are naturally curious. And really, what is the alternative? Do you want your child learning about sex from their classmates or the internet? Don't establish a taboo against talking about sex and romance from a Christian perspective. Your children need your input!

You need to let them know what sex means in God's world. Sexual union is a beautiful reflection of our union with God in Christ (see Ephesians 5:25–33). But contrary to the view of many popular culture works, sex is not the most amazing thing in the history of the universe. Be prepared to tell your children that God gives the wonderful gift of sex, so men and women can enjoy it in completely vulnerable, unashamed, committed, covenant relationships.

You need to gently warn your child that sex outside of that covenant context becomes a powerful idol that can draw us away from God. If we make sex into an idol, it will entrap our souls. And once we are caught, it's hard to break free again. Sex isn't evil, though, and your children ought not be ashamed of their sexual feelings. They need your guidance and wisdom about what sex is for and not for. They need to know they can talk about these questions without shame, for even milder forms of popular culture will raise questions about sex and romance in their minds.

Guideline 3: Be ready to talk about sexual orientation.

A small minority of children will experience unwanted same-sex attraction, whether briefly or more persistently. They will need their parents' patient, unconditional love in their struggles as well as gentle instruction about what the Bible teaches about homosexuality.

Even the majority of people who do not experience same-sex attraction will be curious about the phenomenon, especially because so many works of popular culture tend to normalize homosexual relationships. Parents must be willing to respond biblically and with grace. We need to provide a broader biblical context about *why* God does not approve of same-sex relationships. Let's also study up on how to handle any feelings of same-sex attraction—encouraging any child to be open about these with parents, praying with them, knowing that Jesus still has them. This means we must grasp deeply how sex fits into the ultimate story God has written and is writing—as opposed to the stories we find in popular culture that mix truth and deception in confusing ways. We also must be able to provide the reasons *why* Christians are nevertheless to love homosexuals and point them to Jesus. Appendix B includes a list of Christian resources about popular culture's interaction with same-sex attraction and gender identity, along with some further discussion.

Guideline 4: Encourage your children to accept their bodies.

Your early adolescent child also desperately needs your input about body image. It's normal for kids of that age to be shy or ashamed of their bodies. Unless your boy has the body of a young Greek god, he may feel either skinny and underdeveloped or overweight and flabby compared with his peers. And even *if* your daughter is a budding Aphrodite, she will be self-conscious and hypercritical of her body.

Eating disorders in boys and girls can easily begin at this age. These can be triggered when growing children compare their bodies with other growing children and with media-inspired "norms." Watch your children for harsh self-criticism. Be willing to counter media images with firm, repeated assertions that God has made them the way he wants them to be, and that beauty or handsomeness comes in many forms. Pull alongside your child to instill a healthy skepticism of the ideal body types they find on television, cinema, and in magazines.

Other cultural offerings can actually help. YouTube is full of videos about how photos of supermodels are modified with imaging software. One group employed a professional mannequin maker to craft mannequins to the dimensions of several disabled individuals and then displayed the mannequins in a high-fashion clothing store with custom-made clothing.[3] It is incredibly moving to see people with different-looking bodies being treated with such dignity. When Ted watched this video with his teenage daughter, she got the message: all people deserve to be treated as beautiful and worthy, no matter what they look like. Your worth is not measured in the mirror. To an insecure fourteen-year-old girl, that message is gold—and deeply biblical. "Charm is deceitful, and beauty is vain, but a woman who fears the LORD is to be praised" (Proverbs 31:30).

Guideline 5: Help your child learn to respect the opposite sex.

Popular culture can influence preteenage children by depicting "normal" manhood or womanhood. Too often, cultural works do this in limiting ways for both boys and girls. Boys learn they should be strong and independent. They must never show emotion ("stop crying and be a man!"). And though the #MeToo movement has raised awareness of sexual assault and harassment, a lot of popular culture still associates manhood with sexual conquest. Boys also learn from television, action movies, and video games that they can and should solve problems decisively through violence. Pictures and secular sermons (and even some evangelical sermons) may teach them that some activities are manly, such as sports, and some activities are "for girls," such as music and dance. For some boys, the pressure to conform to truncated versions of manhood can be overwhelming.

Meanwhile, girls may be tempted to view themselves as objects of desire for men. Again, media and popular cultural representations make this seem normal. Girls may come to view any attention as welcome attention, even if they can get it by dressing and behaving inappropriately. They will see and hear repeatedly in shows, movies, ads, games, and magazines that being sexy is powerful, and their bodies are tools to establish their own superiority and their "hotness." Even though the range of activities available to girls is wider than it has been, they will still struggle with subtle cultural pressures that steer girls toward some activities that are "proper" for girls, such as choir and literature, and away from some deemed more appropriate for boys, such as math and science. They too will be trapped in a limiting version of womanhood to which they will feel compelled to conform.

Help your children see that God has made them male or female and that both genders have immense dignity because both equally bear the image of God. Sure, boys and girls have biological and emotional differences. But if your child's gifts and temperament differ from cultural norms for his or her sex, encourage your child's freedom. Don't try to force your child into cultural gender molds—from either popular culture or from some evangelical cultures! Be ready to counter media messages that offer distorted gender norms.

This means not every man has to be an "Esau" with a gun rack. Some men are like Jacob, who prefer to hone cooking skills and help around the house. Some men are like David, who both play the harp *and* slay Philistines. Similarly, some women will be tent-peg-driving women like Jael or savvy businesswomen like the Proverbs 31 woman or Lydia, who was wheeling and dealing with purple cloth.

What if we pressure boys to play sports or pressure girls *not* to play? What if we suggest guys are naturally better at math and girls are naturally better at singing? We end up insisting on overly strict definitions of gender that reflect cultural values more than biblical norms. In fact, some teens feel they just don't fit in church culture because of overly constraining gender expectations and may see in the LGBTQ+ community a more welcoming alternative. The church community should be marked by generosity and warmth, even toward those who don't fit our preconceived notions of manhood or womanhood.

Parents must especially counter the objectification of women in media. Though some shows attempt to "even things up" by treating men as sexual objects, it is still overwhelmingly women who are sexualized for men's viewing pleasure. Treating women as sex objects degrades them and forgets that they too are made in God's image. Instead, teach them to treat women as Jesus treated them: with a respect that exceeded culture's view of them. Teach your sons to protect women and treat them as sisters, with absolute purity (1 Timothy 5:2). And teach your daughters to expect to be treated with respect and purity. Teach them that the gospel sets them free to love and serve however God has gifted them, no matter the norms dictated by popular culture.

For example, as we mentioned before, the Turnau kids have grown up watching the wildly popular anime series *One Piece*. One aspect of the show we have discussed is how all the important female characters seem to have huge chests, as if that were a necessary feature of female heroism. This is true of a *lot* of this subgenre of anime (*shōnen* anime). That's an obvious, not-so-subtle example, but it happens all the time in popular culture, from fashion styles to behavioral expectations. Train your kids to keep their eyes open to it.

Your growing children should express their manhood or womanhood by loving God and loving others in thousands of different ways. Help your child find room for freedom despite the pressures of peers and media. In a world where "normal" is seriously abnormal, teach your child to think critically about media gender stereotyping. The gospel and gospel freedom are the real normal, and your child needs to know that.

CHANGES IN MENTAL PROCESSING

Preteen children's thought processes are also going through massive transformations, moving toward abstract thinking but without much subtlety or nuance. The world to them still looks black and white.

That's why preteens and young teens tend to be obsessed with rules and fairness. If you tell Tommy to clean up his room, he will call you out if you allow Jenny's room to stay messy. It doesn't matter if Jenny had a bad day and is emotionally exhausted. If you don't treat her the same way, you can expect to hear, "But that's not fair!" And the quick retort, "Well, sometimes life isn't fair" won't cut it. You need to fill in the dots and push your early adolescent to think with nuance and compassion beyond a simplistic, "That's not fair!"

Guideline 1: Push your child to think deeper about morality.

Even simple stories of popular culture will provide your child many opportunities to think through moral issues with nuance. Don't be afraid to ask questions like, "Does God promise that the good guys will always win?" If you search hard for quality popular culture, it will often raise such questions for you. Look for stories where characters suffer disappointment and events don't allow for easy solutions. When you find one, don't be satisfied with a response of "That was awesome!" Get your child to dig deeper: "Why was it awesome? What makes the awesome stuff awesome? What are the rules that govern the world of the movie or television show? How do they stack up against God's rules?"

Challenge justice with mercy. You can even graciously throw moral monkey wrenches into your children's neat, clear categories. We Christians know that things are messier than that. Saints are sinners saved by grace. Justice is sometimes long delayed. We learn to live with disappointments, anticipating the day when Jesus will fulfill all our hopes. Until then, we must learn to live in twilight—in a world of mixed light and shadow.

Guideline 2: Help your child behold the glorious gospel of grace.

Through all of this mental stretching, turn your child to the reality of the gospel. The gospel overturns our neat categories, just as Jesus overturned the money changers' tables. The gospel forces us to understand the self-conflicted complexity of human beings, the dignity and worth of those who bear God's image, the common grace woven into the worst of us, and the destroying power of sin that plagues the best of us. Christian parents should be the last on earth to recommend overly simplistic readings of the world to their children (though Christian parents are often accused of doing just that).

Being gospel focused is a powerful apologetic. While your tween or young teen is probably too young to participate in a full-blown popular culture apologetic, you can make a good beginning in that direction. Try proposing conversation starters like these: In what does the main character place his or her hope? Is it a hope worth having? Is it the best hope? Why or why not? What rule does the villain violate? Does he deserve mercy? Does anyone? What would repentance look like for him?

Asking such questions will bring the imaginary world of that popular cultural work alongside the biblical worldview. You don't have to make this a mechanical chore. Rather, allow these questions to arise naturally, and talk about these issues with gentleness, open ears, and an open heart. Let the discussion's tone mirror gospel grace that you want to celebrate before your child's eyes.

This gospel focus means that children start understanding themselves and those around them as shining with created dignity, darkened and distorted by sin but having a solid hope in the unmerited mercy of the Father through Christ. It means life may be disappointing, but their Savior is not. It means life may feel unfair, but their loving Father has never forgotten them. It tilts their minds toward mercy, service, forgiveness, and justice for those ground down by life. It gives them resilience because it grounds their hope beyond the things of this world. It furthers their maturity by training them in the ways of ambassadors of grace. It is key to a flourishing discipleship in a post-Christian culture.

Guideline 3: Help your child consider consequences of actions.

Preteens and early teens have another developmental quirk: they feel invulnerable, especially boys. Both boys and girls might experiment with risky behaviors because they don't think through the consequences of actions. To some extent, they are hardwired for foolishness at this age. Their brains' frontal lobes haven't finished developing.

Again, good popular culture can lead to discussions that help to show how behavior has consequences. Lying and cheating can lead to heartache. Violence devastates the lives of victims. Physical training can lead to excellence.

But even when a popular cultural work *doesn't* show consequences, you can talk about how it glossed over important issues and what the consequences could and should have been. Such conversations also help teach your kids to recognize what makes truly excellent popular culture: nuance, emotional realism, and reckoning with consequences of characters' actions. Help your children project their selves and feelings into lives of fictional characters: "How would you feel if your friend did that to you? Or if you did that to your friend?"

But again, point them to Christ as the Savior who overturns the worst consequences in pure mercy. Help your child ponder how God's mercy, and human forgiveness, can ease the burden of consequences—not for every consequence, to be sure, but to heal the damage of bad actions. The gospel means that, indeed, sometimes life is not fair. And frankly, that's awesome.

GROWTH IN SOCIAL IDENTITY

Of all the changes preteens and early teens experience, this one causes the most fear, pain, and annoyance to parents. Your child begins to pull away to spend more time with friends and less time with family. Is your child rejecting you? Not really. But peers do begin to play a bigger role in your child's sense of self. He or she begins asking: Am I normal? Do people like me? Does that one girl or guy like me? Will I fit in? Who am I, anyway?

Popular culture also starts playing a bigger role in your child's identity. It becomes a kind of social glue because their friends discuss popular culture *constantly*. "Did you hear that new song? Did you see last night's episode of [insert name of awesome television series]? Have you played that new video game yet?" Taste in popular culture becomes a way of finding like-minded peers. This process continues and refines into the later teen years, and even into adult hipsterdom. Especially in a world as media saturated as ours, popular culture plays a huge role during this time in your child's life.

So what can you do as a parent of a child whose popular cultural choices are increasingly defined by peers?

Guideline 1: Become a welcome guest in your child's world.

Parents of older children or preteens have one obvious action: stay in touch with your child's cultural choices. Avoid shoot-from-the-hip rejections of your child's favorite cultural works. These may be identity statements, and you do not want to crush your child's identity. That will only increase the distance between you. Try your best to find what is excellent in your child's choices, even if it's some bubblegum pop star *a la* Justin Bieber (we never said this would be easy). Treat these choices with the same respect you expect from your child. If you really desire relationship with your children, become a welcome guest in their life. Don't let their popular cultural world become a place with gates that shut you out.

Bear in mind that a significant portion of children (as many as 25 percent) develop at least mild depression during these years.[4] Depressed children are often drawn to dark popular cultural works, so be prepared. Entering into their world to engage their culture will help give you insight into your child's emotional life and help you ascertain whether your child might need early treatment.

Guideline 2: Open your home to your children's friends.

It is too easy to make time with your child into a tug-of-war with his friends. Instead of resenting your child's friends and competing with them, invite them in. Make your home a place where your child's friends feel welcome and are allowed to explore popular culture. That doesn't mean everything they want to watch is automatically OK. But clarify to your children and their friends that you don't mind them watching movies or television shows, listening to music, or playing video games while you're around. (Make sure these choices are also OK with the friends' parents.) Make yourself available to talk about what they like and why they like it. This is a time commitment, no mistake, but worth it.

Guideline 3: Let your children develop their own identities.

Preteens want to move beyond being their parent's child and become their own person. And that's fine. It is important for parents to avoid feeling threatened by this; this is how God created the child.

Before, your child's popular cultural choices used to line up with yours. Now as they grow, their taste in popular culture transforms. Let your child find his own identity. Don't let his popular cultural choices become a battleground simply because you don't like his taste in music, movies, television, or games. Of course, if his choices take him into unhealthy territory, you may have to discuss the choices and help find healthier alternatives. ("But Mom, the Nun-Slashers™ are such a cool band!") But stay open to finding the excellence in your child's popular culture, even if you don't agree with all of it.

Give your child an open invitation for further discussion rather than slamming the door in her face. In Ted's case, it stung him a little when his eldest daughter labeled his beloved jazz as "background music." But this didn't stop Ted from listening to her recommendations of what constituted good electronica. It was interesting stuff, and he was able to demonstrate love and respect for her.

Guideline 4: In case of fandom, be ready to "nerd up."

Some older children and teens express identity through intense imaginative and emotional investments into cultural works, also called *fandom*. Fandom has gone more mainstream. It can express itself in many ways: collecting, costuming, writing fanfiction, creating art or videos, chatting about beloved shows online, or attending conventions. Or a fan may just enjoy watching the show, playing the game, reading the novel, or listening to the music.

Whatever form fandom takes, this touches the core of your child's identity. Rejecting a fandom is like rejecting the teen. If you want to critique the work on which the fandom is based, first you must establish your fan "street cred" by logging some serious time watching/playing/reading/listening with your teen. The ensuing discussions can be intense but also a fascinating and rewarding entrance into the heart of your child.

Guideline 5: Speak gospel peace into your child's wild heart.

During this period of identity development, parents often overlook their child's intense insecurity. When your child pushes back in conversations with her own opinions, she may not be rebelling as much as trying to figure out what she actually thinks. When she pushes away from you, it may not be rejection as much as embarrassment or confusion. When she chooses popular culture that pushes boundaries or pushes your button, she may not be trying to annoy you as much as define her own sense of taste.

If your child genuinely struggles with rebellion, you need to deal with it, talking honestly and gently with your child and disciplining in love when necessary. But remember this: your child is very much in process now, unsure of who she is and where she is headed.

It's always better to respond with quiet conversations, gentle challenges, and vigorous encouragements rather than with shouting, rejection, and a judgmental attitude. Look for opportunities to speak into your preteen's or early teen's life, times where they let down their guard. Early-adolescent children might switch between pulling away to assert independence and curling up in your lap like a cat to seek warmth and security. Depending on your attitude, these wild switches can feel terrifying to you (like fighting monsters and trying to keep a lid on the chaos) or exhilarating and fascinating (watching your child gradually reveal his God-given identity). Despite these insecure moments, God calls you to speak gospel grace. Your child is asking again and again, "Who am

I?" You need to keep affirming again and again, "You are God's beloved child. He will never let you go. And neither will I."

Guideline 6: Be ready to engage your teen's social media use.

Few cultural phenomena have impacted early adolescent mental health as much as social media. The lure of instant connection, affirmation, and entertainment is more than many children can resist, especially at a time when their identities are still developing and they are looking for peer approval.

We will discuss social media more when we deal with older teens. But as kids have access earlier and earlier, let us introduce a note of caution. A growing number of studies show that social media has a negative impact on childhood mental development, mostly because of stress. Bullying, the constant search for approval, and even sleep deprivation play a role.[5] Social media is also quite addictive, and young adolescents have few defenses against such addiction.[6] Further, heavy use of mobile devices has been linked to depression and anxiety in teens.[7] Unfettered, unmonitored access to a mobile device is not in your child's best interest.

We are by no means antitechnology. But at this stage more than ever, kids need parents to be engaged and not hands off. For instance, set boundaries that will help your kids value conversation and face-to-face relationships. Ban mobile devices at the dinner table and encourage kids to share their day with you. Have family times, such as game nights or movie nights, when you are engaging together—without the smartphones. Teach them proper etiquette when in the presence of a friend: the flesh-and-blood person takes precedence over their mobile devices. Identity stabilizes when a kid has caring, face-to-face relationships. Of course, your children will look to your example of how you respect people over electronic devices (or don't), so be aware. Their identities need to be shaped by the gospel through relationship, not primarily through the images they project and envy on social media.

Chapter 11

Practice Session for Older Children: *Star Wars: The Force Awakens*

Let's explore a popular movie that can help you and your older child discover age-appropriate moral, spiritual, and imaginative themes. This time, using our five-question template, we'll go a little deeper than we did with *Frozen*. Remember, our goal is to be thorough so that you learn how to respect and understand the origins and themes of this story from one of the most popular franchises of all time. That way, even if you don't share all this information with your children, you will speak from an informed position so that you can better enter this world that your children (and many of us!) may enjoy so much.

After a ten-year hiatus, the *Star Wars* film franchise reawakened with the 2015 release of *Star Wars Episode VII: The Force Awakens*, directed by J. J. Abrams. It continued the original *Star Wars* saga of Luke Skywalker, Han Solo, and Princess Leia Organa, adding to a multibillion-dollar film franchise that includes an extended universe of novels, an animated series, and video games.

STEP 1: WHAT IS THE STORY?

Most parents who know *Star Wars* will have already seen this story with their older children. We know it's important to get the story right! So we'll provide a brief recap.

In the previous film by chronological order, *Star Wars Episode VI: Return of the Jedi*, Jedi knight Luke Skywalker finished his hero's journey. After Luke's great failure, he resisted temptation to evil. He helped redeem his evil father, Darth Vader, and saved the galaxy.

The Force Awakens begins thirty years later. Now the old evil Empire has somehow been succeeded by the First Order, and the old Rebel Alliance has become the Resistance. On the planet Jakku, Resistance pilot Poe Dameron gets a secret map just before the First Order's military ships attack the planet, disgorging hordes of deadly stormtroopers. Poe stores the map inside the spherical droid BB-8 and is captured by the First Order's new dark lord, Kylo Ren. Later, Poe escapes on a First Order ship with Finn, a stormtrooper who no longer wants to fight for the First Order. The ship is hit by a missile and falls to the planet's surface.

Back down there, we meet our third hero, Rey, a scavenger struggling to live on the barren planet. She longs for another life, evidenced by the Rebel helmet and handmade X-wing pilot figurine in her makeshift home. Soon she rescues BB-8 from a desert dweller and later meets Finn. Suddenly, First Order ships attack. Our heroes escape to the only remaining ship, the *Millennium Falcon*. From there they defeat their pursuers and take to space, where they meet original-trilogy heroes Han Solo and Chewbacca. So begins a new adventure to defeat the First Order and discover the hideout of the long-lost hero Luke Skywalker.

Talking with older kids and younger teens about the story

Because of this film's popularity, your kids have likely seen *The Force Awakens* at least once already. Before watching it again, you might suggest pretending this is the first time they've seen the story. Then consider offering discussion questions like these:

- How is *Episode VII: The Force Awakens* similar to *Episode IV: A New Hope* and *Episode V: The Empire Strikes Back*? How are these stories different?
- How did you feel, seeing Han Solo, Chewbacca, the *Millennium Falcon*, Leia, and others?
- What other feelings do you think the filmmakers want us to have, going back into this "galaxy far, far away"? What actions might they want us to do after seeing the film?
- How did you respond to Han Solo's sacrifice? What is really going on between Han Solo and his son on the bridge? What parts of the story are the storytellers not telling us, and why do they withhold that information? Why do stories build suspense like this?
- How did you feel about (spoilers!) Rey finally finding Luke Skywalker at the end? (If you've seen *Episode VIII: The Last Jedi*, you can ask your kids how they feel about Luke's response to Rey handing him the lightsaber. If your kids don't know how they feel, there are *plenty* of *Star Wars* fan-critics on the internet who have opinions about Luke here. In fact, this criticism also comes from the actor behind Luke himself, Mark Hamill, who initially disagreed with Luke's newfound pessimism and anger about the Jedi order.)

STEP 2: WHAT IS THE MORAL AND IMAGINARY WORLD?

The filmmakers plunge us into a faraway galaxy of color, realism, fantasy, spiritual and moral themes, and "small" people who join a great hero's journey. You and your kids can discuss what the story *shows* and what moral or spiritual ideas the story *tells*.

The story world reflects color, realism, and fantasy.

Abrams is an excellent visual storyteller. What the film *shows* reveals the story and its themes even if no one is directly speaking about them. For example, *The Force Awakens* opens with the sight of a new and menacing shadow creeping slowly over a moon, its shape reminiscent of Kylo Ren's new cross-bladed lightsaber. Black and white tones evoke the original-trilogy Empire's corridors and chambers. Flashes of crimson reflect Ren's presence and are particularly stylized during his confrontations with Han and Rey. First Order troops gather in shots framed to evoke Nazi propaganda films. All these serious and darker tones contrast with the film's more pleasing palette, which also recalls images from the original trilogy: lush greens of a forest planet, pale and golden terrains of a desert planet, and blizzard whites and blues of the snow-covered Starkiller planet weapon.

As for our human characters, they've become more diverse. The original trilogy featured white American or British male actors in starring roles. Only near the end of *The Empire Strikes Back* did the story bring in a black actor, Billy Dee Williams, as side character Lando Calrissian. Now the formula is reversed. White male heroes act at the story's margins along with Guatemalan-born Oscar Isaac (Poe Dameron), while female actor Daisy Ridley (Rey) and black actor John Boyega (Finn) take the starring roles. Rey repeatedly subverts the distressed damsel trope by rejecting Finn's well-intended efforts to play the macho hero, saving both herself and him in the process. Maz Kanata is voiced by African actress Lupita Nyong'o, and other characters show a more diverse reflection of humanity, alongside aliens with even more skin tones and textures.

The Force Awakens is also a speculative or fantastical story that is set among spacefaring civilizations. In the world of *Star Wars*, humans live among humanoid aliens and can fly a spaceship between planets as easily as taking a bus. Futuristic tech is common, like light-speed travel and antigravity engines. However, these technologies and their histories are rarely even partially explained, unlike harder science fiction. Instead, *Star Wars* is a space opera—a fantasy adventure set in space. The usual images of fantasy, wizards and enemy castles, become Jedi knights and killer space stations.

But the filmmakers also mean this world to look realistic and lived in. Rey's desert planet feels primitive. Humans and imaginary creatures squabble and barter, Rey keeps her hood up to avoid dust, and beasts make a muddy mess at an oasis well. We clearly see that, on this planet, if you don't scavenge or trade you don't survive. First Order ships gleam as if they've just rolled off an assembly line, while the Resistance's older X-wings are tinged with grime and grease. And Maz Kanata's bar is built inside a stone castle, hinting at a past civilization that we never see or hear about. This is yet another reflection of the appealing ancient-futuristic *Star Wars* universe, which implies hundreds of untold background stories that give the movie's story depth and realism.

The story world explores moral and spiritual themes.

The Force Awakens returns to the religion of the previous films—the hidden power called the Force. In the original trilogy, Obi-Wan Kenobi famously defined the Force as an energy field created by all living things, which binds the galaxy together. Maz Kanata also teaches the audience Force 101: "It moves through and surrounds every living thing," she tells Rey. "Close your eyes. Feel it. The light—it's always been there. It will guide you."[1]

But this power is subject to unspoken moral assumptions. In this imaginary universe, good and evil are real and absolute, and good will eventually defeat evil before the credits roll. (Interestingly, the *Star Wars* films often refer to this victory of good as "balance" between good and evil.) Human life (or sentient alien life) is valuable, and those who murder innocent lives are evil. Loving relationships are good, as shown by several heroes, like Han and Rey.

But anger and abuse are evil, as shown by Kylo Ren and the First Order. Family connections are part of healthy humanity; missing family hurts a person like Rey, while family dysfunction harms a person like Kylo. Values such as freedom and independence are clearly good, as represented by the Resistance. But notions such as the First Order's abuse and authoritarianism are evil and must be fought.

Abrams said he wanted to "make this movie delightful,"[2] and he does not dwell on philosophy. That means we must watch carefully for the story's moral assumptions even as we revel in its fun. The story delights in normal people taking the hero's journey.

The Force Awakens and similar fantastical stories often emphasize people who start in poverty and obscurity but are called to a special, greater cause. For example, in the original *Star Wars* trilogy, Luke Skywalker serves as the hero in a story template popularized by mythologist Joseph Campbell, who called this the *hero's journey* or *monomyth*.[3] As the story's primary hero, Luke starts in a humble place but longs for greater things. He suffers an inciting event, leaves his old life to take a quest, undergoes trials, learns from a mentor, falls, dies (literally or figuratively), then rises to final victory.

The Force Awakens appears to be setting up Rey's story as another monomyth (and the final film confirms this setup). She is a nobody lost on a desert planet. She wants to be reunited with her missing family, but instead an inciting event sweeps her up in a larger quest. At first, Rey resists the call of the Force to become a hero who fights evil and suffers trials. Later movies show more trials, risings, and victories.

Talking with older kids and younger teens about the story world

- Is this a world you would want to live in? What kind of world is it?

- How are this galaxy and its creatures like our own world? How are they different?
- What do good and evil actions look like in this world? Do the consequences make sense?
- Did you notice how the movie uses colors and sounds, especially to represent the bad guys versus our heroes? Why do you think the storytellers made these choices?
- What about the Force? Is it like a biblical concept of supernatural power in the world?

STEP 3: WHAT IS GOOD, TRUE, AND BEAUTIFUL IN THIS WORLD (COMMON GRACE)?

Let's explore the God-given beauty, truth, and goodness in *The Force Awakens*. Before exposing the story's idols, parents can eagerly affirm and praise these graces.

This story's creativity reflects God's own creation.

God wants human beings to imitate him in their creative works. He gives us so many fantastical colors, shapes, and even creatures in our galaxy close, close to home. When humans made in God's image make artistic works, they cannot help but pay tribute to the original Artist through the talents and labor of producers, writers, actors, designers, musicians, and others.

The Force Awakens pays particular attention to meaningful color palettes and style. This alone reflects the organization God put into his created universe. And the use of color and style to reflect simple and natural goodness—versus harsh shades of black and white and crimson—recognizes a clear divide between good and evil.

The film's emphasis on a diverse cast also reflects God's creation of humans in all our diversity. God's image is reflected not in one kind of human being only but in two sexes, as well as different body types, skin tones, and cultures. This marks a welcome improvement over the arguably "monochromatic" casts of films past. As a fantasy set in another galaxy, *The Force Awakens* also reflects a unique picture of God's fantastically diverse world and our longing for adventure, excitement, and exploring new places.

This galaxy far, far away is a deeply moral universe.

The way God lets all people see some truth—part of his *common grace*—is also reflected in the film's moral and spiritual themes. In the real world, God assures us that absolute good should and will triumph over absolute evil and that people will be held to account for how they respond to the moral law they recognize in nature (Romans 2:14–15). *The Force Awakens* also pictures a world in which characters must choose between a clear, absolute good side and an evil side, which war against each other. The film presumes that a righteous "light side" should and will have victory over an evil "dark side." Christians in particular can see how this ongoing drama and battle between good and evil reflects spiritual reality.

Jesus said even evil people can practice common-grace virtues (Matthew 7:11). *The Force Awakens* positively shows flawed heroes who pursue the good. Finn, Rey, and other Resistance fighters fight for human dignity. They implicitly sense the biblical truth that individuals are created in God's image. These heroes also long to be part of a greater story and community—a desire God has placed in our hearts. And when Rey in particular hears about the promise of a higher calling to a spiritual world, her desire to know more reflects our God-given desire to become part of something greater than our own wants.

Our heroes showcase truly heroic sacrifice.

Heroes in *The Force Awakens* often sacrifice their own desires so they can make right choices; in return they find love and goodness awaiting them. For example, Finn forsakes his stormtrooper duties and finds sudden friendship with Poe. Rey forsakes her convenience to save a helpless droid. Han Solo treats Rey with respect and kindness, almost as a father figure, even as he grieves the loss of his own son. All of our heroes are willing to sacrifice their lives to protect the lives of vulnerable friends.

By contrast, Kylo Ren and the First Order are not simply trying to establish order in the universe. They want total, oppressive control, destroying planets and murdering innocents who get in their way. In the world of the film, their evil is easy to recognize.

Even in his private life, Kylo Ren dabbles in literal and spiritual darkness. We see him meditating before a crumpled helmet of his grandfather, Darth Vader. He even "prays" to his infamous ancestor: "Forgive me. I feel it again, the pull to the light. . . . Show me again the power of the darkness."[4] Later, Kylo expresses doubts about the dark side—just before he chooses to murder his own father. Kylo is a picture of complex corruption who might remind us of Romans 3:15–17.

"Their feet are swift to shed blood;
    in their paths are ruin and misery,
and the way of peace they have not known."

Later, in a novel twist, we also see that Kylo is a fool who throws temper tantrums when he does not get his way. His evil is complex only on the outside. Inside he is shallow, petty, and immature. The film goes out of its way *not* to glamorize this evil.

As for the hero's journey, it reflects our God-given longing to rise above ordinary life and join a grand adventure, like an epic quest or a war in the stars. Even better, this hero's journey can reflect Jesus's final sacrifice to save his enemies. Perhaps *The Force Awakens'* most intensely Christlike image is when Han Solo tries to save his rebellious son. Han reflects the love of parents who give good gifts to their children, even at the cost of their very lives. This is a deeply good common-grace gift of our Lord. He himself went to such lengths to save us from being swallowed by the darkness.

Talking with older kids and younger teens about these common graces

Once you have identified common grace—good, true, and beautiful elements—in *The Force Awakens*, you can talk to your older children and younger teens about them. For example:

- In the battle between the First Order and Resistance, who are clearly the "good guys"? How do we know they're good? Can we say for sure, according to the story's own rules?
- What about the Resistance? Can you tell if they stand for an actual galactic government? Why do you think they are resisting? When might it be right to resist or rebel against evil authorities? When might it be wrong, according to Scripture?
- Why do you think Kylo Ren wants the dark side so badly? Why does he intentionally resist the light side, without giving any reason for his evil desires?
- Does everyone have a struggle inside them between a light side and a dark side? Why did Han Solo let his son kill him? Could you do the same thing for someone you loved who was making himself your enemy and turning toward evil? If you turned toward the dark side, what would you think if someone did that for you?

STEP 4: WHAT IS FALSE AND IDOLATROUS IN THIS WORLD?

However, none of the truth and beauty in *The Force Awakens* makes sense without Jesus. If we keep him out of the picture, our sinful hearts only reshape these good gifts into idols.

We might turn the fantastical story into an idol, or we might make baseless morality and Force worship into an idol. We might even turn the human-hero's journey itself into an idol.

Who gets to define good and evil?

For example, film's use of color and style to represent good and evil can feed our desire to classify good and evil in easy, unnuanced rules based on appearance. This makes little sense if pressed to its logical conclusion. Scary-looking people are not always bad, and evil rulers do not always hold Nazi-style rallies with crimson flags, shouting behind large lecterns. Conversely, good people are not always ethnically diverse or easy to identify. In reality, we cannot rely on an artist's use of style and color to interpret good and evil for us. We need some other, higher standard.

The Force Awakens story is also powered by an unseen and *assumed* morality. If the galaxy has no God—no ultimate standard of morality—then how do we know the Resistance is good and the First Order is evil? Yes, the First Order uses a gargantuan space weapon to destroy planets and kill millions of people. But then Resistance fighters arguably respond with "an eye for an eye" to destroy the Order's planet and kill thousands of people in return.

Kylo Ren or Supreme Leader Snoke could confront one of our heroes and raise this point: "Yes, we have killed thousands, but you have also killed thousands. We are not so different, you and I. So embrace the power of the dark side." Rey or another hero would have no logical response. That's because the *Star Wars* world presumes that this eye-for-an-eye approach counts as good justice, or just war, instead of evil vengeance or excessive violence.

We might argue that the Resistance fighters' implied respect for individual freedom, family, and camaraderie gives them the moral high ground. But this point also *assumes* some higher standard to differentiate good and evil. Is freedom an absolute value? Can't individual freedom be twisted into license for selfishness or even the same kinds of tyranny the First Order exercises? Rather, if people enjoy personal freedom without limits, families and beloved allies can become insular and dysfunctional, and even tyrannical, on their own.[5]

After its victory, might the Resistance adopt a "never again" posture toward the First Order and, within another generation or two, turn into just another Empire? In fact, this is exactly the fate of many resistance or revolution movements in our own galaxy. Today's freedom-proclaiming revolutionary may become tomorrow's repressive dictator.

The point is not that freedom or protection of life are evil. But as values, they make no sense in a universe without God as our ally. He alone can name what is truly good and evil.

"My ally is the Force," but it has no will to even *be* an ally.

Instead of God, the *Star Wars* universe gives us the Force. Yoda says in *The Empire Strikes Back*, "My ally is the Force, and a powerful ally it is."[6] But unlike God, the Force has a light side and a dark side and is said to guide the fate of events and people.

The Force, like popular culture itself, is a messy mix. In this case, it blends Western ideas, such as good versus evil, and Eastern notions, such as the Tao. Luke Skywalker actor Mark Hamill himself said, "The idea of the Force is basically 'Religion's Greatest Hits.'"[7]

Star Wars opts for the Force over the biblical God partly because the Force is impersonal. The Force cannot establish moral rules or tell us how to live because it has no authority and no mind. As C. S. Lewis remarked, without even having seen a single *Star Wars* movie,

> One reason why many people find Creative Evolution
> so attractive is that it gives one much of the emo-
> tional comfort of believing in God and none of the

less pleasant consequences. When you are feeling fit and the sun is shining and you do not want to believe that the whole universe is a mere mechanical dance of atoms, it is nice to be able to think of this great mysterious Force rolling on through the centuries and carrying you on its crest. If, on the other hand, you want to do something rather shabby, the Life-Force, being only a blind force, with no morals and no mind, will never interfere with you like that troublesome God we learned about when we were children. The Life-Force is a sort of tame God. You can switch it on when you want, but it will not bother you. All the thrills of religion and none of the cost. Is the Life-Force the greatest achievement of wishful thinking the world has yet seen?[8]

The Force Awakens implies the Force is calling or commissioning someone for a grand destiny. But the Force is not personal and so has no personal identity or moral will. It cannot really call anyone to anything. It cannot reveal right and wrong or lead people. This "god" has no mind *or* heart. It is incapable of love. It cannot fulfill our longing to join the beauty and goodness we see but somehow find ourselves separated from. And finally, this Force has no story of its own. How then can we expect our story to end well or provide us any assurance that our part in saving the universe has been for the sake of good?

The problem of heroism in a me-centered universe

Finally, Rey's heroic journey can reflect God's calling to a Christlike life. But her story can also reflect a self-centered view of the universe. This is the essence of sin. We see ourselves as author, director, and star. We feel no need to look to a divine Savior, a perfect hero who comes into the story *from outside* to save the world (and save his enemies!). Instead we look to a human savior like us—a flawed but moral Chosen

One. Maybe, like Rey, we can also get on the right side of destiny. Can we construct a better origin story to tell about ourselves? Can we act as heroic as the fantasy hero?

So runs our fantasy lives, an escape from our mundane existence of survival, work, and training exercises (which occur in real time instead of movie montages). In our escapist dreams, we can rocket from epic battle to epic battle, fighting for victims and destroying obviously evil Nazilike villains. We can become the saviors of our own worlds.

But even in *Star Wars*, human saviors can't achieve such victories—not permanently. Fireworks fade. Ewoks waddle back to their treehouses. And you're still left with the same sins and struggles against darkness you have always had.

What about Luke's galaxy-saving victory? To quote Mr. Incredible, "No matter how many times you save the world, it always manages to get back in jeopardy again."[9] One minute, throngs of people are shooting fireworks to celebrate your heroism and their freedom. Then years later, some idiot comes along to bring black robes and planet killers back in style, and here we go again. Why won't the victories Rey, Finn, and Poe achieve unravel so that their descendants, a generation later, will need to fight yet another round of star wars?

Talking with older kids and younger teens about idols

Once you have identified idols in *The Force Awakens*, you'll be able to talk to your older children or younger teens about them. For example, consider questions like these:

- If good and evil are constantly warring in the stars, why fight at all?
- Who gets to define good and evil in the *Star Wars* universe?
- If the Force has no mind, why do even our heroes keep talking about the Force as if it can be allied

with any hero, much less summoning Rey to some great adventure?

- When life gets boring or even frustrating with our homework, chores, and family life, do you ever wish you could go off and become a great hero and fight in epic space battles instead? How can this desire to "escape" reality turn into an idol?

STEP 5: HOW IS JESUS THE TRUE ANSWER TO THIS STORY'S HOPES?

Instead of flawed-Chosen-One-saves-the-world promises, what does the gospel offer? Here, you'll want to get quite specific with your older children in challenging them to compare and contrast this story with the truest story, salvation in Jesus.

The gospel transforms this story's color, realism, and fantasy.

C3PO is fond of saying, "Thank the Maker!" The gospel encourages us to say the same.

God has created a real world of color and diversity. On our planet, anyone can behold fantastical creatures and places. But only when we respond *with gratitude to God* can we see such gifts in all their beauty. In fact, if God intends humans to explore all of his renewed creation for eternity, then perhaps someday humans really could travel between new worlds similar to those of *The Force Awakens*. Either way, such fantasy concepts and images can awaken in us a profound sense of gratitude to our Creator, who really has redeemed us from evil and destined us for an eternal adventure for his glory—the greatest beauty of all.

The gospel transforms this story's moral and spiritual themes.

Unlike the ungrounded and unsourced moral laws of the *Star Wars* universe, God has not left us struggling to grasp right and wrong. We need not be plagued by ethical quandaries, vulnerable to potential enemy suggestion that we are not so different from the villains we fight. Instead, God has built his moral law into the universe, and he has revealed in his written Word exactly who he is. His law is clear and unassailable, and it convicts us of an equally unassailable truth: everyone of us has broken his law.

To fulfill this holy standard, God does not send an impersonal Force of spiritual power to be used by us to *try* keeping the law based on our own good or evil impulses. That road inevitably ends in failure and futility. Instead God *himself* comes into our world. Jesus has his own epic origin story as a coequal person of the triune God before time began. Jesus is the perfect, eternal incarnation who is fully God and fully human. He has God's perfections yet suffered the struggles and temptations of humans (Hebrews 4:15). He is not vague and impersonal; he is the final, personal revelation of God. His power does not give us mind control, matter manipulation, or the ability to "let go and use" him. He will not be used. But his power is better and deeper than any Force. He created a universe from nothing, sustains it day by day, and is bringing dead people back to life.

Then as our Savior, who came in from outside to save those who could not save themselves, he also brings his power *inside* us. He sends his Holy Spirit, who is no mere Force, but the active and personal third Person of the Trinity. He dwells in us and constantly points us back to Jesus, while changing us from the inside out to become like our Savior.

God's people know the moral code that *Star Wars* assumes but cannot justify because God has revealed this to us. We know for sure that there is ultimate good and ultimate evil, that good must conquer evil (rather than being balanced by the next generational go-around), and that compassion and mercy are eternal values that hold the universe together.

The gospel transforms this hero's journey.

Finally, human heroes carry their flaws to their deaths and cannot permanently save the galaxy. The best and only complete hero is Jesus Christ. All our hero's-journey stories, all the old and new myths about the dying and sacrificial hero, reflect this ultimate story of stories.

C. S. Lewis calls Jesus's ultimate story the true myth behind all other hero myths:

> "Now the story of Christ is simply a true myth: a myth working on us the same way as the others, but with this tremendous difference that it really happened: and one must be content to accept it in the same way, remembering that it is God's myth where the others are men's myths: i.e., the Pagan stories are God expressing Himself through the minds of poets, using such images as He found there, while Christianity is God expressing Himself through what we call 'real things.'"[10]

Jesus came from a humble background, lived a human life, perfectly resisted the temptation of the dark side, died, and rose again to secure an eternal kingdom and save the galaxy *permanently*. Because of his heroism, we needn't fear that our lives will revert to what they were before Jesus arrived. No empire or dark lord can ever undo Jesus's final victory! Instead we live in the light of his victory, fight the remaining spiritual darkness within and without, and await the consummation. When Jesus returns and brings the new heavens to the new earth (Revelation 21), the fireworks and celebrations will be here to stay. And when he glorifies his people with spiritual bodies immune to decay and temptation, there is no chance we would ever want to go back to the dark side.

Now, thanks to Jesus, we need not feel burdened to live like fictional heroes or to make up our own hero's-journey stories so we can save the world. We need not feel the vacuum of boredom or depression when we fail to live a life of repeated epic awesome hero moments. Instead, Jesus makes our ordinary lives extraordinary. Every moment of non-montage training work and every person we meet become eternally significant. Jesus is showing us the greatest and most intricately plotted story of all, and every little detail and plot turn in our galaxy matters. He makes his people into heroes in his drama, and we *can* await an eternal life of adventure. Now and forever, we're thrilled to journey with the greatest hero of all.

Talking with older kids and younger teens about the true hero: Jesus

Finally, here's where you can get excited showing how Jesus Christ, our real and personal Savior, fulfills every good hope the story has reflected but can't fulfill apart from him. For example, when exploring *The Force Awakens*, revisit the idol questions like this:

- How does Jesus define good and evil, such that even if a story's heroes (or villains) couldn't answer what's good and what's evil, we the movie fans can answer this?
- Why is Jesus a better hero than the Force or even the good heroes of this story? (Examples: Jesus has a mind and is not an impersonal "magic." He wants us to know him. He clearly reveals to us his true story about how he has defeated evil and is saving the universe. He has assured us that he will *defeat* evil once and for all and not just put it in time-out until the next version of the Empire comes along!)

- How can Jesus fulfill our desire to be called away from mundane life into a grand hero's-journey type of adventure? (Example: In real life, Jesus *has* called us to an adventure. It does start off slow, as if we are living in the "deleted scenes" of the movie, those parts we don't see when Rey is living day to day. Or maybe we aren't Rey at all. Maybe we're an "extra" or a hero who doesn't appear on the film poster. But God has promised us a future life of excitement and adventure as we fulfill his epic callings in the eternal new heavens and new earth. And even today, we can get little glimpses of the excitement and dangers of living in Jesus's quests for us.)

As helpful as these starter questions might be, let's also remember that we needn't make every discussion with your older children or younger teens about obvious truths, Jesus-like hero's journeys, or serious reminders that the Force does not exist. Remember also to live out the joy of God-given imagination for his sake. Fantastical stories are not for children only but for godly adults. Their magic can aid us in our own "awakening" to the deeper magic of the gospel.

Chapter 12

Engaging Popular Culture with Older Teens and Young Adults

One parenting adage asserts, "We are not raising children; we are raising adults." This is especially true in the later teen years (about ages fifteen through nineteen). It can be a time of many "declarations of independence" that are perfectly normal in the transition into adulthood but that can be deeply unsettling for parents used to more dependent, submissive children.

It's also a time when childhood faith either sticks or evaporates. In some churches, this is the time when many kids stop coming.[1] In a post-Christian culture, it is easy to understand why parents would want to shelter their kids. Sheltering kids at this age, however, ironically makes things worse. A faith that fears the culture around it feels stifling. A church that allows for no expressions of doubt, loneliness, pain, and struggle is a straitjacket.

Older teens need more than a list of rules. They need room to explore the beauty and meaning of the big picture. They don't need shelter. They need a mentor—someone to walk with them through the transition, asking tough questions and helping them find real answers.[2] This can happen organically, not just by discussing the sermon on the drive home but also by discussing popular culture when you watch TV or play a video game.

Older teens have a lot of questions, and they live in a culture that is increasingly skeptical about Christian beliefs and moral values. At this age, popular culture carries huge weight, and teaching kids how to think it through *as Christians* helps bolster their faith. One survey shows that a significant reason why young adults chose to stay in their church was an attitude of engagement rather than fear regarding popular culture: "In many ways, pop culture has become the driver of religion for Millennials, so helping them think and rightly respond to culture should be a priority."[3]

Let us take a look at the messy challenges older teens and young adults will face.[4] Then we'll discuss how you can help meet these challenges as you engage popular culture with your teenage son or daughter.

Growth in Sexual Awareness

In the last chapters, we explored these changes in summary form. Now we need to take more time with each one.

Body image dissatisfaction. Teen bodies change a lot between ages fifteen and nineteen, and body image is huge for this age group. Many teens obsess over their looks. They may bathe in waves of body-image dissatisfaction and can develop eating disorders.[5] Popular culture doesn't help, with its images of airbrushed bodies on magazines and impossibly glamorous stars and starlets in makeup and good lighting who have full-time trainers on their payroll (not to mention the unattainably perfect computer-generated bodies that populate many video games). Who wouldn't be dissatisfied?

Sex on overdrive and pornography. As older teens mature sexually, sexual attractiveness and dating become major concerns. Ted remembers sitting in his tenth-grade health class when the teacher announced a disturbing statistic: "Teen boys typically think about sex every fifteen seconds." All the girls' eyes widened, and they turned to us, "Is this true?!" The boys blushed and sank into their seats. It didn't matter that the statistic was almost certainly false; it *felt* true.

The prevalence of pornography makes it worse. In the West and many other parts of the world, most teens—both boys and girls—use porn.[6] Pornography is not harmless entertainment. It alters the chemistry of the pleasure centers of the brain, so it's highly addictive. Over time, porn changes attitudes about normal sexual behavior and sexual partners—for the worse.[7] And that's not even to mention the guilt and isolation that haunt Christian teens who stumble into sin because of porn.

Pornography is not only more accessible but also more acceptable in mainstream culture. (Ted has actually seen "I ♥ porn" stickers on lampposts and on a teen's backpack). Some mainstream popular culture reflects this increased acceptance with elements that are soft-core porn or reference pornography. This occurs in films (such as the *Fifty Shades of Grey* series), music videos, television (*Game of Thrones*), and even video games (such as *The Witcher 3: Wild Hunt*). Culture-engaging parents need to be committed to open communication and have lightning-quick reflexes for fast forwarding when necessary!

The messy truth about sexual orientation. There's also the prospect of a teen, or one of his friends, "discovering I'm gay." This is seldom as simple as it tends to be portrayed in popular culture. Recent research reveals a more fluid and messy picture of sexual orientation.[8] Attraction, behavioral habits, and sexual identity don't always overlap and often shift over time. A young woman may identify as heterosexual but find herself attracted to a female friend, and even act on that attraction. Or a young man who identifies as gay may find himself developing a crush on a young woman. A teen who is solely same-sex attracted is the exception. Bisexual and shifting attractions are more common, and young people in particular may flip-flop between same-sex and other-sex attraction. It isn't always set for life, regardless of a teen's chosen identity. Popular culture that strongly affirms "gay identity," as if this were unchangeable, only adds to the confusion.

The painful truth about gender identity. *Transgender* is an umbrella term including everyone who feels uncomfortable with their own biological sex (1 in 215 males, 1 in 300 females). A smaller number of people are diagnosed with actual gender dysphoria, an intense discomfort caused when biological sex does not line up with gender identity.[9] This unease can appear quite early in childhood, but it becomes clearer in the later teen years. Even here, though, there is fluidity. For teens who suffer from gender dysphoria (including the notorious "rapid onset gender dysphoria"), about three in four will find that those feelings lessen or go away entirely (though some end up struggling with same-sex attraction).[10]

Risk to teens is real, and they need our support. For kids who struggle with these issues, suicide rates and other risky behaviors skyrocket.[11] These kids need loving support and guidance in a confusing time. Rather than turning to monolithically LGBTQ+-affirming popular culture and support groups, they should be getting guidance from caring Christian parents and youth workers. Our advice: stay calm and loving. Patiently offer gospel grace to your children. These struggles can actually drive them *deeper* into relationship with Jesus, and with you, if they know that grace is available to strugglers. We have a golden opportunity to address a whole myriad of issues with gentle, biblical wisdom if we can respond with trust in God's provision rather than desperation or judgmental anger.

Here are specific guidelines for responding to these many changes in older teens.

Guideline 1: Help your teen appreciate the goodness of creation and true inner beauty.

Teen body dissatisfaction can be unhealthy, even dangerous. The deeper problem with body dissatisfaction is that it allows a twofold lie to flourish: that God's creation isn't good enough and that our real beauty is tied to how good we look. But God's Word gives us the truth. First, it says we are created by God, and God doesn't make junk. We need to learn contentment and gratitude for the bodies he gave us, even if they aren't Hollywood ready. Parents can model contentment for teens by being content with their own changing and aging bodies and not criticizing teens about their bodies.

Second, God's Word tells us that true, lasting beauty resides inside. While the Bible affirms the goodness of bodies, we also are so much more than our appearance, weight, and muscle mass. Samuel, in choosing the next king after Saul, needed a reminder from God not to be dazzled by looks (1 Samuel 16:7). The Lord values the heart more than the hairdo and character more than charisma.

As you engage popular culture, be ready to counter images of outer hotness with stories of inner contentment and inner beauty. For example, at the Christian school where Ted teaches, a new student made a snarky comment about another young woman's weight. Her classmates rushed to her defense: "You can't say that about her! You don't know her like we do!" Ted was really proud of those students because they got it.

By engaging popular culture with teens, parents have many opportunities to address what is real and true—what lies beneath. The effects of a beautiful heart aren't as immediately apparent as a beautiful face, but a repeated, consistent exposure to the gospel helps cultivate a beautiful heart. Theologians call these habits the *means of grace*—Bible study, prayer, preaching,

sacraments, and relationships with other Christians. Be ready
to lead your teen to what is real and lasting.

Help teens also see the hidden beauty in others. A culture that focuses on appearance judges without mercy, and its
hierarchies are unassailable. No one knows this better than
teens: the popular, good-looking kids rule, and the rest drool.
Teach your teens how to opt out of that game, how *not* to
appraise their peers on their babeness or hunkitude. Help
them participate in an alternative economy where what is
valued is love, joy, peace, patience, kindness, gentleness, and
self-control (Galatians 5:22–23). Let them hear you appreciate who they are *inside*.

Guideline 2: Help teens understand sex in an increasingly pornified culture.

Given the easy access to pornography, some parents
might be tempted to move to a cave until their kids are thirty.
Nevertheless, engaging popular culture together with teens is
still a better option than withdrawal.

Of course, parents can prevent access to online pornography with filtering software because some works are inappropriate for *any* age. But we need more. For one thing,
pornographic elements *don't* stay filtered. They seep into
the style and stories of popular cultural works that are well
written, creative, culturally influential, and otherwise worth
engaging. Must we withdraw and restrict older teens to culture made for eleven-year-old children? That response leaves
teens unprepared for young adulthood, and it turns any cultural depiction of sexual relationship into extra-tempting forbidden fruit. Is there a better way? We think there is.

First, watch favorite shows or movies together, always
ready to skip past the parts that are too explicit. If you have
a good relationship, most teens will appreciate a genuine
willingness to engage their culture with them, and they will

find it more difficult to indulge lust while a parent is sitting right there. Your presence guards them in a way that may be simultaneously unnerving *and* comforting. You have created a safe zone of sorts.

Second, maintain open communication and seize teaching opportunities within that safe zone. Teens need guidance about sex that goes beyond saying, "Just say no (until you're married, and then it's OK)." Invite shame-free, no-taboo, gospel-centered conversations about this most delicate of subjects: what sex is truly for. Teens need to understand the meaning of this wonderful, incredibly powerful drive God created in them. Messages they get from secular culture don't amount to much: "Well, Billy, it's just instinct, the need to breed," or "When you love someone very, very much, and you really want to, why not?" Biblical Christianity offers a much richer perspective that actually gives them a reason to wait and tread carefully.

Ted's story: What's the big deal about sex?

When I served as a youth pastor to a group of teen boys, we sometimes had open discussion sessions. One time, they wanted to talk about sex and why their parents thought it was such a big deal. They thought sex was like a sport played for entertainment—fun but not particularly meaningful.

I explained what sex was about: communication, a God-given path to intimacy, a way to share yourself with a woman in the most vulnerable way possible. I saw raised eyebrows. No one had ever explained how serious sex is or how easily they could damage a loved one. Now they understood the need to surround sex with promises of protection, lifetime commitment, and covenant. God isn't a killjoy. He's a wise Father looking out for his children. He knows that our joy is made complete only by glorifying him and reflecting his love of intimacy.

My wife and I had a similar conversation with our seventeen-year-old daughter as we watched the episode "Innocence" from *Buffy the Vampire Slayer*, season 2. In this story, teenage Buffy decides it's time to lose her virginity, and she sleeps with her boyfriend (who happens to be a vampire). She wakes up to find out that he is different, distant, and she feels terribly used. Popular culture often idolizes sex and romance, but it also sometimes provides avenues for talking about issues teens wouldn't necessarily bring up themselves.

****

One final thought: gospel grace should cover all. Given the permissive attitudes and temptation in today's culture, we should be prepared to extend genuine forgiveness and support when teens stumble. We want our children to be wise about sex, but we need to be emotionally and spiritually prepared to pick up the pieces if they are not. It is not the end of the world. Make it clear that God wants to continue a relationship with them and to heal where they are broken, and that you want the same. The alternative is shaming and shunning, which will drive your teen away from the God of grace.

Guideline 3: Help teens navigate a culture that celebrates alternative sexualities.

Many works of popular culture add to sexual confusion by presenting strongly gay-affirming storylines and characters that glorify (or at least normalize) alternative sexualities. This has gone on for decades, and it's had a significant effect on social attitudes.[12] A new sexual orthodoxy has been created: the only people worthy of stigmatizing are those who don't accept and celebrate the individual's absolute right to whatever sexual self-expression the individual deems good and right.[13] It is tempting to become alarmed and withdraw from gay-affirming culture, but that would miss an opportunity to guide teens at a confusing time.

Popular culture often assumes that a person's LGBTQ+ identity is fixed, like race (echoing civil rights themes). To quote Lady Gaga, gay people are "born this way," end of story—and this means sexual orientation can give us a stable identity, it is believed. But as we've mentioned, that's a vast oversimplification. The fluidity of sexual attraction can be disconcerting for teens, but it also shows the need for biblical wisdom and truth. Sexual desire—shifting or stable—cannot tell us who we are. It cannot give us our true self. Only Christ can do that by naming us adopted sons or daughters of the King. This God-given identity can guide our teens' behavior even when unruly desires shout for attention. Identity rooted in Christ gives freedom: we are more than what we want.

Trusted adults can share biblical wisdom with struggling teens: "Sexual desire doesn't define you or dictate behavior. Where you stumble, grace is ever available. If you allow sex to forge your identity, it will become a prison. We were made for a deeper purpose and identity." This is life-saving truth.

Be careful not to have a double standard, forgiving teens who struggle with heterosexual sin while shunning those who struggle with homosexual sin. Perhaps we can learn from popular culture here. When a character comes out as gay, he or she is embraced and accepted. We don't ever want to affirm sin, but we do want to support and encourage those who struggle with sin. Can we embrace and encourage those who struggle with same-sex attraction even while maintaining that the Bible condemns homosexual behavior as sin? Befriending teens who struggle with same-sex attraction demonstrates what the gospel means in the realm of sexual identity. Paul extends that kind of grace and encouragement to people who came out of that lifestyle but who may still be struggling. He warns them against it, but he also affirms that is no longer who they are (1 Corinthians 6:9–11).

Guideline 4: Be ready to walk teens through increasingly confusing gender-identity issues.

Many popular culture creators have already moved past the trend of being gay affirming and now seek to affirm people who struggle with transgenderism and other confusions. As of this writing, "trans" themes have gone full mainstream. Even shows intended for young teens and older children, such as *Supergirl* and other series based on DC superheroes, have begun adding transgender characters. Similarly to the addition of same-sex-attracted characters and subplots, these cast additions frequently gain the attention of geek and fan websites, who write excited headlines about the casting and what it means for this next sexual frontier.

Christians should be ready to extend the same grace and biblical wisdom to teens who struggle with transgender and gender dysphoria. This is a complex issue, one on which Christians of good will can disagree. (Even the authors of this book don't see eye-to-eye on a few aspects of this issue. For more about our differences, please see appendix B.) But it is a vital issue and one very much in play in popular culture. Here is what we agree on:

1. God has a created norm governing male and female, and that ought to frame our identity. We live within a created binary of sexuality, and the Bible affirms this as good (see Genesis 2:21–24; Deuteronomy 22:5).

2. A disconnect between gender identity and biology reflects a fallen world rather than (necessarily) a deliberate, consciously sinful choice on anyone's part.

3. Kids who struggle with gender identity need the gospel and support within the church community rather than marginalizing and shame.

When it comes to sexual issues, many teens' consciences are haunted by failure. They doubt God's love, patience, or power to change them. They don't know why their choices or their gay friends' choices are wrong. They become orphans in what they feel is a sea of judgmental (and sometimes hypocritical) adults. When the faith becomes nothing but a web of rules they feel they cannot keep, it makes sense to walk away and adopt a live-and-let-live or anything-goes attitude. Give teens a burden and no help to bear it, and they will flee.

Instead, we need a clear enunciation of the gospel, especially how God restores the sexually broken and confused. Teens need a chance to hear why God's law is in fact wisdom *and* a chance to hear about God's grace and patience with those who stumble and struggle to find their feet. Real transformation begins only as idolatrous heart desires are dethroned and the heart is wooed to new affections by the gospel of grace.[14] Older teens need to understand the deep relevance of the gospel to this most messy of human arenas, sex.

GROWTH IN MENTAL PROCESSING

Mid-adolescence into early-adulthood is an exciting time intellectually. Older teens handle abstract thinking better and need less concrete imagery. They are better at logic, though they use it selectively. Teens are moving away from black-and-white thinking into more nuanced analysis, seeing shades of gray and sometimes reveling in that ambiguity. They can see issues from multiple angles. They can handle more complex information and analysis, including the five-question model for engaging popular culture presented earlier. (Ted actually asks high school seniors in his apologetics class to use them to analyze a movie clip.)

This increased mental capacity makes it easier for adults to relate to teens, but it also raises challenges. Teens can poke holes in parents' and teachers' arguments. They may doubt and challenge worldviews. Some may reject some aspects of their faith traditions during teen or young adult years and yet continue to believe the gospel. Others depart their childhood faith.

This new intellectual defiance could be a sign of teen rebellion. Or it could be how teens naturally test new ways of thinking. They discover new belief territories nearly every day as they read books, watch movies, and play games—as if the world has laid out twenty-five new stunning and radically different outfits. Teens want to try them all. And they want to know if the clothes they were raised with are really worth wearing. Are their old beliefs really true to who they are? Are they really true to the way the world is?

For many teens, these new intellectual abilities outstrip wisdom. The parts of the brain linked to self-regulation and risk assessment develop later (around ages twenty-two to twenty-five).[15] So teens will be tempted to break rules. When Harry Potter sneaks around after hours, this is not only heroic; it's also classic teen behavior.

All in all, a child's mid-to-late teen years are among the most exciting *and* challenging for a parent. How should a caring adult respond, and how does engaging popular culture fit in?

Guideline 1: Allow room for wrestling together.

Consider mid-to-late teens as young martial arts students in a kung-fu film just starting to hone their skills (cue training-montage music). The students don't need shackles; they need a wise sensei and sparring partner. God has given them you.

The attitude you bring into the dojo makes all the difference. Will you draw a teen into deeper relationship or push her away? A wise and patient sensei should be slow to show offense. Remember: teens are trying out alternatives and testing limits. You may feel shocked at storylines they find fascinating or characters they root for, but keep in mind your relationship with them.

If you ask teens what they like about storylines or characters, you will open avenues of exploration and deepen your relationships. But if you come down with bare assertions of authority rather than reasoned discussion, you will likely frustrate teens and "provoke your children to anger" (Ephesians 6:4), increasing the distance between you. Instead, discussion might show you both that any upset response wasn't necessary in the first place. Certainly, your parental authority still matters, but your role is changing. You are no longer just a guardian and guide but now also a partner. Your teens don't need you less; they need you differently.

Here's one practical tip for wrestling together when you engage popular culture: instead of giving quick answers, use questions. Make your teen think through ideas and express them. Questions drive deeper engagement with an issue—and throw a monkey wrench into runaway trains of thought. Most of all, questions help teens own their thought experiments and follow them to conclusions.

Guideline 2: Do the homework. *Be* the homework.

Of course, asking leading and provocative questions assumes you've thought through these issues on your own. Leading questions don't work if you don't know where they lead. Some teens abandon Christianity because they feel it is shallow, anti-intellectual, anti-science, and doesn't give them answers to questions they face outside church.[16] The bumper-sticker attitude of "The Bible says it, I believe it, that settles it," doesn't help inquisitive teens. They need to see the *why* and *how*. They need to see that the Christian faith can hold its own in the marketplace of ideas. They need us to do our homework.

But before we can do our homework, we must *be* the homework. This sounds Zen, but we mean that your teens need models of intelligent, thoughtful Christians. Do they see you searching the Scriptures, trying to live them out, and wrestling with their meaning in today's world? Do you wrestle in prayer over things that matter? Do you love God not with your heart only but with your mind? They need to see models of intellectual integrity.

Parental homework means we must also learn apologetics, especially worldview critique—understanding how non-Christian worldviews fall apart when pushed to their logical limits. Just because something *sounds* rational (or freeing or morally just) doesn't mean it actually *is*. Worldview apologetics give us a set of tools to deconstruct unbelief. In Ted's worldview class at a Christian high school, he can always tell the atheists because they have the best questions. He relishes the opportunity to give them answers—and ask them questions—that make them think.

Even if you don't have formal apologetics training, you can find many resources—websites with colorful names like Choosing Hats, the Poached Egg, Saints and Skeptics, the Wee Flea, and Apologetics 315. The Gospel Coalition, Christ and Pop Culture, the *Pop Culture Coram Deo* podcast, and many other websites also deal with worldview issues from a Christian perspective. So you will find no shortage of answers. However, if your teen stumps you, there is no shame in saying, "That's a *great* question. Know what? Why don't we research that together?" And voilá, you have formed a study group *and* treated your teen as a fellow scholar. You have laid the groundwork for a deeper relationship.

It is vital to have a strong doctrine of creation that understands that Christ "is before all things, and in him all things hold together" (Colossians 1:17). Teens are curious about everything, and too often Christians seem to be anti-this or that. A strong doctrine of creation provides a healthy antidote. If Christ is Lord of all, everything is fair game for discussion:

Q: Is Christianity against science?

A: How *could* it be? God created nature, and science simply interprets structures and processes found in nature. How could Christians oppose good science? Just as theology interprets God's Word, science interprets God's world. They need not be in conflict. Unless, of course, you're dealing with bad theology or bad science.

Q: Is Christianity antisex?

A: How *could* it be? God created sex. He created plants to pollinate and created animals and humans to be male and female. Sex was *his* idea. But he also created it to be surrounded with promises and covenants.

Culture's messages contain mixtures of truth and error, insight and deception. Be ready to ask questions, discuss the claims, and think through issues, images, and stories on offer from the popular cultural dream factory. It is time to do some serious (and seriously fun) thinking with your teen.

GROWTH IN SOCIAL INTERACTION AND IDENTITY

Questions about identity drive older teens: "Who am I besides my parents' son or daughter? How do I find out who I am?"[17] This inner questioning can lead teens to be self-absorbed, hyperaware of their own wants and needs. But as their identity settles, they will become more aware of others' needs as well—loved ones, peers, and all society. Social justice issues such as racism and sexism may become relevant in a new way. In the mid-to-late teen years, teens typically move from self-involvement to other-involvement.

This period is a time of uncertainty, discovery, and anxiety, a time when teens can develop depression or anxiety disorders.[18] If you notice a profound change in mood or behavior, talk to your teen and figure out what is going on. It might stem from substance abuse, harassment or bullying, or a depression/anxiety disorder. Do not mess around; seek treatment if necessary. Many instances of depression do not stem from sin. Even when they do, kids who suffer from it cannot just snap out of it. They need help. Paying attention to your teen's favorite entertainments can help give clues that may indicate the early stages of depression and give you an opportunity to talk about what's going on inside.

In their search for identity, older teens may spend more time away from family and with peers. Peers are a family you get to choose (this is a common theme in popular culture aimed at teens). However, once young adults move out, they may long to reconnect with family and what is literally *familiar*. This is all part of the search for identity. Teens cluster with those who share their perspective, who can provide a safe space for self-discovery.[19]

Just as teens migrate to new peer groups, they also migrate to new cultural tastes, discovering new sounds, styles, and stories that resonate with them. These cultural products can become "friends"—an abiding and comforting presence in the teen's life. Teens express identity through cultural choices. They are what they love. They might latch on to a fandom, displaying affections that seem too deep and weird to outsiders. It is all a part for this search for identity.

Older teens may also become obsessed with social media because this too gives them a sense of identity. Almost 50 percent of American teens say they are on social media "almost constantly."[20] Their main reason is to "appear interesting, popular and attractive" to peers. They carefully select the images, words, and videos they post and often ask friends to comment favorably to boost their online persona.[21] In other words, they are trying to create and maintain an identity, one that will out-compete their peers in "likes." And often, their actual, inner sense of self cannot measure up to their friends' online personas—or even their own. So while social media can help teens connect with peers, paradoxically it can also make them feel more isolated in the highly competitive world of social media.

How can parents and other caring adults help teens negotiate this delicate journey toward an independent identity?

Guideline 1: Negotiate health and peace.

In their quest for independence, teens can get themselves into trouble. They need limits and guidelines, even if they don't admit it. But parents who simply impose rules as they would on small children will stoke resentment. Rather, communicate and negotiate reasonable expectations regarding chores, homework, time with friends, curfews, screen time (computer or mobile device), and so on. Even their popular cultural diet needs negotiation, for the problem with much popular culture is that it depends on a sedentary audience. Sometimes teens need to be reminded that they need exercise in real life. Because bright screens can disrupt healthy sleep patterns, teens need to be reminded when to switch off.[22] Teens need parental guidance.

How you deliver your guidance makes all the difference, particularly when it comes to social media. If parents simply issue a decree, teens have deceptive ways of circumventing them. Confiscate a device, and they'll get access to another. Demand their Instagram password, and they'll give you one to a fake account.[23] Instead, engage with your teens. Ask about their favorite videos. Visit their favorite sites together and talk about what they are posting.[24] Build your relationship with them *in this area of their lives* so that when you have to have a difficult talk—about sexting, cyberbullying, limiting screen time—they will understand and buy in.[25] They need to know you are for them. And as a Christian parent, you know where true, stable, life-giving identity is found. It is not in a mask, a fragile online persona that must be constantly maintained or it falls apart. Teach your teen to know the difference.

Guideline 2: Open doors and hearts by getting to know their friends.

Try not to force your teens to choose between friends and family. Instead, make your home a welcoming place for their friends. No teens enjoy hearing parents judge their friends, especially when the parents know little about them. So get to know them. Understand their situations and characters, and let their friends get to know you.

What about when your teen chooses the wrong crowd? As hard as this is to swallow, even here your teen needs support and gentle guidance rather than a decree from on high. Unless your teen is being drawn into immoral or illegal behavior, refrain from forbidding contact with friends. That hasn't ever worked, as far back as the days of *Romeo and Juliet* ("And stay away from those dang Capulets!"). You only give your teen a reason to sneak behind your back.

Open communication about your concerns is a better path. Step into your teen's world and try to see that friend through his or her eyes. If your teen is trying risky behavior, negotiate rules and consequences. And talk about what real friendship means, and when other loyalties (such as to the Lord) should run deeper. Loyalty to friends is a huge theme in popular culture. Engaging popular culture together gives you a chance to bring biblical wisdom to bear.

Guideline 3: Let teens make their own cultural mistakes.

Some years back, the term *helicopter parents* came into vogue. It refers to parents who are so anxious to see their kid succeed that they hover, monitoring every decision. The result is a generation of kids who have never made a mistake that required them to pick up the pieces and push through (unless they hid their mistake from Mom and Dad). It creates a fragile generation governed by fear.

Sometimes, kids need to make their own mistakes so they can learn to make wise choices. This also applies to cultural choices. It's how teens learn cultural discernment.

Ted remembers, as a teenager, asking for and *receiving* two Pink Floyd albums for Christmas. His parents shook their heads and said they didn't endorse what Floyd stood for. He understood and thanked them. Then many months later, he realized how Floyd's music altered his mood, forming cynicism in him toward Christian brothers and sisters. He needed to put away the music for a couple of years until he was mature enough to handle the sardonic attitudes of acid rock. But this had to be his choice, and he's glad his parents let him make the choice. It was a watershed moment in his process of learning discernment.

Guideline 4: Learn to understand and value your teen's cultural tastes and choices.

Allowing your older teens latitude in their cultural choices lets them establish an independent identity and a healthy transition to adulthood. Parents might interpret their teens' choices as rejection of the parent's values, aesthetic sensibilities, or of *them* personally. After all, isn't the teen replacing familiar culture with an inferior, subversive alternative? But parents need not respond this way *if* we strive to understand the appeal and (often) the real excellence of their teens' cultural choices.

You can't support your teen and also dismiss their cultural tastes with an attitude like, "The garbage kids watch and listen to these days." You can either walk with teens through their cultural worlds or indulge in snap judgment and push your teens away.

Engaging with your teen's cultural choices does not mean you agree with every message and image in those works. It means you understand these choices are part of your teen's identity, and you care enough to want to understand what resonates with that identity—what he or she finds excellent.

When Ted teaches classes on popular culture, he often tells his students that *this* is the golden age of television, which has matured as its own art form. Cinema has been going strong for decades and shows no signs of flagging, especially if you don't dismiss whole genres of film, such as action-adventure. Music developments are fascinating, particularly electronica, but also neo-folk and lo-fi. The success of the Harry Potter series has boosted sales of young adult fiction (and popular fiction in general). Video games from major or independent studios have improved depth and nuance in writing, gameplay dynamics, graphics, and art styles. It is a fantastic time to enjoy popular culture.

By letting his teens make their own cultural choices, and enjoying their shows, games, and music, Ted has been alerted to cultural creativity he would have otherwise missed. And he's been able to give his teens the affirmation they crave but wouldn't dare request out loud.

As Your Child Becomes an Adult, Pursue the Relationship

We cannot promise that if you follow all these guidelines you are guaranteed your teen will maintain a solid Christian faith through these years. That's not how this works. Sometimes parents do everything right, and a child still wanders away. This is not about guarantees; it's about putting yourselves in a position of genuine relational depth from which you can share and reflect that depth of God's grace available in Jesus. A child may walk away, but a solid love relationship provides a foundation of hope.

Another foundation of hope: God alone is Lord of the heart. He alone can reshape desire and melt the hardest heart to draw a teen to himself. So, obviously, pray! Pray for and with your kids often. Even alienated teens appreciate parents who show love through prayer.

Now let's explore a concrete example of popular culture aimed at older teens.

Chapter 13

Practice Session for Older Teens: *Fortnite Battle Royale*

Let's apply what we've learned about teenagers and popular culture to a practical example a teen might enjoy. We will explore a wildly popular online video game, *Fortnite Battle Royale* (2017). But first, we offer two disclaimers.

This game is aimed at older teens. However, many younger kids are also drawn to this game. Stephen can cite examples in his church and extended family alone. We urge caution in allowing children and even teenagers unsupervised access to the game. For example, *Fortnite* employs a series of rewards in the form of digital currency used to buy items that change the appearance of the player's in-game avatar. It can be very tempting for younger kids who have little resistance to hard sell, "for a limited time only!" types of marketing. Different teens have different strengths, weaknesses, and levels of maturity. In training ambassadors for Christ, some works will be beneficial for one child but not another: "'All things are lawful,' but not all things are helpful" (1 Corinthians 10:23). That's a judgment call you need to make together.

Also, we're going to spend more time exploring this game's origin story and history. This isn't because we're geeks obsessing over details. Rather, we do this for two main reasons.

First, we want to show by example how we respect the creative works of God's image-bearers. That goes double for this medium of video games. In the past, some Christians have dismissed video games as being especially frivolous (more so than movies) or only suitable for immature men. No doubt, you've seen the ditch-video-games-and-man-up articles from some Christian authors. Even if your game-enjoying teenage child has not seen these, he might catch this condemnation from the Christian-cultural winds.

Second, we also spend more time with this example because, as your teenager grows, she needs even more to see that you are respecting her cultural worlds enough to understand them before you enter them alongside her. This applies beyond video games to pop cultural pursuits that may seem even stranger, like gaming tournaments, fanfiction, or K-pop. Either way, you should want to do your homework. Here's how we did ours with this game.

FORTNITE BATTLE ROYALE (2017)

We'll start with context to help parents understand the game's massive cultural impact.

In July 2017, Epic games released the long-awaited *Fortnite*.[1] This free-to-play game is most popular in its Battle Royale mode, which pits each player, duo, or squad against all others to be the last player or last team standing. *Fortnite Battle Royale* has been wildly successful, becoming the biggest online game across all platforms in terms of monthly players and revenue generated.[2] Because it uses Epic's Unreal Engine, a "platform agnostic" program that powers games, it can be played on any console, mobile device, or computer.[3] It has been a critical success, too, being nominated for or winning numerous awards.[4]

The game leapt to public attention around midnight, March 14, 2018, when professional *Fortnite Battle Royale* player "Ninja" (Tyler Blevins) livestreamed a session with rapper Drake, NFL wide receiver Ju Ju Smith-Schuster, and other celebrities. That event broke the record for the number of concurrent viewers in a nontournament stream with 628,000.[5] It was all the more impressive because there was no promotion outside of word of mouth.

Industry analysts estimate that *Fortnite* earned Epic $318 million in May 2018 alone, and more than $1 billion and counting in total.[6] And this is from a free-to-play game funded solely through microtransactions (more on that below). At last count, the game has 250 million players and shows no signs of slowing.[7] It is a bona fide cultural phenomenon—or what one magazine called "The Most Important Video Game on the Planet."[8] It is truly an unusual and multifaceted game.

STEP 1: WHAT IS THE STORY (OR DRAMA)?

Some games start with a movie to introduce players to the drama they're about to enter. But instead of a story, *Fortnite Battle Royale* has rules, a mood, and narrative elements.

What are the rules? The original *battle royale* phrase comes from the title of a Japanese novel and movie. In computer games, the term refers to a game format that pits one hundred players against one another, with variants allowed for team play. The last player or team standing wins. *PlayerUnknown's Battlegrounds* (PUBG) was the first to score a major commercial success with the battle royale format in 2017.[9] *PUBG* was gritty and tried to be battleground realistic. Blood indicates a hit, and explosions send adversaries flying. It tries to make players feel as if they have entered a war zone.

Epic noticed *PUBG*'s success and, that same year, adapted the format into a lighter mood. *Fortnite*'s graphics are cartoon eye candy, *not* realistic—more fun than gritty. Players ride in on a blue Battle Bus suspended from a hot-air balloon. They enter the game by parachuting or paragliding from the bus to their destinations. After a mad dash to find weapons, ammo, and building materials, they hunt for other players. But there is no blood; eliminated players simply disappear, de-pixelated. It's more like a fast-paced game of tag.

Another important factor is the storm (also borrowed from *PUBG*). The storm is a damage-dealing atmosphere that begins on the edges of the battleground island and encroaches into player territory. It always leaves a safe zone in the eye of the storm, but that circle narrows every couple of minutes, forcing players into a tighter and tighter arena. If you move too slowly and get caught out of the eye, you take damage and die. But if you move into the eye, you're likely moving into a fight. Therefore, the player cannot stay passive. *That's* the heart of the battle royale format.

However, *Fortnite Battle Royale* is also a *crafting* game. Each player starts with a pickax-like collection tool. By whacking various objects, players collect building materials. Chop at a tree, you get wood. Chop at a building, you get brick. Chop at a car, you get metal sheeting. The player uses those materials to build walls that block bullets (for a while), bridges to cross into different territory, or ramps to gain a high-ground advantage over another player. It's an interesting concept: a first-person-shooter game crossed with a building game, as if *Counter-Strike* met *Minecraft* and they had a baby. The game has no real story in the traditional, adventure-game sense. Instead, it has interesting rules set in a fun, vibrant, ever-changing world that hints at a larger story going on behind the scenes.

Epic changes the rules and landscape every week to keep things interesting. Pop culture trends change the game. For example, in 2018 developers added a unique weapon, the Infinity Gauntlet from Marvel's *Avengers: Infinity War*, which makes the wearer superpowerful, like Thanos.[10] There's also a working golf game, a go-kart game, and other mini-games within the game.[11] You know, in case you get bored of killing people.

Fortnite is not superserious. It's about having fun by collecting materials, building structures, playing games, and improving on your skills by beating other players. It's about as goofy and innocent as a first-person-shooter game can get (with the exception of *Splatoon*).

Though the game has no full-fledged story, narrative elements *are* woven into the world itself, creating what game designers call *environmental storytelling* that implies a story. Gamers find areas with goofy names like Tilted Towers and Wailing Woods. Or they'll find a secret villain's lab with a missile silo hidden in the basement of a house in Snobby Shores. Each season of gaming ends with an event that moves the story of this world along, leaving the environment changed. *Fortnite* gives enough story to let players speculate about what's going on, how to explain the changes.[12] For example, in May 2018, players found the game map altered. A meteor had crashed, leaving a huge crater filled with purple rocks that players could pick up and use to jump extra high. Then two months later, a rocket launched, and players stopped playing just to watch it go up, come down, and disappear into a space-time rift—which teleported the spaceship to another part of the map, only to disappear into another rift. All of this rifting left huge glowing cracks in the sky. Players noticed that the cracks were growing and appearing elsewhere on the map, swallowing certain landmarks. This changed gameplay. If you found a rift near you, you could run into it and reappear hundreds of feet in the air—helpful for gaining a tactical advantage in a fight. One journalist, playing during the rocket launch, remarked, "It reminded me a bit of watching the season finale of *Lost*: no one actually understood what was happening, but we were all in it together, sharing the moment."[13]

The latest season-ending event (at the time of this writing) broke all previous records for online audiences for Twitch's streaming platform (1.6 million watched live).[14] After a rocket launch that again went awry, rifts opened and disappeared, creating duplicate rockets that aligned with a meteor that had been suspended over the map's central energy source. Together, they penetrated the energy sphere, sending all the players hurtling into outer space, only to be sucked back into a black hole. And then the online game switched off for an unprecedented forty hours. When it came back, there was a new name (*Fortnite Chapter 2*), a new map, new game mechanics (including swimming, carrying allies to safety, and fighting while driving boats), and new weapons. It became a whole new game. And who knows what changes further seasons will bring? This is all part of the charm of the game.

Step 2: What Is the Moral and Imaginary World?

In a game with so much environment-based storytelling, the line will appear fuzzy between the story and the imaginary world. Still, let's explore the game-world's style and assumptions.

First, *Fortnite*'s world is fun to play. The world is colorful and retro with *The Incredibles*–style architecture but sillier, like a toned-down *Pee-wee's Playhouse*. It's a fun world to explore, full of hidden surprises: treasure chests, ammo stashes, old tires that let you bounce ten feet into the air. Game controls are complex and not easy to master. Fortunately, the game's playground mode lets you practice and explore. You get a pressure-free environment to become competent at in-game mechanics, such as how to switch from weapons to building mode.

In the competitive mode, things happen fast. You learn quickly or die. But it's the only way to gain experience points toward the next level. Once you lose, you cannot respawn until the next game. But you can observe the game through the eyes of the player who eliminated you, which can be an education in itself if you were killed by a competent player. Learning the game is a lot of fun, and we imagine the fun increases once a player gets a feel for the game.

Fortnite Battle Royale also offers a form of social media— a way of displaying a player's style. The free-to-play game makes its money through *microtransactions* using V-Bucks, *Fortnite*'s in-game currency. For ten dollars a player can purchase a thousand V-Bucks. Players can also earn V-Bucks by purchasing a seasonal Battle Pass (for 950 V-Bucks) and completing challenges and leveling up. Leveling up unlocks new, rarer items for purchase, as well as earns V-Bucks. You may be tempted to buy cool stuff, but with a Battle Pass you can also earn V-Bucks in-game—even enough for your next Battle Pass. If you play well and wisely, you can have a lot of fun and earn items without spending more than ten dollars.

Players use V-Bucks to purchase *skins*, *emotes*, and other accessories. Skins change the look of your in-game character, your *avatar*, into a soldier, spaceman, disco dancer, guy in a frog costume, or many others. Emotes are dance moves your character can do in the game: the Robot, Dab, Breakin, and so on. Using V-bucks, you can also buy different designs for your glider or parachute, weapon modifications, or bling for your characters. Each affects only the appearance, not the gameplay.

Here's where the world of competitive gaming and competitive social media meet. Each emote, skin, and accessory says something about your in-game competence. An especially coveted skin in season 3 was the John Wick skin, earned only by completing all one hundred tiers, which represents a time investment of anywhere from 75 to 150 hours of gameplay (if you're good).[15] In other words, V-Bucks reflect *two* separate currencies: money *and* time invested in the game. Your avatar's skin, emotes, and accessories, as well as the cleverness and style with which you kill competing players, are all channels through which the player broadcasts his or her status: winner or loser, in-game god or hopeless noob (file us under the latter category). Underneath the easygoing, colorful, playful vibe of the game, some serious competitive display is going on.

The game is still technically free to play. Ted has played and has not yet spent a single, slim dime on the game. But that's only OK if you don't mind wearing the starter skins and emotes, traipsing around like a fashion disaster. In *Fortnite*, style is everything. And that makes the game potentially quite addictive for a teen. As *New York Magazine*'s Brian Feldman put it, "*Fortnite* is a candy-colored video game populated by friends and celebrities, with quantified metrics for success tucked into every corner, constantly updated, highly social, usable anywhere, dopamine-releasing, and extremely competitive. In other words, the way to think about *Fortnite* isn't *Halo*, but Instagram. Not *Call of Duty*, but Snapchat. What's the difference between racking up kills and racking up likes?"[16]

It's still a game, but it's also a hybrid that has broken new ground in the gaming world.

STEP 3: WHAT IS GOOD, TRUE, AND BEAUTIFUL IN THIS WORLD (COMMON GRACE)?

As Christian parents, where can we find God-given common grace in this game?

Fortnite expresses creativity in several ways.

Epic's game developers have put effort into making a world that is fun, colorful, and ever-changing. Logging in to see what's new is part of its appeal. Feldman noted: "It feels less like a thing you log in to every few days to waste some time and more like an app that you're constantly pulling to refresh, always something new to see."[17] That can only occur because programmers, writers, and artists are committed to ongoing experimentation and innovation, creating more and better and goofier ideas. In this commitment to creativity, they image the Creator. And the result is a ridiculously entertaining game, a world that's fun to be in.

It's not only the game developers who are creative; the players are as well. By combining a first-person-shooter with a crafting game, *Fortnite* forces players to create in order to succeed. You must literally build something new if you want a shot at winning, or even not immediately dying. The building strategies of successful players are complex and executed at lightning speed. That creativity can be digitally preserved. Players are able to record their best in-game moments and post them online, including creative builds, innovative play (such as riding on a teammate's rocket-propelled grenades), and inventive kills. In this way, the game has created its own subculture.

Players can also contribute to *Fortnite*'s cultural imprint in other ways. Players create many of the emotes by videoing themselves doing silly dances, hoping Epic animators will notice—and sometimes they do. Players might edit in-game clips into a montage and synchronize it to music, creating a game music video. Players have also created skins and submitted their ideas to Epic.[18] In-game events, such as the rocket launch, provoke players to write theories and share them with other players. All of this builds a sense of community among *Fortnite* player-fans. As with all online communities, this can be both healthy and unhealthy.

Fortnite also feeds a genuine sense of curiosity and exploration.

It gives the player a big, diverse map with lots of hidden features that is frequently updated with new items and features. Curiosity is a God-given desire, the "glory of kings"

(Proverbs 25:2). Curiosity is the engine that drives science, philosophy—any learning whatsoever. Video game–provided curiosity doesn't undermine the goodness of curiosity, especially if players learn to also direct this curiosity toward other arenas outside the game world.

Fortnite's design reflects the rule-bound order of the universe.

Fortnite Battle Royale's rules are admirably simple but allow for huge variations in individual player styles, skill levels, and engagements. This imaginary, rule-bound world is a reflection in microcosm of the world at large created by God. It too is bound by rules—gravity, conservation of energy, moral laws, wisdom—that still allow for an amazing amount of creative variation among individuals. *Fortnite*'s rule-bound order also gives players a clear sense of direction that mimics the larger life purpose we crave. That sense of purpose is itself a gift of God. We were meant to find a purpose that fits with the rule-bound world. In this way, *Fortnite* gestures toward what it means to live in God's world.

The game reflects good competition, which is also a gift of God.

Whether in virtual reality or in organized sports, games are inherently competitive. Part of their fun lies in the fact that you are playing against others. Games allow players to test their levels of accomplishment, hone skills, deal with disappointment, and learn how to win or lose with grace. Paul uses competitive athletics as a model for pursuing the Christian life: "An athlete is not crowned unless he competes according to the rules" (2 Timothy 2:5). This implies that competition in itself is a good gift and not sinful. Of course, competition without restraint or perspective can indeed cause great harm, but there's nothing wrong with games or with winners and losers.

In fact, if we tried to remove competition from life, we would leave teens with an unrealistic perspective on life and overinflated self-esteem. It's far better to take healthy pride in real accomplishment and in victories we have honestly won.

Common grace, the insight and creativity God gives to everyone, believers and unbelievers alike, shines in the curiosity and competition surrounding *Fortnite Battle Royale*. There's a lot to love about the game.

STEP 4: WHAT IS FALSE AND IDOLATROUS IN THIS WORLD?

The same elements that make *Fortnite* wonderful can also be twisted into idols. Remember, idols are parasites, using creation's good things to seduce the heart to false worship. It's great fun to enjoy a vividly colorful, entertaining, super-competitive, never-boring world. But in the eyes of a teen, this game world can also become more important and more rewarding than the real world.

How can a parent tell if a teen is idolizing the game? Ask the following questions: Does the teen's desire to live in that world overwhelm other desires and responsibilities? Does this desire take up homework time so that grades suffer? Does it eclipse family time so that relationships suffer? And most importantly, does your teen play the game freely or because he is driven? Does he hold the game with a light hand, or is it more like a death grip? If he doesn't feel free to put the game down, he may be in happily forced servitude to an idol.

What gives *Fortnite Battle Royale* such potential to become an idol?

Idol 1: The game's creativity makes it addictively entertaining.

Fortnite Battle Royale is bright, colorful, fast paced, and always gives the player something new to see. It is utterly unlike the tedium teens face in doing daily chores, sitting in boring classes, studying what feels like pointless homework. By contrast, *Fortnite*'s uber-stimulating environment draws in the player. If you don't log in every week, every day, you're bound to miss something exciting. You are trained to want something new and have a fear of missing out (FOMO).

Idol 2: A sense of purpose apart from the real world.

The rules are simple and the objective is clear: gather, hunt, kill, win. Be the last one standing. There is no ambiguity, no difficult and nuanced moral choices to make. Imagine you're a teen who must choose which parent to live with, whether to cheat on a test, or whether to cross that line with a girlfriend. It would be bliss to escape into a world where things are simple and direct. You don't have to think, only react. A simplified world cleansed of the need to wrestle with choices can become an unhealthy refuge from the ambiguities and struggles of real Christian life.

Idol 3: A sense of success apart from the real world.

Fortnite displays metrics that constantly show how many experience points a player has earned and how long until the next, achievable goal. Ted has only played a few times and has yet to score a kill because he's pretty slow and still learning. But hey! He's at level 4, and he gained 285 XP toward the next tier at 400 XP. He's doing OK! Surely, he'll continue to climb and get better, and maybe someday soon *he'll* be the one to pwn some noobs!

This is so unlike real life, where markers of success are rarer and not always positive. Teens face daily the creeping and unshakable suspicion that they are *not* OK. Every word of criticism, especially from adults, rings in their ears for an eternity. They seldom hear enough praise, affirmations of love, or pride in who they are becoming. It feels like a relief to escape into a world that shows you are doing OK, or better than OK—you're awesome and only getting awesomer!

This idol of success is especially tempting in *Fortnite* because it is woven into the game's fabric. You don't have to be satisfied with great gameplay. You can display to other players how great you are by sporting the latest skin, emote, or accessory. You can make other players take note and say, "Wow, that looks cool!" Remember back in middle and high school, how you had to have those shoes, that brand of jeans, that kind of mobile phone, or the other kids would tease you and make you feel like dirt? This is the same impulse, transposed to a digital domain. But make no mistake: the goods are as meaningful and real as any article of clothing or physical accessory you could name. The Joneses are now playing *Fortnite*, and one *must* keep up with the Joneses. We may talk of it being "mere aesthetics," but in *Fortnite*, the aesthetics of success is king.

In this way, *Fortnite*'s idol of success combines greed ("Ooooh! I want that!"), envy ("Ooooh! I want what *he* has!"), and what the Puritans called vainglory ("Hey, dude, look what *I* got! Isn't it cool? Don't you wish you had one too?"). This idol shapes a teen's social networking and identity just when those are most in flux. Teens can effectively believe that a person's worth *is* measured by how much he or she owns, even if you've taught them that "one's life does not consist in the abundance of his possessions" (Luke 12:15). Instead they start thinking in line with the old adage that "he who dies with the most toys [or skins or emotes or bling] wins." Some teens exhaust themselves to get this success and, more importantly, to project an image of success to their peers. They will spend too much time and money trying to get hold of those V-Bucks and all that V-Bucks riches represent. Epic counts on this for its enormous profits.

You may notice that these idols of entertainment, purpose, and success are no different than the idols worshiped by some adults—the idols that power consumerism. We *all* sometimes want to be entertained to alleviate the tedium of our jobs. We want a clear, uncluttered sense of purpose in what we do. We want to succeed *and* be seen as succeeding. And we will exhaust ourselves trying to attain these things. The impulses that drive teens to play video games aren't alien; they're human.

But these virtual idols are even more potent than their real-world cousins because the virtual idols are supported by formidable behavioral technology. Internet tech firms have invested millions into what are called *persuasive technologies*—ways of weaving patterns of stimulus and reward to shape player or user behavior and keep players or users hooked on particular apps or games.[19] Rewards include senses of accomplishment and a little hit of dopamine to the brain's pleasure centers whenever the player levels up, unlocks a treasured item, or wins a round. Or these games can use negative stimuli, such as the fear of peer rejection, looking like a loser, or FOMO. For teens who are developing their identities, to whom peer acceptance means the most, the pull can be almost irresistible.

How do we topple these powerful idols?

Start by admitting these idols are not only the *kids'* problem. Own your own idols—career goals, reputation, comfort, or whatever—and let teens know that you too struggle with them. But beyond that, you need to draw alongside your teen and give guidance. Show him or her that these idols are Emperors Who Have No Clothes. They are fragile and unworthy of the teen's worship (as expressed in an inordinate investment of money and time). Here are some ways you might talk with your teens about this idol worship.

First, note that these three idols each puts the self in the center of life.

These idols are about keeping *me* entertained, fulfilling *my* goals and sense of purpose, bringing *me* success. This self-centeredness reveals what Martin Luther called a heart curved in on itself. This is the default setting of fallen humanity, and it distorts what God originally made to be beautiful. Self-centered, greedy living is *ugly*, no matter how much we dress it up with beautiful things like expensive cars or cool emotes. Because we lack perspective, the self-centered heart looks large to the self, but actually it is small and shrunken.

When we follow the desires of a self-centered heart, we also create an ugly world where we become blind to the needs of others. It becomes easier to abuse others to get what we want. Left to themselves, our cravings to gratify the self would make the world a living hell. This is the ugly and evil consequence of following a self-centered, greedy heart.

Not so a heart of love. The heart of love sees the humans around him as humans, valued by God. Love's heart flows out for the good of others, as Christ's did. In flowing out toward others, the heart of love creates beauty. Selfish greed turns a garden into a ruin, but love can turn a ruin into a garden. Greed is love's kryptonite and vice versa. You cannot harbor both greed and love consistently in the same heart. You cannot sell your soul to a system of greed *and* say that you follow the Lord of love. Deep down, your teen already knows this truth. Your job is to remind him of it.

Second, show how fragile, vapid, and insatiable these idols will become.

Entertainment can get boring. Or it can turn addictive, diverting attention from what's truly important, such as human relationships. In-game purposes (of gather, hunt, kill, win) don't really translate to anything of value in the outside world unless you are one of the talented few who can earn a living as a professional gamer. It might give you boasting rights in your school lunchroom, but that never lasts long. And really, how loving is an identity based on boasting?

There is a practical downside to finding your ultimate purpose in the game. If in-game purpose looms too large, if that's all a teen cares about, it can sabotage purposes and goals outside the game (such as by hurting grades). It can deafen the teen to God's call to the *real* adventure.

Third, consumerist idols are fragile and always need upkeep.

In the end, this idol will fail you. If you ground your identity and self-worth in the number or quality of things you possess, you will never feel really secure. There will always be more to buy. Teens already feel insecure about who they are, and that makes them easy marks for ads that entice them to buy the Cool Thing. But it's a bad bargain and a never-ending game.

Here's the catch: how much do you need to feel truly secure? In the television drama *Breaking Bad*, when Jesse Pinkman asks Walter White how much money he would need to feel secure, Walter answers without hesitation, "More." Welcome to the treadmill of consumerism, a greed that always needs to feed. The *illusion* of success must be maintained to keep insecurity and self-doubt at bay. In this way, the idol of consumer "success" enslaves, promising security and contentment but never quite delivering. The love of V-Bucks can be the root of all kinds of evil.

There is another way, however: "Godliness with contentment is great gain" (1 Timothy 6:6). Perhaps the most effective way of countering the addictive pull of the idols of a combined game/social media platform like *Fortnite* is to make sure teens are grounded in the reality of something better that actually delivers contentment. And that leads to our last question.

STEP 5: HOW IS JESUS THE TRUE ANSWER TO THIS STORY'S HOPES?

The gospel presents far better fulfillment than the idols of *Fortnite*. Jesus offers his followers a vision of the world that transcends mere entertainment. This life purpose leads to wisdom and to an identity grounded in Christ's success rather than our own "success." Each of these is deeper and more grounded than anything the game can give.

Jesus promises a colorful new creation beyond entertainment.

It is true that the world of the Christian can be less than entertaining. Sometimes, it can be downright boring. But by engaging the occasional tedium, a Christian learns perseverance of faith. Faith in what? Because Jesus broke the back of death and futility, we know that the path of patient obedience leads somewhere, that our service to God is never in vain. God is in the process of renewing the world, starting with the resurrection. According to 2 Peter 3:11–12, "You ought to live holy and godly lives as you look forward to the day of God and speed its coming" (NIV). Notice that this is not passive waiting. In following Jesus, we participate in and even speed along the renewal of creation that God will, in his time, bring to fruition an earth that will flow with more color and energy than any computer game. This doesn't mean we should tell our kids "Never play entertaining computer games," but rather, "Always remember where your true hope lies; don't ever make entertainment an idol." The gospel offers something better than entertainment. It offers the new creation to which entertainment gestures.

Jesus promises real purpose in a confusing world.

It is true that finding purpose in this world is difficult and filled with uncertainty. A teen's head is filled with questions: "What am I good at? Will I ever find my place in the world? How do I navigate the choices I'm faced with?" *Fortnite*'s clarity of purpose looks appealing, but Jesus offers a better path.

Teens can actually develop wisdom and dependence on God when they learn to live within the confusion, sorting good from bad, and find their place. These challenges give teens an opportunity to wrestle with the fundamental question: "Is God for me, or am I on my own? Can I trust God?" The gospel's good news is that God has declared in the most startling terms that he *is* for those who take refuge in him. This promise should drive us to Scripture, to prayer, and to seek counsel from fellow travelers on Christ's path. It's an unnerving place to be, but it is healthy: it undercuts the illusion of autonomy, that we are self-sufficient. It makes the teen accustomed to a life of dependence on God and his guidance.

Teens understand God primarily through the model of their parents. Not only do they look to parents to see what faith in practice looks like, but they also base their understanding of God on parents. The question "Is God worthy of my trust?" is directly connected to "Are my parents (especially the father) worthy of my trust?" Your character as a parent plays a huge role in the teen's larger search for purpose and meaning. Make yourself a transparent lens for the gospel to shine through.

Jesus promises his own success, giving us free identities in him.

Finally, success and identity look quite different in light of the gospel. *Fortnite* offers an identity that needs to be constantly maintained by buying digital items that project success to peers within a system of competitive status display. It is, at base, a fiercely performance-based identity: you are what you've earned or bought.

Jesus offers a better identity that is based not on the player's performance but based on *his* success, *Christ's* perfect performance on our behalf. In Christ, we've already won the war. In the cosmic battle royale, he was the last man standing. We benefit from his victory, for he is our champion. Battles remain that we must fight, but win or lose, they have no power to shake the core victory and the identity we have in Christ. And that sets us free. We don't have to build up our own image before others.

It is tough to convince teens that, because their identity is anchored in Christ's victory, they are fundamentally OK in Christ. They spend so much time feeling not OK. They face so much evidence in their lives that makes them feel like losers: desires and fears pulling them this way and that, guilt over moral failings, social defeats great and small. But this is the parent's job—to remind your teen of the gospel, how it sets us free *despite* what we see around us and feel inside. This is the nature of faith grounded in the cross and resurrection. Christ has declared us free. It doesn't matter what others think about us, or even what we ourselves think. The only One whose opinion matters already loves us as his own children, seeks our best, and will not let us go. That identity flows from Jesus's victory.

If we don't have to obsess about our own image because God has declared his unchangeable love for us in Christ, then we are free to follow Jesus into the true grand adventure: his "love conquest" of this earth. We are free to live as God's beloved children who seek to spread his *shalom* by loving and serving others. Biblically speaking, love for God and others is the deepest expression of freedom.

Convincing a teen that he has been set free to love, and that love and freedom are two sides of the same coin, is a tough sell. A life of love often involves *dying* to self—and in whose dictionary does death equal victory? But that's the paradox Jesus expects his followers to embrace when he tells us to pick up our cross and follow him: "For whoever would save his life will lose it, but whoever loses his life for my sake will find it"

(Matthew 16:25). We can either indulge selfishness and lose ourselves by inflating ourselves to death, or we can renounce greed and gain what truly matters by dying to self, freeing ourselves to be part of God's "love initiative" in the world.

When we understand how freedom and love for others are intertwined in Christian discipleship, it weakens the game's addictive grip. Getting that newest skin or emote might be fun, but on the deepest level, *it just doesn't matter*. What is essential is "faith working through love" (Galatians 5:6). Fun is good. Entertainment and competition are good. But *love* is the ultimate quest that we seek to win, the ultimate victory that we *already have won* in Christ. Knowing this gives a teen the freedom to enjoy the game without the game controlling her.

But when teens face such persuasive technologies, your mere words may not be enough. You need to help the teen build *new patterns of habit* that challenge the reward patterns built into the game. Start with patterns of accountability. Ask your teen questions about how she is doing with the game, with her heart. Create spaces for honest conversation. And be vulnerable about how the idols of consumer culture can sometimes override your own loyalty to Jesus. Let her know that you are two sinners who need to watch out for each other.

Parents should also teach, model, and reward good habits that build character. Does your teen want money for that season pass? Then he can earn it by helping around the house, by doing homework on time, or waiting for Christmas. Parents and teen together can decide how best to proceed in a balanced, healthy way. One word of warning: parents should take care that they don't make building character into another performance-based idol that replaces the game's idols. The point is not about your teen earning something, but rather about the character he develops in the process: the patience, the endurance, the wise management, and the contentment that comes with delaying gratification. Your goal is not to create a "successful" teen, but rather a teen whose heart and habits please the Lord.

MORE TIPS FOR ENGAGING *FORTNITE BATTLE ROYALE* WITH YOUR TEEN

Fortnite Battle Royale is not *necessarily* a path to idolatry. We do not want to leave the impression that *Fortnite* is (to borrow an expression from Obi Wan Kenobi) "a wretched hive of scum and villainy."[20] It's a fun game that has inherent temptations and pokes at teens where they are weak, so you will need to engage it in a way that's larger than, "C'mon kid, get in touch with reality. You've got to prepare for college!" That would simply be replacing in-game idols of success with real-life idols of success. Your frame must be, "How do I relate to this game in light of the gospel and the freedom Christ has won for me?"

What about gameplay? Does a Christ-shaped, love-shaped identity change the way a player approaches the game? We need to be careful here because the player cannot simply change the rules. You have to "kill" rival players to win. But this is only a game. The killing involved is about as far from real killing as you can get—avatars dissolve as the player goes back to the waiting area—about on par with a game of tag. Parents who get hung up on the perceived violence of the game may be missing the point. There are games where violence is a concern, but the violence is tame in this one. For most teens, the greater danger of *Fortnite* probably lies in the way the game can shape identity and self-worth along the lines of greed and self-glory.

But Christian love can and should shape the way a player approaches *Fortnite*, if we also admit that Christian love can and should shape the way a player approaches ping-pong or chess. The game's rules don't remake themselves because you are a Christian, but *within the rules*, a Christian plays with basic habits: don't cheat, don't verbally abuse other players, encourage others rather than cut them down, and so on. *Fortnite* makes verbal abuse difficult because you can only chat with teammates and not other players. Competent players can have decent conversations while building, hunting, and killing. So a player can love his teammates by listening well and being interested in them—similar to demonstrating love over social media. In fact, when we approach the game from a Christian perspective, the game can become a classroom for learning how to relate to a consumer culture in a godly way by cultivating patience, humility, even generosity. A player can show love by sharing V-Bucks with players who have few, letting that kid who's struggling get that cool skin. This is simple generosity, but it can be profound. Greater love hath no *Fortnite* player than that he lay down his V-Bucks for his friend.

More Discussion Questions

Rather than hearing sermons about video games, teens need space to think, breathe, and explore an issue with you. Here are some more questions you might use.

- What do you like best about the game?
- What do you think God likes best about the game?
- If you had the option to live in the world of this game, would you? Why or why not?
- What do you want to get from a game like *Fortnite*?
- What's your purpose in the game? What's your purpose in real life?
- What roles do greed, envy, and boastfulness play in the game? What are some ways of short-circuiting those?

- Is it ever hard to stop playing? Why do you think that is?
- How has *Fortnite* affected your relationships?
- What difference does being a follower of Jesus make in the way you approach the game or what you want from the game?
- What similarities or differences do you notice between the world of the game and the real world?
- What are trustworthy signs that you've gotten too invested in the game and need to take a break? What are trustworthy signs of freedom?
- What habits or limits do you think could keep you from being controlled by the game—or being controlled by consumer culture in real life?
- Why invest time and energy in the real world *over* the game's world? Why is real life more important? (Hint: What arena does Jesus call us to?)
- How do you use words in-game? Do they build others up or tear them down? How can you practice generosity in-game?

Consider this practice session a launchpad for exploring the particular types of popular culture your teen enjoys. Note that your tone is crucial. Try to have teens think for themselves rather than being spoon-fed the answer. And when they have a counter-question—such as, "Well, why *should* I prefer the real world to the game world? Real world's pretty messed up!"—be prepared to give an honest answer. Let them search, let them explore, and let them bounce ideas off you as a guide. In this way, they grow in wisdom as you deepen your relationship with them.

Chapter 14
Final Ideas on Pop Culture Parenting

In this book, we explored the biblical purposes of children, popular culture, and gospel-centered parenting. We compared these with two unhelpful responses—the hands-off and endless-childproofing approaches to parenting and popular culture. We proposed a better approach with five steps to exploring popular culture with children. Finally, we explored three broad stages of children's growth and offered different case studies of age-appropriate stories, songs, films, and games.

We haven't covered everything—for example, specific content challenges like sex or violence, specific fiction genres such as fantasy or horror, or specific cultural forms like phone apps or sports. That would take a whole other book or even a series of books.

Instead, consider this book an orientation to the lifelong journey of gospel-centered parenting in popular culture. From here the journey becomes more challenging as you and your children actually live it out day to day. We believe the material we have presented is solidly biblical. We encourage you to engage with our views in the same way you'd engage with any other work of Christian literature. Look up our texts and references. Discuss the topic with Christian friends and leaders. And compare what we say not with opinions or traditions but with Scripture, which always gets the last word.

We have six final words of encouragement and practical guidance for the path ahead.

1. REMEMBER THAT THIS JOURNEY ISN'T EASY.

Some readers might think we suggest all parents should become full-time popular culture critics. You might say what Luke said when Yoda asked him to force lift his X-Wing out of a swamp: "You want the impossible."[1] The kind of interpretation and everyday theology required may make engaging popular culture seem out of reach to ordinary Christians.

Ted remembers teaching an early version of this type of popular cultural engagement at a Christian conference in Europe. Ted stated, "This method isn't rocket science, but it does require some careful reflection." A man raised his hand and replied, "Look, I'm an engineer for the European Space Agency, so you could say I *am* a rocket scientist. And I'm still having a hard time getting it!" So the group spent more time workshopping and practicing.

That's the key. Like any other skill, it requires practice. Most of the time it feels easy to us because we've been doing it for many years. We might assume that everyone finds this journey as obvious and straightforward as we do.

But here's the good news: At first this approach to engagement will feel awkward and forced. It will feel as if you're overthinking stories, songs, shows, and games. You may even feel like you're doing what Christian writer Jonathan Acuff calls a "Jesus juke"—that is, when someone takes a fun conversation and completely reverses direction so it becomes about Jesus.[2] But eventually, like breaking in a pair of new shoes, this kind of engagement will feel natural and even fun. And all the while, you will be strengthening relationships with your kids, having surprising conversations, respecting them by making them think and voice their thoughts out loud, equipping them for the life ahead.

2. Find Ways to Train Kids in Solid Biblical Doctrine.

A key ingredient for this method to work is a foundation of solid biblical doctrine. If you plan to engage popular culture from a Christian perspective and want to teach your children to do the same, you had better know the Christian perspective top to bottom.

This doesn't necessarily mean studying theology at a seminary, but it does mean study of some sort. Read good books about Christian thought and practice (the Bible first and foremost!). Listen to good preaching. Get involved in a Bible study or adult Sunday school at your church. If your church doesn't offer much by way of adult theological education, talk to the pastor and volunteer to help find people who have studied the Bible and sound theology and create a forum where they can share what they've found. In other words, if you want to equip your kids with a biblical vision, you yourself need to be equipped. Of course, you should be reading and discussing the Bible with your kids. Your engagement of popular culture should *expand on* regular biblical engagement as they see how the gospel is applied in a variety of imaginative contexts.

3. Draw on Resources from Your Local Church and Become a Resource Yourself!

Christian pastors and youth ministry leaders can certainly help share a more gospel-centered approach to parenting and popular culture. But what about you? Do you have teaching gifts or organizational skills? Do you feel alone in this call to engage and need help? Be proactive in finding resources from your local church. Consider starting a small group with other parents and individuals to explore the parenting journey together, parental iron sharpening iron. Work through *The Pop Culture Parent* or other materials about gospel-centered parenting and popular culture. Form a group with parents to watch a movie every so often, and try the five questions among yourselves. You might find more resources from our website, www.thepopcultureparent.com, and from other gospel-centered ministries.

Once you've gotten the hang of engaging stories and songs among adults or among your children at home, why not try a similar gathering with children at your church? Invite parents and children for a movie night, listening club, book-reading group, or video game session. Try a few discussion questions, such as our five questions. Stephen has done this at church with films as well as fantastical fiction, including many novels from excellent Christian authors. We invited people of all ages—younger children, older children, parents, and grandparents—to enjoy and explore these stories and images together. Remember to be sensitive to children's developmental and spiritual level. Some stories or songs might be more appropriate to share only among guests of a certain maturity level.

The point is to strengthen and encourage the church in its discipling mission. Parental engagement should not end at home. It must continue in the church as we spread God's glory to the ends of the earth, taking every thought captive and loving our neighbors.

4. As you learn and work, be sure to enjoy the journey.

Our goal is to help you raise your kids to explore popular culture, training them to be astute cultural observers and apologists for the task of missions. But this brings a potential risk: that we turn every moment of cultural enjoyment into an ultraserious teaching exercise. Nothing saps the joy out of engagement faster than a family atmosphere of perpetual spiritual gravitas. But it doesn't have to be this way. Popular culture is meant to be *enjoyed*.

Humans are naturally drawn to the awesome. So a big part of engaging culture with your children is to show them the connections between the awesome and the Awesome, the Lord God of All Awesomeness. That's a lofty privilege, but don't overdo it either. It is OK just to enjoy small-*a* awesomeness with your kids. That's why we recommend you not force a conversation about theology, mission, and culture *every* time you watch, listen to, or play something. Instead, use your God-given wisdom to find opportune moments of openness for talking about important stuff. Do so in ways that will strengthen relationship, build understanding, and engage the desires of the heart. Make it a natural part of your life together. The gospel is not a weird religious add-on; it is the answer to the deepest human ache and need, the answer to our deepest questions. And you get to do this with your kids! What a privilege!

5. Always be praying for and with your children!

In a sense, this book has been a call to spiritual warfare. We are encouraging you to engage the idols and unbelief of the culture around you and to wrestle. This battle is not won by superior strength but by a Spirit-guided wisdom. In other words, by ourselves, we simply don't have what it takes to win. We draw aid from one another in our churches, but the help we most need is from God. Engaging with culture and with your children's hearts is a dizzying responsibility. Happily, Scripture has promised that God gives wisdom to those who ask (James 1:5). So don't be shy about asking God for wisdom in your parenting. Ask often, and trust God to deliver what he's promised for the good of your children and his world.

6. In your parenting, always anticipate the new creation.

In all of our discussions, it's easy to fix your eyes only on the now: today's church missions, today's threats to Christian families from political or legal developments, competing religions, or popular games and streaming shows that we fear might corrupt our kids.

But let's not neglect the big picture—the new creation, bearing down with an unstoppable momentum, the new heavens and new earth "in which righteousness dwells" (2 Peter 3:13). This is the eternal universe that Jesus will renew and where he will at last dwell with his people forever.

It's so easy for us to reduce our vision of this coming world with vague terms like *heaven*, a fuzzy and mostly white place that we don't think much about. Or we allow ourselves to imagine only ghostly outlines of some dimension unlike earthly life, an eternal place that is so "spiritual" it could not possibly capture imagination or bring anticipation. God promises otherwise. Jesus will make all things new (Revelation 21:5). Until then, it is both lawful and healthy to *imagine* what eternity will be like, as long as it is in harmony with Scripture.

This means that Christian parents must strive to see past the urgent now, the present daily grind, as if this stage of life will last forever.

Our children won't stay children forever. We will not act as their full-time parents forever.

Even after your children grow to become adults, you and your children will not pursue family life, vocations, and new-family raising forever. All these life stages will end. After all this—family, career, aging, and death—will come eternity. Unless Christ comes first. Unless glory springs on earth even sooner than we expect. *That* is the future we should imagine while we parent and engage popular culture's stories, songs, images, and games.

If our children are redeemed in Christ, they are destined to rule this world as God's regents. They will be ambassadors of the King. Imagine that reality! Imagine the children you helped disciple for eighteen-plus years on this earth redeemed for eternal life in that future new creation! You will literally rule *alongside* your children in the eternal kingdom, going on adventures and serving Jesus by filling the earth, subduing it, stewarding and enjoying this restored paradise as redeemed humans, all in a universe without sin.

How will today's parenting relationships resonate into eternity? We cannot know for sure, but we do know that our present identities and memories will continue. We know that every redeemed person will have a Spirit-reformed and empowered body. We will be not only immortal but perfect. Imagine having *perfect* relationships with your children. No more evil. No more lost tempers. No more temptations. No more family divisions or quarrels. No more sin, ever again.

But we get to *keep* the good habits we have taught our children in this life. For eternity, we get to keep exploring theology, mission, stories, images, songs, and games. We'll have all the benefits and not a single detriment. And we would never have been able to reach paradise without passing through the day-to-day parenting challenges we face. They are significant, part of the picture that sets up eternity. Remember: none of your efforts now will be wasted in the new creation.

Now *that* is an eternal future worth living for. And despite all of today's challenges, fears about children, and fears about popular culture, that's a future that Jesus lived for and died for and was raised again to secure for his people, God's children. Lean into that promise every day and every hour. Resist giving into fear, but instead entrust yourself *into* the arms of Jesus, the giver of all good things—of children and of popular culture. And remember: in the process of raising your children, our heavenly Father is also raising us. May this book encourage you and your children to grow into grace together.

Appendix A:
The Eternal Future
of Popular Culture

Christians may believe we oughtn't spend so much time getting to know popular culture because we believe popular culture won't last for eternity anyway. Even if we understand that God gave humans the call to make culture, including popular culture, and that redeemed Christians can help redeem these gifts and teach their children to do the same, won't it all someday fade away forever? Once Jesus returns and we enter the new creation, won't popular culture be forgotten? If our stories, songs, and games don't endure for eternity, why bother with them now?

For many of us, the answer seems clear: "Yes, popular culture may have eternal effects because popular culture will influence our souls for good or bad. But someday popular culture itself will pass away. Our stories, songs, and anything else will have no part in eternal life." Many Christians have assumed that God will burn up, or annihilate, planet Earth and everything on it, including human culture, and replace his creation with a different, a-cultural existence for eternity.

Of course, the Bible does not give us every detail about exactly how eternity will operate. But several clues from Scripture point in a different direction. They suggest that popular culture will not be destroyed but rather will survive into the next age, perhaps even with its sinful elements intact. Let's look at some of the evidence and the various possibilities.

1. THE BIBLE WILL LAST FOREVER, INCLUDING POPULAR CULTURE QUOTES.

As we've seen, the Bible itself includes examples of popular culture. This includes Jesus's masterful adaptation of popular storytelling techniques (parables) and the earlier Israelite cultural works, such as the Psalms, Proverbs, and Song of Solomon. But even pagan popular culture makes it into the Bible. Paul seems to have memorized and quoted pagan poets, such as Aratus (Acts 17:28), Menander (1 Corinthians 15:33), and Epimenides (Titus 1:12). These quotes will last forever if only because they were immortalized in Scripture, which God has promised will last forever, even into the new creation (Psalm 119:89; Isaiah 40:8). If these fragments of pagan popular culture will endure into the new creation, why not the entire works? Why not also selections of contemporary popular culture?

2. GOD WILL RESTORE AND RENEW HIS CREATION, NOT DESTROY IT.

Some Christians believe that God will simply destroy the creation and replace it with an immaterial kingdom called "heaven." If that is true, then logically, the only eternal things worth bothering about are God's written Word and human souls. The rest will burn.

But does the Bible actually teach this? In short, no. The Bible's view of redemption is stubbornly material and cosmic in scope. God will be satisfied with nothing less than the redemption, renewal, and transformation of not only our souls but his entire creation.

In Romans 8:19–23, Paul pictures nonhuman, fallen "creation itself" groaning, longing to be released from its "bondage to decay" (NIV). And creation shall indeed be released when God redeems his people. To be sure, Christ's redemption starts with his people, but he also extends this redemption to the whole of creation. This includes not just our souls but our physical bodies (see 1 Corinthians 15:35–54) and even the whole cosmos! God does not "free" creation from its bondage by suddenly destroying it.[1]

What about other texts, such as 2 Peter 3:10? You may recall the warning (in the King James Version) that in the end "the earth also and the works that are therein shall be burned up." But the key phrase *burned up* comes from a less-reliable manuscript from the Middle Ages. Newer translations based on older, more reliable manuscripts promise a different fate for earth: "The earth and the works that are done on it will be exposed" (ESV). Peter's language is not about annihilation. It's about unveiling and purifying, refining, purging unwanted elements to refashion something new and good from the original material. The language points not to destruction but to renovation.

Following the same promises in the Old Testament, the New Testament points to the judgment and destruction of God's enemies. Yes, the Day of the Lord will be awe inspiring and terrifying. But God will *not* trash his own creation; he believes creation is worth saving.

3. GOD WILL RESURRECT HIS PEOPLE TO A FULLY HUMAN EXISTENCE, INCLUDING AT LEAST SOME HUMAN-MADE CULTURE.

Even if God preserves his creation after judgment day, does this mean culture will likewise survive? Won't God wipe the earth of everything human made because we won't need culture anymore in our "spiritual" existence? Wouldn't we be too busy for culture-making anyway because we are only praying, singing, or being "lost" in the infinite worship of God?

We reject this concept for this simple reason: Scripture constantly emphasizes *continuity* between this world and the next. If we accept that new earth will be a real and physical place and God has given us the Cultural Mandate, then we have no biblical reasons to suspect that God will let the Cultural Mandate expire for eternity. Then, as now, Jesus our Savior is also Jesus the King over all creation. As his subjects, we will still have work to do: not to be passively "lost" in God's presence but to worship him by following his ongoing call for us to steward his creation for his glory. That includes cultural development.

In light of Christ's glory, Earth's *good* things won't actually "grow strangely dim" (to quote the hymn "Turn Your Eyes Upon Jesus"). As Joe Rigney suggests, these good things will actually "grow strangely bright" to the eyes of redeemed people whom God creates to worship him in creaturely, *finite* ways. Rigney says, "Our existence in time, space, and bodies is not a bug; it's a feature, designed by infinite wisdom for the communication of the unfathomable riches of [God's] glory. . . . As creatures, we never do anything infinitely. To be a creature is to be finite and limited. We have no infinite capacity for anything. To seek to love God infinitely is to place upon ourselves an impossible burden."[2]

Scripture gives us another picture: the possibility that we will make even more culture in the new creation as acts of worship to our Creator—as we would have before the fall.

The Bible's central hope of resurrection is woven into every book of the New Testament. But this promise of resurrection means we will be raised not in spirit only but in body as well. We will have glorified bodies that are genuinely physical. In our bodies, we will eat meals (Luke 24:41–43) and even enjoy feasts (Revelation 19:9; 22:2). We will not be raised into a ghostly "spiritoid" existence, as if the spiritual body Paul promises is an immaterial body. Instead, we will have a Holy Spirit–powered existence that is imperishable and fully physical (see again 1 Corinthians 15:35–55). We will be raised to the fullest possible experience of humanity. This includes our ability to make and enjoy culture.

Isaiah prophesies that Gentile kings will carry the treasures of their cultures into the New Jerusalem. Later, John references Isaiah 60 in Revelation 21:24–26 when he says kings will bring into the city the glory and honor of the nations. Isaiah goes into more detail than John in describing this glory and honor as "the wealth of the nations" (60:11) that flows into the redeemed city. It includes all kinds of cultural goods: Lebanese lumber of several kinds, flocks of various animals, gold and silver (probably minted coins), frankincense—and, of course, the kings themselves, who previously had been their enemies. Richard Mouw points out that these kings are not simply political figures. Instead, they were patrons who represented whole cultures.

> Ancient kings served as the primary authorities over the broad patterns of the cultural lives of their nations. And when they stood over against other nations, they were the bearers, the representatives, of their respective cultures. To assemble kings together, then, was in an important sense to assemble their national cultures together. The king of a given nation could bear, singly, a far-reaching authority that is today divided among many different kinds of leaders: the captains of industry; the molders of public opinion in art, entertainment and sexuality; educational leaders; representatives of family interests; and so on. This is why Isaiah and John could link the entrance of the kings into the City with the gathering in of the "wealth of the nations."[3]

Isaiah speaks elsewhere of culture enduring into the redeemed life of God's people in the new creation: We can expect to "plant vineyards and eat their fruit" (Isaiah 65:21).

We will cultivate the ground to grow actual grapes. But after people harvest the grapes, what comes next? With acts of culture, we would make grapes into wine (see also Jeremiah 31:5 and Amos 9:14). After that, God's people would enjoy the wine along with good things that Scripture associates with wine: feasting and celebrations with friends in the age of God's glory and sharing stories, songs, games, and other delights—in other words, popular culture. We will continue fulfilling God's original Cultural Mandate. As Mike Wittmer observes,

> The cultural mandate is the one biblical command that our fallen race has kept the best (Genesis 1:28; 2:15). . . . Our works have staying power. When Jesus returns, he will not take out a giant eraser and wipe out several thousand years of human history. He will not send us back into a pristine garden to start from scratch. He will start us out in a well-developed city, the New Jerusalem that descends from heaven. The difference between a garden and a city is culture, so it seems we will enter the new earth with whatever cultural level we have achieved.[4]

Today, as Christ's people, we certainly glorify God through prayer and singing (which, by the way, are themselves unique cultural forms). But we also should worship him with our other creative works as stewards of his world. In the future, after Jesus returns, we have no reason to assume this task will end. Instead, our human practices that honor our Creator will get better and better. This worship will continue through cultural means, filling new earth not only with songs but with other works for God's glory.

Culture has a definite role in the new creation. So does popular culture—the common culture we make for celebration and recreation.

4. What about Popular Culture from before Jesus's Return?

Based on these biblical hints, we believe Christ's people in the new heavens and the new earth will go on making new songs, stories, and games forever. But what about today's popular culture? What will happen to the movies, television shows, popular songs, computer and board games, and books that we and our children have enjoyed as we've built relationships with one another and others? Will these gifts simply be lost in God's judgment fire?

Some Christians might say yes. Even if they accept a renewal of the physical universe, they may still emphasize nonearthly aspects of the new heavens and the new earth. For example, they might still suggest that even if we *could* worship God in human ways for eternity, why would we care? Why have anything to do with old, flawed popular culture when we can make better creative works? For example, why bother with the old *Lord of the Rings* epic, when a resurrected J. R. R. Tolkien could craft an entirely new fantastical mythology?

However, Scripture never indicates human progress will be lost or "reset" after King Jesus renews all creation. Wheels will still be wheels, and we needn't reinvent them. Music scales and mathematics are part of this universe's unchanging laws. The "hero's journey" will still be a basis of many stories. Thus, if we have no reason to suspect our genres and styles will be reset, we also have no reason to suspect we would disregard specific and good creative works that glorify God. Sure, J. R. R. Tolkien may create even better Middle-earth tales. But surely we will always remember his first stories of Beleriand, the Elves, and the hobbits.

Humans will likely continue to enjoy today's culture—including popular culture—in some form for the rest of our Christ-exalting eternal lives. How so? Here the Bible gives hints rather than details, but we can speculate on three options.

First, maybe only culture with Christian or moral content may last forever. For example, Randy Alcorn suggests, "Many current movies celebrate sin and therefore won't have a place [on new earth]. But good movies, like good books, tell powerful stories. Movies on the New Earth might depict sin, as the Bible does, showing it to be wrong. But for any portrayal of sin, there would be a greater emphasis on God's redemptive work."[5]

This view is possible but seems overly narrow. What would be the purpose? Immortal, perfected saints don't need to be protected from bad teaching. Or what theological test would be applied? Would we suppose that a story must portray goodness at least 1 percent more often than it portrays sin? Must it feature a gospel presentation?

If this view is true, most beautiful and honest portrayals of the human existence will burn. What about the long-lost age of preflood culture and music of Genesis 4? Would a tune composed by ancient celebrities such as Jubal be doomed because it has theologically inaccurate lyrics? What about works that don't articulate theology at all, such as an instrumental jazz piece or Howard Shore's incredible score for *The Lord of the Rings*? What about works that deal honestly with human pain and loss without any clear redemption, as in Psalm 88? Are excellent human creations worthless if they do not mention Jesus?

Second, perhaps God will clean up certain cultural works before they enter the new creation. We might speculate that these sinful works will be radically transformed in God's judgment process. All sin-causing elements could be simply deleted or replaced by more suitable content. However, this also seems unlikely because it reduces God's divine renewal of creation to a sort of holy censorship. It is difficult to imagine the Almighty stooping to bleep out the bad words, especially when he has already defeated the devil, renewed the world, and glorified his children so they can never give in to temptation again. But perhaps the transformation of fallen cultural products will be so radical and unexpectedly beautiful (like how our lowly bodies change into our resurrection bodies, that Paul talks of in 1 Corinthians 15) that we can't yet discern what this would be like.

Third, God may simply renew our eyes and ears. Our culture would not change as much as we would change—so changed that popular culture simply could no longer tempt, stain, or sadden us. We experience this in part even now as we grow into the mind of Christ. In this view, we could expect to see many popular cultural works carried unaltered into the new creation, but they would be repurposed and reoriented because God has already glorified us.

Lest this seem crazy, remember that even the most flawed human still dimly reflects God's image. Similarly, a flawed story, song, or game reflects the glory of God, albeit with a faded and distorted image. How much more clearly will our glorified eyes see this reflected glory shining in manmade things! After all, if we see a reminder of sin today, this doesn't make us sin today. We only fall into sin when our own idolatry latches on to these depictions. But in eternity's tomorrow, those idols and twisted desires will be no more. We will be literally incorruptible. Even our memories of sin will only move us to gratitude and worship because of our redemption. (Remember that Scripture offers no support for some "memory wipe" at the resurrection. Otherwise, we would not be able to recognize Jesus, recall the ways he helped us in our sufferings, or even read portions of Scripture that describe evil.)

These three options are not mutually exclusive. Surely some works will be judged and destroyed. One obvious example: we would not expect to find pornography in the new creation! Some works may be transformed in ways that we cannot yet fathom. And some may be brought in whole to be enjoyed with new, incorruptible eyes, ears, and hearts.

Regardless, popular culture in some form will likely endure as part of new earth life. When we deal with popular culture today, we may well be dealing with something that is actually eternal.

Appendix B:
More Resources
for Pop Culture Parents

When three coauthors write a book, you just might see three times as much research going into it! Happily, many of the works that helped us will also be helpful to you, our reader. In this list we also include our own relevant works.

- Of course, visit our own website for this book, www.thepopcultureparent.com. You'll find more information and links to our existing resources to help you and your kids together engage specific kinds of popular culture.
- Ted Turnau's first book helps present a biblical understanding of popular culture and how Christians might react to popular culture in questionable ways. In this book, Ted first outlined his five-question method for helping us analyze and discern a popular cultural work. See Ted Turnau, *Popologetics* (Phillipsburg, NJ: P&R Publishers, 2012).
- E. Stephen Burnett's magazine *Lorehaven* serves Christian fans, including parents, by finding biblical truth in fantastic stories. Free web issues offer flash

reviews, articles, and news about Christian fantasy, science fiction, and other fantastical genres. Visit www.lorehaven.com to subscribe to the magazine for free. You'll also find the *Fantastical Truth* podcast, which explores Christian-made fantasy novels, and your kids (and you!) can join a thriving community of fans who love sharing (and sometimes creating!) published fantastical novels that are intended to glorify Jesus for readers of many ages.

- Jared Moore cohosts a podcast (with Jeff Wright) called the *Pop Culture Coram Deo* podcast. In this series, these two pastors explore specific new movies and other popular cultural works, analyzing the story and working through questions similar to our five-question method in this book. They may also do a little geeking out (especially for the stories they love). Find the podcast to subscribe at www.pccdpod.com.

- The webzine *Christ and Pop Culture* shares a diet of essays and podcasts to help Christians engage popular culture with nuance and integrity. Stephen and Ted have also written for this site. Explore these resources at www.christandpopculture.com.

- A Christian resource specifically for gamers and other "nerds" (as well as their families) is Love Thy Nerd: www.lovethynerd.com.

- For movie fans, there's Hollywood Jesus at www.hollywoodjesus.com.

- Tedd Tripp's and Paul Tripp's parenting books help parents focus on children's heart-level idolatry that can only be resolved by the gospel of Christ. See Tedd Tripp, *Shepherding a Child's Heart* (Wapwallopen, PA: Shepherd Press, 1995), and Paul Tripp, *Age of Opportunity: A Biblical Guide to Parenting Teens* (Phillipsburg, NJ: P&R, 1997).

- Randy Alcorn's works, especially his book *Heaven*, help Christians reboot their beliefs about heaven and especially the new heavens and the new earth with in-depth yet readable biblical teaching, complete with necessary and biblically based speculation about the afterworld that awaits us— and will likely include popular culture in some form! See Randy Alcorn, *Heaven* (Carol Stream, IL: Tyndale House Publishers, 2004).

- For more details concerning our hope in the new creation, see N. T. Wright, *Surprised by Hope: Rethinking Heaven, the Resurrection, and the Mission of the Church* (New York: HarperOne, 2007); and J. Richard Middleton, *A New Heaven and a New Earth: Reclaiming Biblical Eschatology* (Grand Rapids: Baker Academic, 2014).

- The Turnau family found three helpful resources for parents who want to engage with the Bible during their family routines: *The Beginner's Bible: Timeless Children Stories* (Grand Rapids: Zondervan, 2016) for preschool into elementary school ages; Starr Meade, *Training Hearts, Teaching Minds: Family Devotions Based on the Shorter Catechism* (Phillipsburg, NJ: P&R, 2001) for middle school and young high school; and Philip F. Reinders, *Seeking God's Face: Praying with the Bible through the Year* (Grand Rapids: Baker Books, 2010).

- For good practical advice about being engaged with your child's (and your own) use of electronic devices, see Andy Crouch, *The Tech-Wise Family: Everyday Steps for Putting Technology in Its Proper Place* (Grand Rapids: Baker Books, 2017).

- For some good insights about how face-to-face conversation shapes us, see media scholar Sherry

Turkle's *Reclaiming Conversation: The Power of Talk in a Digital Age* (New York: Penguin, 2015).

- For an excellent resource for understanding how the gospel relates to sexual struggle, see Paul David Tripp's *Sex in a Broken World: How Christ Redeems What Sin Distorts* (Wheaton, IL: Crossway, 2018).

- The best depiction of depression we have found is in the writing and art of Allie Brosh and her blog on *Hyperbole and a Half*, specifically "Adventures in Depression," http://hyperboleandahalf.blogspot.cz/2011/10/adventures-in-depression.html, and "Depression, Part 2," http://hyperboleandahalf.blogspot.cz/2013/05/depression-part-two.html. Do be aware that she uses coarse language.

RESOURCES FOR CRITIQUING NON-CHRISTIAN WORLDVIEWS

Worldview apologetics really helps when you are trying to identify a culture's idols and false salvation stories. Apologetics is the art of defending and commending the Christian faith in a context of unbelief (like secular culture). Good resources for critiquing non-Christian worldviews would include

- Greg Bahnsen, *Always Ready: Directions for Defending the Faith* (Nacodoches, TX: Covenant Media Foundation, 2011 [1996]), https://www.scribd.com/doc/159423767/Always-Ready-Greg-Bahnsen.

- William Edgar, *Reasons of the Heart: Recovering Christian Persuasion* (Grand Rapids: Baker, 1996).

- Os Guinness, *Fool's Talk: Recovering the Art of Christian Persuasion* (Downers Grove, IL: InterVarsity Press, 2015).

- Randy Newman, *Questioning Evangelism: Engaging People's Hearts the Way Jesus Did* (Grand Rapids: Kregel, 2004).

- Francis Schaeffer, *The God Who Is There: Speaking Historic Christianity into the Twentieth Century* (Downers Grove, IL: InterVarsity Press, 1998 [1968]).
- James Sire, *The Universe Next Door*, 5th ed. (Downers Grove, IL: InterVarsity Press, 2009).

RESOURCES ABOUT SAME-SEX ATTRACTION

Over the past two decades, same-sex attraction and gender identity have become huge topics in popular culture. It's no exaggeration to say this is a central theme in contemporary youth culture, or that the Christian church has not generally handled these issues with clarity and compassion. Parents and youth workers need information and insight about this aspect of popular culture because kids you know and love will struggle with these issues.

Here is what we affirm about same-sex attraction as Bible-believing Christians:

First, as Christians, we must go against the grain of a culture that largely affirms and celebrates gay sexuality. The Bible clearly calls out homosexual lusts and behavior as disobedient and sinful. For example, 1 Corinthians 6:9–10 says, "Or do you not know that the unrighteous will not inherit the kingdom of God? Do not be deceived: neither the sexually immoral, nor idolaters, nor adulterers, nor men who practice homosexuality, nor thieves, nor the greedy, nor drunkards, nor revilers, nor swindlers will inherit the kingdom of God."

Second, the gospel teaches us to love and embrace those who are broken, who struggle, rather than shun those who are messed up before God (which includes *all* of us). God loves and accepts us not because we have our act together, but because Jesus died and rose for us and is our advocate before the Father. First John 2:1–2 says, "My little children, I am writing these things to you so that you may not sin. But if anyone does sin, we have an advocate with the Father, Jesus

Christ the righteous. He is the propitiation for our sins, and not for ours only but also for the sins of the whole world." If God accepts us, we should accept one another, messy though we may be (Romans 15:7).

Within these broad and biblical areas of agreement, some Christians still differ about how best to address these issues—including this book's authors! Therefore, the resources we suggest will offer differing perspectives on these important issues.

Ted believes that the Bible calls same-sex behavior (including imaginative behavior, such as lust) sinful but not necessarily same-sex orientation, which many did not choose and find it impossible to change, even after much prayer, effort, and counsel. Ted recommends these Christian resources for parents facing these issues:

- Christian pastor Sam Allberry does not call himself "gay." He prefers to talk about "same-sex attraction" precisely because his orientation is not his identity. His real identity comes from Christ, not from patterns of sexual desire. For a great short introduction to his approach, see his book *Is God Anti-Gay? And Other Questions about Homosexuality, the Bible, and Same-Sex Attraction* (Surrey, UK: The Good Book Company, 2013).

- Mark Yarhouse is one of the few evangelicals who has studied both theology and the science of sexuality. He is a treasure trove of thoughtful, biblical, scientifically accurate material on these issues, in books such as *Homosexuality and the Christian: A Guide for Parents, Pastors, and Friends* (Bloomington, MN: Bethany House, 2010); *Understanding Sexual Identity: A Resource for Youth Ministry* (Grand Rapids: Zondervan, 2013); and with coauthor Olya Zaporozhets, *Costly Obedience:*

What We Can Learn from the Celibate Gay Christian Community (Grand Rapids: Zondervan, 2019).

Jared believes that sexual orientation is a habit of desire that can be sinful or holy. Anything contrary to God is sin, whether this is human nature, inclinations, desires, thoughts, or actions. As such, Christians who find themselves same-sex attracted must strive to fight these sinful desires as a part of their day-to-day struggle for holiness. Jared recommends

- Jared Moore, "A Biblical and Historical Appraisal of Concupiscence, with Special Attention to Same-sex Attraction" (PhD dissertation, Southern Baptist Theological Seminary, 2019).
- Denny Burk and Heath Lambert, *Transforming Homosexuality: What the Bible Says about Sexual Orientation and Change* (Phillipsburg, NJ: P&R, 2015).
- Denny Burk and Rosaria Butterfield, "Learning to Hate Our Sin without Hating Ourselves," Public Discourse, July 4, 2018, https://www.thepublicdiscourse.com/2018/07/22066.

RESOURCES ABOUT GENDER DYSPHORIA AND IDENTITY ISSUES

Likewise, gender identity issues have provoked a lot of discussion and confusion in today's culture, among both Christians and non-Christians. These are major issues in popular culture and youth culture and will likely only grow in prominence.

We understand the Bible to assert the following:

1. God's creation plan includes two human genders: male and female (Genesis 1:27; 5:2). This plan deserves our honor; to violate this plan is sin.
2. We live in a fallen world, and this warps and distorts many aspects of created existence, including gender. We should expect some people to struggle with their gender identities.

260 THE POP CULTURE PARENT

3. Because we are sinners who are welcomed into
    God's presence only by grace, we must treat people
    who struggle with the effects of the fall—including
    gender dysphoria—with compassion rather than
    condemnation.

Ted finds in the work of Mark Yarhouse a good balance
in a difficult situation. Yarhouse has clinical experience as a
therapist who works with people who struggle in this way. His
goal is to bring such people into mental health (and often out
of suicidal depression) using as little intervention as is possible.

- Mark Yarhouse gives his fullest treatment of the
  issue in *Understanding Gender Dysphoria: Navigating
  Transgender Issues in a Changing Culture* (Downers
  Grove, IL: InterVarsity Press, 2015).
- For a summary of some of Yarhouse's findings,
  see his article "Understanding the Transgender
  Phenomenon," *Christianity Today*, June 8, 2015,
  https://www.christianitytoday.com/ct/2015/
  july-august/understanding-transgender-gender-
  dysphoria.html.
- Yarhouse also wrote a more accessible book for
  parents and youth leaders: *Understanding Sexual
  Identity: A Resource for Youth Leaders* (Grand Rapids:
  Zondervan, 2013).
- Finally, Rev. Steve Froehlich has written
  a wonderful pastoral response to gender
  identity issues: "Christian Faithfulness and
  Gender Dysphoria: Navigating Pastoral
  Care for People Living with Gender Identity
  Conflict," Ransom Fellowship, May 2,
  2018, http://ransomfellowship.org/article/
  christian-faithfulness-and-gender-dysphoria.

Jared believes that while we must lovingly walk alongside these image-bearers and brothers and sisters in Christ as they seek to turn from this lifestyle, it is impossible for someone to cross-dress and also be a faithful Christian (see Genesis 1:26–28; Deuteronomy 22:5; and 1 Corinthians 11:2–16). It is also impossible for someone to deny his biological sex and embrace the opposite sex as a chosen gender while continuing to be a faithful Christian. Embracing a gender identity other than one's biological sex is a sinful desire. Therefore, the church must not treat gender-confused people according to their chosen gender but according to their biological sex. Otherwise, the church encourages sin and unrepentance. These results will be messy, and the church must be longsuffering because people will struggle. But those seeking to turn from their sinful desires must be embraced, forgiven, and encouraged.

Robert Gagnon and Mark Yarhouse have briefly debated back and forth on this subject. Jared commends Gagnon's two responses to Yarhouse.

1. "How Should Christians Respond to the Transgender Phenomenon?" First Things, October 16, 2015, https://www.firstthings.com/web-exclusives/2015/10/how-should-christians-respond-to-the-transgender-phenomenon.
2. "Gender Dysphoria and 'Practical Application': A Rejoinder to Mark Yarhouse," Robgagnon.net (blog), August 28, 2016, http://www.robgagnon.net/Yarhouse%20Rejoinder.htm.

MORE RESOURCES FOR FAMILIES TO EXPLORE GOD'S DESIGN

We also recommend these materials to help parents and their older kids together consider the biblical truths of God's design for women, men, and families:

- Stephen commends the *Adventures in Odyssey* audio drama series from Focus on the Family, and regarding these issues of family and identity, the best story arc is "The Ties that Bind." Longtime *Odyssey* writer Paul McCusker scripts this fourteen-episode storyline. It explores God's design for boys, girls, and families in a manner perfectly suited for children ages eight through twelve. Christian heroes such as Mr. Whittaker, Connie, Eugene, Katrina, and Wooton show not only the ideas of this cultural struggle but also the missional heart of faithful Christians who engage with people who believe differently from them. This story arc is available in the 2014 CD album release. Or you can download it, along with the longtime audio drama's entire library, via the Adventures in Odyssey Club audio streaming app at www.oaclub.org.
- New Growth Press (this book's publisher) offers several resources, including Marty Machowski's book *God Made Boys and Girls* (2019) and David White's book *God, You, and Sex: A Profound Mystery* (2019). You can also find booklets exploring tough practical questions, such as Tim Geiger's *Explaining LGBTQ+ Identity to Your Child: Biblical Guidance and Wisdom* (2018) and *Your Child Says, "I'm Gay"* (2013).

Endnotes

Chapter 1

1. Ted Turnau compares popular culture to an airlike substance in his book *Popologetics* (Phillipsburg, NJ: P&R, 2012).

2. Casey Liens, "Americans Are Becoming Less Religious," *U.S. News and World Report*, April 11, 2017, https://www.usnews.com/news/best-states/articles/2017-04-11/americans-are-becoming-less-religious. Liens draws her data from a Pew Research Center study, "America's Changing Religious Landscape," May 12, 2015, https://www.pewforum.org/2015/05/12/chapter-1-the-changing-religious-composition-of-the-u-s.

3. "British Social Attitudes 36, Religion," NatCen Social Research, 2019, http://www.bsa.natcen.ac.uk/latest-report/british-social-attitudes-36/religion.aspx. NatCen Social Research has tracked religious attitudes in Britain from 1983 to 2018.

4. Benjamin Fearnow, "Conservative Christian Group Accuses University of Iowa of Discrimination against Religious Clubs," *Newsweek*, February 6, 2019, https://www.newsweek.com/university-iowa-christian-sex-morality-lawsuit-religious-watch-list-1320393.

5. Charles Spurgeon, "Sheep Among Wolves" (sermon, Metropolitan Tabernacle, Newington, August 19, 1877), sermon 1370, Spurgeon Gems, http://www.spurgeongems.org/vols22-24/chs1370.pdf.

Chapter 2

1. Carl R. Trueman, "The Rise of the Anti-Culture," *First Things*, May 4, 2016, http://www.firstthings.com/blogs/firstthoughts/2016/05/the-rise-of-the-anti-culture.

2. Timothy Keller, "Why Culture Matters," *Q Ideas* speech, September 6, 2015, https://www.youtube.com/watch?v=XWynJbvcZfs.

3. Turnau, *Popologetics*, 73–74.

4. Andy Crouch, *Culture Making* (Downers Grove, IL: InterVarsity Press, 2009), 107.

5. Turnau, *Popologetics*, 48–60.

6. William Edgar, *Created and Creating: A Biblical Theology of Culture* (Downers Grove, IL: IVP Academic, 2017), 176–77.

7. Christian screenwriter and cultural critic Brian Godawa calls this "cultural anorexia." See "Sex, Violence and Profanity," in his *Hollywood Worldviews: Watching Films with Wisdom and Discernment*, 2nd ed. (Downers Grove, IL: InterVarsity Press, 2009).

8. Albert M. Wolters, "Discerning Structure and Direction," in *Creation Regained: Biblical Basics for a Reformational Worldview* (Grand Rapids: Eerdmans, 1985).

9. Edgar, *Created and Creating*, loc. 3,638–75.

10. Edgar, *Created and Creating*, chaps. 10–11.

Chapter 3

1. "*Westminster Shorter Catechism* question and answer 1," Westminster Shorter Catechism Project, BPC.org, http://www.shortercatechism.com/resources/wsc/wsc_001.html.

2. The whole perspective of parenting by engaging the heart owes a huge debt to the brothers Tripp. Please see Tedd Tripp, *Shepherding a Child's Heart* (Wapwallopen, PA: Shepherd Press, 1995), and Paul Tripp, *Age of Opportunity: A Biblical Guide to Parenting Teens* (Phillipsburg, NJ: P&R, 1997). For general guidance on parenting, we know of no better resources.

3. Thomas Chalmers, "The Expulsive Power of a New Affection," sermon, https://www.monergism.com/thethreshold/sdg/Chalmers,%20Thomas%20-%20The%20Exlpulsive%20Power%20of%20a%20New%20Af.pdf.

Chapter 4

1. The term "cheap grace" was first used by German theologian Dietrich Bonhoeffer in his seminal book, *The Cost of Discipleship* (New York: Macmillan, 1966 [1937]).

2. Daniel Eakin, "We need for television shows to be as they were in 1950," comment, PureFlix Facebook page, August 5, 2019, https://www.facebook.com/PureFlix/posts/2773701772646416.

3. *I Love Lucy*, "The Seance," IMDB plot summary, http://www.imdb.com/title/tt0609382.

4. The Andy Griffith Show, "Three Wishes for Opie," IMDB plot summary, http://www.imdb.com/title/tt0798990.

5. Elevenofus, "I have had books from A Beka that I have liked," review of *Song of the Brook* by Matilda Nordtvedt, June 25, 2014, http://www.amazon.com/review/RTCUXBAYQM6MK/ref=cm_cr_pr_perm?ie=UTF8&ASIN=B0006EXIXG.

6. Alan Noble, "Franz Kafka and McGee and Me," *Christ and Pop Culture Magazine*, #20, http://christandpopculture.com/franz-kafka-mcgee.

Chapter 5

1. Rod Dreher, "The Cult of Transgender," *The American Conservative*, August 10, 2016, http://www.theamericanconservative.com/dreher/the-cult-of-transgender.

2. Mike Cosper, *The Stories We Tell: How TV and Movies Long for and Echo the Truth* (Wheaton, IL: Crossway, 2014), Kindle edition, locs 673-75.

3. "Frequently Asked Questions," the Center for Barth Studies, Princeton Theological Seminary, http://barth.ptsem.edu/about-cbs/faq. The quote has also been attributed to the famous preacher Charles Spurgeon.

4. Herman Ridderbos, *Paul: An Outline of His Theology* (Grand Rapids: Eerdmans, 1975), 304. Ridderbos draws a connection between Ephesians 5:11 and 2 Corinthians 6:14 ("Do not be unequally yoked").

5. John R. W. Stott, *God's New Society: The Message of Ephesians* (Downers Grove, IL: InterVarsity Press, 1979), 199–201.

6. See for instance Gordon D. Fee, "Concluding Exhortations," *Philippians*, the IVP New Testament Commentary Series (Downers Grove, IL: InterVarsity Press, 1999), http://www.biblegateway.com/resources/commentaries/IVP-NT/Phil/Concluding-Exhortations; A. H. Snyman, "Philippians 4:1–9 from a Rhetorical Perspective," *Verbum et Ecclesia* 28, no. 1 (2007): 237–38, 241; and Moisés Silva, *Philippians*, 2nd ed., Baker Exegetical Commentary on the New Testament (Grand Rapids: Baker Academic, 1992, 2005), 197.

7. Fee, "Concluding Exhortations," *Philippians*.

8. See Daniel B. Wallace, "1 Thessalonians 5:22—The Sin Sniffer's Catch-All Verse," Bible.org, June 30, 2004, https://bible.org/article/1-thessalonians-522%e2%80%94-sin-sniffer%e2%80%99s-catch-all-verse; and Colin Brown, ed., *The New International Dictionary of New Testament Theology* (Grand Rapids: Zondervan, 1975), vol. 1, 703–4, cited by Bob Hayton, "The Real Meaning of 1 Thessalonians 5:22," *Fundamentally Reformed* (blog), May 5, 2010, https://www.fundamentallyreformed.com/2010/05/05/the-real-meaning-of-1-thessalonians-5-22/.

9. M. Joseph Young, "Appearances," Christian Gamers Guild Chaplain's Corner, December 2001, http://www.christian-gamersguild.org/chaplain/faga009.html.

10. Todd Friel, "Magic and wizards in fiction," *Wretched TV*, June 21, 2018, http://www.wretched.org/magic-wizards-fiction.

11. Todd Friel, *Wretched Radio*, July 19, 2011. Transcription provided by Stephen.

12. John MacArthur, "Treating the Symptoms, Not the Sin," *Grace to You* (blog), May 8, 2015, https://www.gty.org/library/blog/B150508. MacArthur refers to Proverbs 1:22, 32; 14:15, 18; 22:3; 27:12.

Chapter 6

1. Turnau, *Popologetics*, chaps. 10 and 11.

Chapter 7

1. For a good overview of media violence studies up to 1999, see W. James Potter, *On Media Violence* (London: Sage, 1999). For a newer survey of recent studies, see the research brief "Media and Violence: An Analysis of Current Research," Common Sense Media, February 13, 2013, https://www.commonsensemedia.org/research/media-and-violence-an-analysis-of-current-research. For a critical response to some of the influential studies, especially the ones that found a long-term effect from violent media, see Gerard Jones, *Killing Monsters: Why Children Need Fantasy, Super Heroes, and Make-Believe Violence* (New York: Basic Books, 2002).

2. Kevin J. Vanhoozer, "What Is Everyday Theology? How and Why Christians Should Read Culture," in *Everyday Theology: How to Read Cultural Texts and Interpret Trends*, ed. Kevin J. Vanhoozer, Charles A. Anderson, and Michael J. Sleasman (Grand Rapids: Baker Academic, 2007), 29.

Chapter 8

1. Some of this research about elementary-age child development comes from Karen DeBord, Childhood Years: Ages Six Through Twelve (Raleigh, NC: North Carolina Cooperative Extension Service, 1996), https://extension.tennessee.edu/centerforparenting/TipSheets/Childhood%20Years%20Ages%20Six%20through%20Twelve.pdf.

2. For one resource, see Michael K. Laidlaw, "Gender Dysphoria and Children: An Endocrinologist's Evaluation of *I am Jazz*," *Public Discourse*, the Journal of the Witherspoon Institute, April 5, 2018, https://www.thepublicdiscourse.com/2018/04/21220. For a child-friendly exploration of embracing our own gender identities based on biological sex, we also recommend Ellie Klipp, *I Don't Have to Choose* (self-pub., CreateSpace, 2018).

3. See Kyung-Seu Cho and Jae-Moo Lee, "Influence of Smartphone Addiction Proneness of Young Children on Problematic Behaviors and Emotional Intelligence: Mediating Self-Assessment Effects of

Parents Using Smartphones," *Computers in Human Behavior* 66 (January 2017): 303–11; and Rikuyu Hosokawa and Toshiki Katsura, "Association between Mobile Technology Use and Child Adjustment in Early Elementary School Age," *Plos One*, July 25, 2018, https://journals.plos.org/plosone/article?id=10.1371/journal.pone.0199959.

4. On the Greek term *perichoresis*, see Timothy Keller, "The Dance of God," in *The Reason for God: Belief in an Age of Skepticism* (New York: Penguin Books, 2008). But see also Larry Perkins, "The Dance Is Not *Perichōrēsis*," Northwest Baptist Seminary, April 6, 2007, https://nbseminary.ca/the-dance-is-not-perichrsis.

Chapter 9

1. Beatrice Verhoeven and Cassidy Robinson, "30 Highest Grossing Animated Movies of All Time Worldwide," *The Wrap*, September 27, 2019, https://www.thewrap.com/30-highest-grossing-animated-movies-of-all-time.

2. For a more technical explanation of the software created to animate snow in *Frozen*, see the video presentation by Alexey Stomakhin, et al., "Disney's *Frozen*: A Material Point Method For Snow Simulation," January 26, 2014, https://www.youtube.com/watch?v=O0kyDKu8K-k.

3. See Charles Taylor, *Secular Age* (Cambridge, MA: Harvard University Press, 2007), especially "The Age of Authenticity." Readers new to philosophy will appreciate the much shorter and more accessible summary found in James K. A. Smith, *How (Not) to Be Secular: Reading Charles Taylor* (Grand Rapids: Eerdmans, 2014).

4. Ron Clements and Jon Musker, dir., *Aladdin* (Burbank, CA: Walt Disney Pictures, 1992).

5. See Rob Lowman, "Unfreezing *Frozen*: The Making of the Newest Fairy Tale in 3D by Disney," *Los Angeles Daily News/Pasadena Star News*, November 19, 2013, http://www.pasadenastarnews.com/arts-and-entertainment/20131119/unfreezing-frozen-the-making-of-the-newest-fairy-tale-in-3d-by-disney.

6. Kierran Petersen, "Disney's *Frozen* and the Gay Agenda," *BBC News*, March 27, 2014, http://www.bbc.com/news/blogs-echochambers-26759342.

7. Jess Denham, "*Frozen 2*: Idina Menzel Backs 'Great' Fan Campaign Demanding Disney Make Elsa Its First Lesbian Princess," *The Independent*, May 24, 2016, http://www.independent.co.uk/arts-entertainment/films/news/frozen-2-idina-menzel-backs-great-fan-campaign-asking-disney-to-make-elsa-its-first-lesbian-princess-a7044401.html.

8. Gregory Mertz, "Disney: No Princess for Queen Elsa #CharmingPrinceForElsa," *Citizen Go*, May 23, 2016, http://www.citizengo.org/en/fm/34400-disney-no-princess-queen-elsa-charmingprinceforelsa.

9. Augustine, *The Confessions of Saint Augustine*, trans. Hal M. Helms (Brewster, MA: Paraclete Press, 2010), https://www.paracletepress.com/samples/exc-confessions-of-augustine-essential.pdf.

10. Benjamin Franklin, *Autobiography of Benjamin Franklin* (Philadelphia: J. B. Lippincott & Co., 1869), 228–30.

Chapter 10

1. Much of this chapter's information was culled from the following online sources: "Stages of Adolescent Development Chart," Cornell University eCommons, http://ecommons.library.cornell.edu/bitstream/1813/19311/2/StagesAdol_chart.pdf; "Understanding and States, Ages 10–14," *Keep Connected*, an online resource of the Search Institute, https://keepconnected.searchinstitute.org/understanding-ages-and-stages/ages-10-14/; and "Parents and Teachers: Teen Growth and Development, Ages 11 to 14," Palo Alto Medical Foundation, https://www.sutterhealth.org/health/parenting-preteens-teens/physical/teen-growth-development-ages-11-to-14. Ted found other information from the experience of raising three kids through their tweens and early teen years with his wise and insightful wife, Carolyn. She provided a lot of input for this section.

2. Maggie Jones, "What Teenagers Are Learning from Online Porn," *New York Times*, February 7, 2018, https://www.nytimes.

com/2018/02/07/magazine/teenagers-learning-online-porn-literacy-sex-education.html. Be advised: the article contains very sexually explicit language.

3. "Because Who Is Perfect?" *ProInfirmis*, YouTube post, December 2, 2013, https://www.youtube.com/watch?v=E8umFV69fNg.

4. Jerry L. Rushton, Michelle Forcier, Robin M. Schecktman, "Epidemiology of Depressive Symptoms in the National Longitudinal Study of Adolescent Health," *Journal of the American Academy of Child and Adolescent Psychiatry* 41, no. 2 (2002):199–205, cited in National Institute for Health Care Management, "Improving Early Identification and Treatment of Adolescent Depression: Considerations and Strategies for Health Plans," NIHCM Foundation Issue Brief, February 2010, http://www.nihcm.org/pdf/Adol_MH_Issue_Brief_FINAL.pdf.

5. George Bowden, "Social Media Affects Child Mental Health Through Increased Stress, Sleep Deprivation, Cyberbullying, Experts Say," *The Huffington Post* UK, February 18, 2016, https://www.huffingtonpost.co.uk/2016/02/12/social-media-affects-child-mental-health_n_9202460.html.

6. Claire McCarthy, "The Latest Dangerous 'Addiction' Parents Need to Worry About: Mobile Devices" (blog), Harvard Health Publishing, May 10, 2016, https://www.health.harvard.edu/blog/latest-dangerous-addiction-parents-need-worry-mobile-devices-201605109680.

7. Markham Heid, "We Need to Talk about Kids and Smartphones," *Time*, October 10, 2017, http://time.com/4974863/kids-smartphones-depression; and Terri Williams, "The Role of Social Media in Adolescent/Teen Depression and Anxiety," Center for Digital Ethics and Policy, April 3, 2018, https://www.digitalethics.org/essays/role-social-media-adolescentteen-depression-and-anxiety.

Chapter 11

1. J. J. Abrams, dir., *Star Wars: Episode VII, The Force Awakens* (San Francisco: Lucasfilm, 2015).

2. Scott Dadich, "Lucky VII: Superfan J. J. Abrams on Directing *The Force Awakens*," interview with J. J. Abrams, *Wired*, November 2015, http://www.wired.com/2015/11/star-wars-force-awakens-jj-abrams-interview.

3. John Higgs, "The Hero's Journey: The Idea You Never Knew Had Shaped 'Star Wars,'" *Salon*, November 8, 2015, http://www.salon.com/2015/11/07/the_heros_journey_the_idea_you_never_knew_had_shaped_star_wars.

4. Abrams, *The Force Awakens*.

5. See Timothy Keller, "Why Can't I Be Free to Live as I See Fit as Long as I Don't Harm Anyone?," in *Making Sense of God: An Invitation to the Skeptical* (New York: Viking, 2016). Keller does a masterful job showing how empty freedom is, as an absolute value, unless it is contextualized within a larger understanding of what human beings are ultimately for.

6. Irvin Kershner, dir., *Star Wars: Episode V, The Empire Strikes Back* (San Francisco: Lucasfilm, 1980).

7. Mark Hamill, "Biography," IMDB.com, accessed September 24, 2019, http://www.imdb.com/name/nm0000434/bio.

8. C. S. Lewis, *Mere Christianity* (New York: Macmillan, 1952), 35.

9. Brad Bird, dir., *The Incredibles* (Emeryville, CA: Pixar, 2004).

10. C. S. Lewis, *Letters of C. S. Lewis*, ed. W. H. Lewis (Orlando: Harcourt, 2003), 288.

Chapter 12

1. See Barna Group, "Six Reasons Young Christians Leave Church," Barna Research, September 27, 2011, https://www.barna.com/research/six-reasons-young-christians-leave-church; and Scott McConnell, "Reasons 18- to 22-Year-Olds Drop Out of Church," Lifeway Research, August 7, 2007, https://lifewayresearch.com/2007/08/07/reasons-18-to-22-year-olds-dropout-of-church/.

2. Ed Stetzer, "Dropouts and Disciples: How Many Students Are Really Leaving the Church?" *Christianity Today*, May 14, 2014,

http://www.christianitytoday.com/edstetzer/2014/may/dropouts-and-disciples-how-many-students-are-really-leaving.html. The article cites a Lifeway survey that found a significant factor determining whether teen faith survived into adulthood was "At least one adult from church made a significant investment in me personally and spiritually (between ages fifteen and eighteen)."

3. Barna Group, "Five Reasons Millennials Stay Connected to Church," Barna Research, September 17, 2013, https://www.barna.org/barna-update/millennials/635-5-reasons-millennials-stay-connected-to-church#.V2LStbt95D8.

4. Many of the thoughts here, and in the "Growth in Mental Processing" and "Growth in Social Interaction and Identity" sections of this chapter, are drawn from Sedra Spano, "Stages of Adolescent Development," *ACT for Youth Research Facts and Findings*, May 2004, http://www.actforyouth.net/resources/rf/rf_stages_0504.pdf and https://ecommons.cornell.edu/bitstream/handle/1813/19311/StagesAdol_chart.pdf;jsessionid=2D6C4A57F1B3F65DE02F9C60E6DCC7A5?sequence=2; "Understanding and Stages, Ages 15–18," *Keep Connected*, an online resource of the Search Institute, https://keepconnected.searchinstitute.org/understanding-ages-and-stages/ages-15-18/; and "Parents and Teachers: Teen Growth and Development, Ages 15 to 17," Palo Alto Medical Foundation, https://www.sutterhealth.org/health/parenting-preteens-teens/physical/teen-growth-development-ages-15-to-17.

5. See K. R. Merikangas et al., "Lifetime Prevalence of Mental Disorders in U.S. Adolescents: Results from the National Comorbidity Survey Replication-Adolescent Supplement (NCS-A)," *Journal of the American Academy of Child and Adolescent Psychiatry* 49, no. 10 (October 2010): 980–89. See also "Eating Disorder Statistics & Research," Eating Disorder Hope, http://www.eatingdisorderhope.com/information/statistics-studies.

6. See M. Mattebo et al., "Pornography and Sexual Experiences among High School Students in Sweden," *Journal of Developmental and Behavioral Pediatrics* 35 (April 2014): 179–88, http://www.ncbi.

nlm.nih.gov/pubmed/24695119.

7. Normal Doidge, "Brain Scans of Porn Addicts: What's Wrong with this Picture?" *The Guardian*, September 26, 2013, https://www. theguardian.com/commentisfree/2013/sep/26/brain-scans-porn-addicts-sexual-tastes; and Ana J. Bridges's fine overview of research on pornography's effects, "Pornography's Effect on Interpersonal Relationships," http://www.socialcostsofpornography.com/Bridges_ Pornographys_Effect_on_Interpersonal_Relationships.pdf.

8. Lisa Diamond, "Lisa Diamond on Sexual Fluidity of Men and Women," presentation, Cornell University, October 17, 2013, https:// www.youtube.com/watch?v=m2rTHDOuUBw. Diamond's presentation is fascinating and looks at some of the most complete data sets. She was frankly surprised by her findings. Well worth a watch.

9. See Mark Yarhouse, "Understanding the Transgender Phenomenon," *Christianity Today*, June 5, 2015, https://www.christianitytoday.com/ct/2015/july-august/understanding-transgender-gender-dysphoria.html. Rapid onset gender dysphoria (ROGD) is a hotly debated condition that strikes some teenage girls, causing acute discomfort with their own gender, and then often simply dissipates after some months or years.

10. Yarhouse, "Understanding the Transgender Phenomenon."

11. R. Garofalo, R. C. Wolf, S. Kessel, S. J. Palfrey, R. H. DuRant, "The Association between Health Risk Behaviors and Sexual Orientation among a School-Based Sample of Adolescents," *Pediatrics* 101, no. 5 (May 1998): 895–902, the US National Library of Medicine, https://www.ncbi.nlm.nih.gov/pubmed/9565422; Stephen T. Russell and Kara Joyner, "Adolescent Sexual Orientation and Suicide Risk: Evidence from a National Study," *American Journal of Public Health* 91, no. 8 (August 2001): 1,276–81, the US National Library of Medicine, https://www.ncbi.nlm.nih.gov/pmc/articles/ PMC1446760/; Cecilia Dhejne et al., "Long-Term Follow-Up of Transsexual Persons Undergoing Sex Reassignment Surgery: Cohort Study in Sweden," *Plos One*, February 22, 2011, https://journals. plos.org/plosone/article?id=10.1371/journal.pone.0016885.

12. Angela Watercutter, "How Pop Culture Changed the Face of the Same-Sex Marriage Debate," *Wired*, June 27, 2013, http://www.wired.com/2013/06/pop-culture-same-sex-marriage.

13. Alastair Roberts, "Five Principles of the New Sexual Morality," The Gospel Coalition, August 15, 2014, https://www.thegospelcoalition.org/article/the-principles-of-the-new-sexual-morality.

14. Chalmers, "The Expulsive Power of a New Affection."

15. Arthur Allen, "Wild Teenage Behaviour Linked to Rapid Cognitive Change in the Brain," *The Guardian*, September 5, 2014, http://www.theguardian.com/science/2014/sep/05/teenage-brain-behaviour-prefrontal-cortex.

16. See Barna, "Six Reasons Young Christians Leave Church"; Brian Housman, "Why Are Teens Leaving the Faith?" Apostolic Information Service, July 20, 2007, https://www.apostolic.edu/why-are-teens-leaving-the-faith/; and Fuller Youth Institute, "What Makes Faith Stick During College?" Fuller Youth Institute, September 6 2011, http://fulleryouthinstitute.org/articles/what-makes-faith-stick-during-college.

17. The following paragraphs draw extensively from Sedra Spano, "Stages of Adolescent Development," *Research Facts and Findings*, ACT for Youth Upstate Center for Excellence, http://www.actforyouth.net/resources/rf/rf_stages_0504.pdf; and "Parents and Teachers: Teen Growth and Development, Years 15 to 17," Palo Alto Medical Foundation website, http://www.pamf.org/parenting-teens/health/growth-development/growth.html.

18. National Institute of Mental Health, "Any Anxiety Disorder," updated November 2017, https://www.nimh.nih.gov/health/statistics/any-anxiety-disorder.shtml; and "Major Depression," updated February 2019, https://www.nimh.nih.gov/health/statistics/major-depression.shtml.

19. For more on youth clustering, see Chap Clark, "Peers," in *Hurt 2.0: Inside the World of Today's Teenagers* (Grand Rapids: Baker Academic, 2004, 2011).

20. Monica Anderson and JingJing Jiang, "Teens, Social Media and Technology 2018," Pew Research Center, May 31, 2018, http://www.

pewinternet.org/2018/05/31/teens-social-media-technology-2018.

21. University of California-Irvine, "Teens Post Online Content to Appear Interesting, Popular and Attractive, UCI Study Finds," *UCI News*, February 12, 2018, https://news.uci.edu/2018/02/12/teens-post-online-content-to-appear-interesting-popular-and-attractive-uci-study-finds/.

22. See Stephani Sutherland, "Bright Screens Could Delay Bedtime," *Scientific American*, January 1, 2013, http://www.scientificamerican.com/article/bright-screens-could-delay-bedtime.

23. Ana Homayoun, "What Teens Wish Their Parents Knew about Social Media," *Washington Post*, January 9, 2018, https://www.washingtonpost.com/news/parenting/wp/2018/01/09/what-teens-wish-their-parents-knew-about-social-media.

24. These and other practical tips come from "How Parents and Teens Can Help Reduce the Impact of Social Media on Youth Well-being," *The Conversation*, December 7, 2017, http://theconversation.com/how-parents-and-teens-can-reduce-the-impact-of-social-media-on-youth-well-being-87619.

25. Homayoun, "What Teens Wish Their Parents Knew about Social Media."

Chapter 13

1. "Release Timeline," *Fortnite Wiki*, https://fortnite.gamepedia.com/Release_Timeline.

2. Blake Hester, "*Fortnite* Now Largest Free-to-Play Console Game of All Time," *Variety*, April 26, 2018, https://variety.com/2018/gaming/news/fortnite-worlds-top-battle-royale-game-1202788425.

3. Brian Feldman, "The Most Important Video Game on the Planet," *New York* magazine, July 9, 2018, http://nymag.com/selectall/2018/07/how-fortnite-became-the-most-popular-video-game-on-earth.html. Feldman's long-form article is by far the most extensive treatment of *Fortnite* at the moment.

4. Gil Kaufman, "JAY-Z, RuPaul, Lady Gaga, Katy Perry and Kourtney Kardashian Among 2018 Webby Award Winners: See the

Full List," *Billboard*, April 24, 2018, https://www.billboard.com/articles/news/awards/8373458/2018-webby-awards-jay-z-rupaul-lady-gaga-katy-perry-kourtney-kardashian; and Steve Watts, "Resident Evil 2 Wins Top Honor In E3 Game Critics Awards," *Gamespot*, July 5, 2018, https://www.gamespot.com/articles/resident-evil-2-wins-top-honor-in-e3-game-critics-/1100-6460135/.

5. Feldman, "The Most Important Video Game on the Planet."

6. Dustin Bailey, "Epic Games Banked $3 Billion in Profit this Year Mostly Thanks to *Fortnite*," PCGamesN.com, December 27, 2018, https://www.pcgamesn.com/fortnite/fortnite-revenue-2018.

7. "Number of Registered Users of *Fortnite* Worldwide from August 2017 to March 2019 (in Millions)," *Statista*, 2019, https://www.statista.com/statistics/746230/fortnite-players.

8. Feldman, "The Most Important Video Game on the Planet."

9. Rhodri Marsden, "Battle Royale: The Story Behind the Phenomenon that Is *Fortnite*," *The National*, June 21, 2018, https://www.thenational.ae/arts-culture/battle-royale-the-story-behind-the-phenomenon-that-is-fortnite-1.742749.

10. Ben Kuchera, "Thanos Is the Best Thing in *Fortnite* Right Now," *Polygon*, May 8, 2018, https://www.polygon.com/2018/5/8/17332600/fortnite-thanos-infinity-gauntlet-is-the-best.

11. Ben Kuchera, "Calling *Fortnite* a Battle Royale Game Misses the Point," *Polygon*, July 13, 2018, https://www.polygon.com/fortnite/2018/7/13/17568900/fortnite-battle-royale-cultural-phenomenon.

12. For an example of a player piecing together events and changes into a coherent story, see TheSmithPlays, "The Entire *Fortnite* Storyline You Didn't Know Explained! (Seasons 1–10)," August 8, 2019, YouTube, https://www.youtube.com/watch?v=bRD6KZPyJs4.

13. Andrew Webster, "*Fortnite* Has the Most Interesting Video Game Story in Years," *The Verge*, July 2, 2018, https://www.theverge.com/2018/7/2/17525200/fortnite-storytelling-rocket-launch.

14. Oscar Gonzales, "*Fortnite*'s Black Hole Event Was a Serious

Game Changer," C/Net, October 16, 2019, https://www.cnet.com/news/fortnites-black-hole-event-was-a-serious-game-changer.

15. Daniel Mackrell, "How to Get the John Wick Skin in *Fortnite*," Metro, April 15, 2018, https://metro.co.uk/2018/04/15/get-john-wick-skin-fortnite-7469035.

16. Feldman, "The Most Important Video Game on the Planet."

17. Feldman.

18. Scott Duwe, "Some of the Best Fan-Concepts for Fortnite's Skins," Dot Esports, September 12, 2018, https://dotesports.com/the-op/news/fortnite-best-community-fan-skin-concepts-21619.

19. See Richard Freed, "The Tech Industry's War on Kids," *Medium*, March 12, 2018, https://medium.com/@richardnfreed/the-tech-industrys-psychological-war-on-kids-c452870464ce.

20. George Lucas, dir., *Star Wars: Episode IV, A New Hope* (San Francisco: Lucasfilm, 1977).

Chapter 14

1. Kershner, *The Empire Strikes Back*.

2. Jon Acuff, "The Jesus Juke," *Stuff Christians Like*, November 16, 2010, http://stuffchristianslike.net/2010/11/16/the-jesus-juke.

Appendix A

1. See Randy Alcorn, *Heaven* (Carol Stream, IL: Tyndale House, 2004), chap. 15.

2. Joe Rigney, *The Things of Earth: Treasuring God by Enjoying His Gifts* (Wheaton, IL: Crossway, 2015), Kindle edition, loc. 1,230–32, 1,429–30.

3. Richard Mouw, *When the Kings Come Marching In: Isaiah and the New Jerusalem* (Grand Rapids: Eerdmans, 2002), Kindle edition, loc. 457–61.

4. Michael E. Wittmer, *Becoming Worldly Saints: Can You Serve Jesus and Still Enjoy Your Life?* (Grand Rapids: Zondervan, 2015), 168.

5. Alcorn, *Heaven*, 406.